Advance Praise for *WILDFIRE*

"Ralph Ryan's *Wildfire* is a first-hand and exciting account of one of America's last great true-life adventures—Smokejumping. Live it and feel it from inside as the smokejumpers themselves do. Fly in over a fire, survey the scene below, jump from the plane, soar above the timber, and experience the passion, the pride, and the sheer guts of parachuting to wildfires amidst the grandeur of the mountainous West and Alaska."
—Murry A. Taylor, author of Jumping Fire: A Smokejumper's Memoir of Fighting Wildfire, and The Rhythm of Leaves.

"A vivid and compelling account of one man's career as a wildland firefighter and smokejumper in the 70's and 80's. *Wildfire* is closely recorded, finely observed and full of interesting characters and unforgettable stories. Ralph Ryan doesn't just take you into the epic blazes, fiery winds and dangerous tree landings, but also into the lives of the heroic firefighters who risked everything to protect our national forests."
—Kevin Grange, author of *Beneath Blossom Rain*

WILDFIRE

WILDFIRE

Memories of a Wildland Firefighter

RALPH RYAN

WILDFIRE

www.ralphryan.com

First Printing 2013

ISBN-13: 978-1484024430

ISBN-10: 1484024435

For all my firefighting brothers and sisters and dedicated to the memory of Luke Sheehy, a five-year California Smokejumper who died while fighting the Saddle Back Fire in the Warner Wilderness, Modoc National Forest, June 10, 2013. Ride on Pale Rider. Rest in peace, bro.

FOREWORD

"I'm willing to take a chance on most any kind of proposition that promises better action on forest fires, but the best information I can get from experienced fliers is that all parachute jumpers are crazy, just a little bit unbalanced, otherwise they wouldn't be involved in such a hazardous undertaking."
— Evan Kelly, Regional Forester, 1939

CHAPTER 1

Load Up, Let's Go

Village Fire, Angeles National Forest
November 23, 1975

Fanned by the strong wind, spot fires erupted into a solid wall of flame. It leapt wildly one-hundred plus feet into the night, long tapestries of fire separating from it and whipping above the brush. I pulled out my Instamatic camera and took a few shots just before the reality of our situation hit. We're trapped; the flames had cut off our escape route. I'm thinking, '*we're going to burn to death*,' when Harold yells, "Get into the burn, and get 'em off your backs!"

I couldn't believe it. Just five hours earlier, I'm at home with my military brat roommates and my girlfriend, Sarah, celebrating the Thanksgiving holiday with a bottle of Old Number 7 whisky, plenty of beer, and the Doors blaring through our eight-speaker stereo system. The Santa Ana winds—those in the wildland firefighting business call them the 'Devil Winds'—were rocking the house outside when the fire call came in. Sarah's disappointment quickly turned into her most seductive look, one I couldn't pass up, and twenty minutes later, I'm tucking my shirt and scrambling out the door with Jim Morrison singing behind me, *"Try to set the night on fire!"*

I had a strange feeling about this mission when I arrive at the work center. Harold, our roughneck, tough as nails foreman, stepped out of his office with a dead serious look and yells, "Load up boys, time to go." Within minutes, I'm sitting in my gear in a crew carrier racing on I-15 toward Mt. Baldy. The chaotic radio chatter created a grim and somber atmosphere. Rising above the darkly silhouetted mountain range before us, the blaze on top of Mt. Baldy burned like a golden orb.

Keith, a stout, red-haired Irishman who'd been practicing with his band—Rattlesnakes and Eggs—when the call came in, whistled beside me, "Holy Jesus! Please tell me we're not going there."

Harold poked his head through the opening to the crew compartment and said, "You men are going to earn your pay tonight. The fire is totally out of control. It's threatening Mt. Baldy Village."

The crew cab went silent. I checked my gear one last time. C-rations, jacket, gloves, water canteens, fusses, safety glasses, earplugs, chainsaw wrench, extra spark plug, air filter, chain, fire shelter, and hardhat. I savored the scent of Sarah on my body, and for back up, I had a picture of her taped to the inside of my hard hat. I couldn't stand to leave her. Then again, my obsession to feel flames licking at my body overpowered every other thought. I'd found a passion that trumped every interpersonal connection I'd experienced. Maybe, too, being a military brat made it customary to walk out a door never expecting to walk back in. My worse childhood memories consisted of packing up and leaving everyone behind.

Visions of Sarah danced in the advancing flames. She was always on my mind with hot flesh on flesh, and a smile that could melt snow. She could turn heads in the darkest light. I often wondered while sleeping on the ground between shifts, am I good enough for her? Will she be faithful while I'm out here busting my ass and eating smoke? The reality that I may have just walked out that door frightened me.

After hours of intense line construction, we'd made good progress until the weather changed. A strong up-slope wind eddied back onto itself at the ridge top blowing ash and cinders down the mountain. Everyone's tools fell silent, thirty sets of eyes watched in horror as a bright trail of embers floated over our heads and settled in the brush below us, lighting spot fires wherever they landed. Harold yelled into his radio, "Crew 7-Charlie to the Engine Company on Mt. Baldy Road, come in!" No reply. He tries again, "Crew 7-Charlie to the engines on Baldy

Road! Do you copy? Answer Goddamn it!" The radio remained silent. Harold's face contorted with tension and the veins on his forehead seemed about to burst. He looked like a cornered animal and it frightened me. "Why aren't they putting out those fires? What the hell are they doing down there?" he shouts to no one in particular.

As the order shot down the line, firefighters around me ran into the burn. Harold ordered us to deploy our fire shelters, little aluminum tents designed to offer protection against radiant heat and intended for life-threatening situations only. They're referred to as a 'shake-n-bake; you shake it open, cover yourself with it and prepare to bake. Our engine foreman had warned us when he'd taught us how to deploy them, 'If you ever have to use these, somebody screwed up big time.'

Super-heated air burned my nose and throat, the roar of the fire grew so loud, I couldn't think. I knew we were fucked, it's now or never to get my shelter out. I kicked aside hot embers, ripped the tab open and in seconds the aluminum tent is flapping wildly in the wind.

Beside me, John, our assistant foreman, had trouble with his shelter. The release tab broke off while he pulled on it. He calmly asked, "Anybody got a knife?" When no one responded, he frantically began shredding the plastic with his bare fingers as he glanced at the advancing fire: he knew his life depended on getting that shelter open.

I fought the wind to get my boots into the anchor straps at the shelter's bottom, my hands into the upper corners. I fell to my knees, made sure John had his open too, and lay on the ground. The fire sucked the oxygen out of my tent, pulling at my lungs. I clawed open a small hole in the ground, stuffed my bandana in it, soaked it with water from my canteen, and buried my face in it. Cool air filled my lungs. I heard a voice fading in and out on the blasting wind. Someone's singing:

"Oh, the weather outside is frightful,
But the fire is so delightful,
And as long as you love me so,
Let it snow, let it snow, let it snow."

I knew that poor guy had lost his mind. Am I next? The rancid smell of Nomex, the fire resistant chemical our fire clothes were saturated with, began filling my shelter. The radiant heat was baking the chemical right out of my clothing! My mind began to reel. *I'm about to burn. To die! What did I do to deserve this?* At the sound of rain pelting my shelter, I lifted my head in hope and saw bright orange and yellow light through every crease and seam. It wasn't rain at all, it was firebrands!

The head of the racing inferno reached me with a vibration as intense as a freight train. I felt sure it would crush me. I ached to get up and run, but could only manage a lung-draining yell. My body's pulsating, I feel like a naked heart pounding on the dirt. I see Sarah beckoning me, just out of reach. I yell, "Please God! Don't let me die like this! I'll be a better son! A brother! A boyfriend! Please don't let me burn to death!"

I had no idea how much time passed before I heard Harold's voice hollering in answer to my prayers, "Everyone all right?"

Firefighters began calling out in reply. I sheepishly raised a corner of my shelter to see thick smoke billowing past. I pulled the shelter back down. I wanted to stay in that womb-like cocoon forever.

Harold's voice rang out again, this time closer. "Those worthless sons-of-bitches!" he seethed. "Why didn't they get those fucking fires out? All right, men. Get out of your shelters and line out."

I stood slowly, keeping the shelter wrapped tightly around me to shield myself from the blowing smoke. All around me, firefighters stumbled out of their shelters hollow-eyed, looking as though they'd lost the power of thought. Like zombies, we formed a line and followed Harold down the mountain. The once wild brush below became a barren field of smoldering stumps, ash rose as we crossed it, blinding me. Finally, we stumbled down onto solid pavement. Our once enthusiastic 'Can Do' attitude; completely gone. We walked along the road log-jammed with emergency vehicles. The solemn crowd that had gathered gave us a wide berth. By the sheer number of ambulances, I figured the Fire Boss had written us off as a body recovery mission.

Harold took us to the first aid station and immediately marched to the command post to get answers. Where were the engine crews responsible for anchoring the road? He wanted to know. Moreover, where in the hell are they now? His voice boomed through the staging area. A few minutes later, he came back to where we waited and said flatly, "The bastards fell asleep. They've been pulled off the fire. A bus is coming to take us to the main fire camp in Glendora."

News of our ordeal spread quickly through camp. The servers in the chow line wouldn't meet my eyes. Had we done something wrong? Had it somehow been our fault? While scrubbing up at a wash station, I realized why the servers weren't able to look at me. In the mirror, I saw a haunting face cloaked in black ash. The whites of my eyes, hellfire red surrounded by piercing blue. My own face frightened me.

Harold ordered us to bed down. I flopped on a field cot totally exhausted from the fear I'd felt on the mountain. The crushing sound of the fire beating down on me wouldn't go away. I kept asking myself, 'Why would you subject yourself to such danger? It's fucking insane!' But another part of me rejoiced. I gazed up at the stars. Death had made me feel more alive than at any other time in my life.

When my nerves finally settled down, I took an analytical approach, looking for answers. The engine crews had fallen asleep, but due to the village being threatened, the overhead team may have acted without considering the Ten Standard Firefighting Orders, the firefighters' Ten Commandments. If one or more of these orders is broken, the chances of dying on a fire are greatly increased:

1. Know what your fire is doing at all times.

2. Base all actions on the current and expected behavior of the fire.

3. Keep informed on fire weather conditions and forecasts.

4. Post a lookout where there is possible danger.

5. Have escape routes for everyone and make sure they are known.

6. Be alert, keep calm, think clearly, and act decisively.

7. Maintain control of your men at all times.

8. Give clear instructions and be sure they are understood.

9. Maintain prompt communication with your men, boss, and adjoining forces.

10. Fight fire aggressively, but provide for safety first.

I knew how lucky I was to be able to review our mistakes from the comfort of a cot. Firefighters had gone to their deaths by compromising only one of the orders. I noticed a few of the Standard Orders were broken.

I drifted in and out of sleep that night. In my dream, Sarah bit her lower lip in the way that drove me crazy. She whispers, 'You can't have me if you're dead!'

At breakfast, humble, haggard faces ate silently in ash-covered clothes. Harold found us, took a seat, his mood subdued as he explained our assignment for the day: "A bus is coming to get us. We're going to collect our fire shelters and whatever else is left on the mountain. After that, we're on the fire line again."

We rode in silence back to where we'd nearly died. In the light, I saw the once thick brush field reduced to a gray, pitiful field of smoldering stubs. Skeletal remains of the big trees stood out like grave markers, plumes of ash whirled listlessly in the breeze. In the middle of the moonscape dashes of silver glinted in the sun. I found where I'd discarded my fire shelter; it immediately disintegrated into powder in my hands. I followed the fire line looking for my cherished chainsaw. When I found it, I almost cried, it's reduced to a twisted chunk of charred metal.

Keith yelled out, "My Pulaski handle is gone!"

The fire had burned the wooden handles off our tools, our heavy-duty gallon canteens, clumps of melted plastic. By that afternoon, Crew 7-Charlie took to the fire line. The Mount Baldy blaze—later named the Village Fire—would eventually burn over 100,000 acres. But just before we headed down to fight it again, I sat for a moment on the spot where only a few hours earlier, I'd felt sure I would die. Now, the sun shone bright on my spot, there wasn't a cloud in the sky. If the fire had taken us, I knew where they would've set the memorial markers.

CHAPTER 2

Firefighters From The Sky

Flat Fire, Sequoia National Forest
August 30, 1975

I had all winter to reflect on my life as a firefighter. I didn't tell my family about the burn-over in order to spare myself a barrage of concern. Instead, I spent as much time with them as possible. My relationship with Sarah grew stronger. The first time I saw her, her big brown eyes and long black hair with the bangs cut straight across like Cleopatra, and her tight body, mesmerized me. Her family and I became close also. Her dad, Roger, surprised me one day by saying, "Ralph, we have to talk. I'm taking my retirement in a month and I'm not leaving my daughter at the base unless she's married."

An uneasy sensation settled into my stomach, a dormant anger rose up. I'm not listening to his words, just hearing the commanding tone, the condescending ring of authority coming from another man in a military uniform towering over me and telling me I couldn't see his daughter, unless. Marriage? Hell, I didn't even know if I knew love yet. Nevertheless, Roger planned on relocating his family to Alabama and Sarah adamantly told me she didn't want to go. When we made our decision, it all seemed simple enough. Roger let me borrow his dress shoes, and Sarah and I married before the Justice of the Peace in Lancaster.

We settled in a little rental house near the base, and quickly fell into a marital routine.

I had one more college class to complete that winter for my Natural Resource Management Degree, and wanting to have more options that just firefighting, I applied to Humboldt State's Forestry Program. I also had a dream I'd carried with me from my brainwashed military brat childhood: I saw myself as a Green Beret, a "Greenie," as the grunts called them, crazy men who parachuted from the sky. Though my yen to enlist had faded as I observed all the bureaucratic bullshit my dad had endured over his thirty-year career, I never lost the desire to jump out of planes. I used to fashion parachutes out of my dad's handkerchiefs, attach my GI Joe's to them, and sneak to the top of our three-story apartment building and throw them off. My dream in life floated down with them.

When I first became a wildland firefighter in 1973, I learned about an elite group of men in Redding, California, who parachuted into fires—the near-mythical 'smokejumpers'. Maybe my dream could still be realized; maybe I could jump with a tool instead of a gun. I focused on mastering the tool—a chainsaw— and after two seasons on an engine crew, in 1975, I'd taken the next step and joined 7-Charlie helicopter crew to get experience in aircraft safety and technical operations.

My early training had been conducted by 7-Charlie's team pilot, a tall, lanky man with a mustache that curled to the bottom of his jaw. The first time I stood in front of his chopper, I liked him. His eyes sparked with confidence, a jaunt to his step. At our first session, he looked us over and said, "Just call me 'Dusty'." He patted the nose of his helicopter like a loved pet. "The Army drafted me in '67, about the same age as many of you here. Even with the war heating up and the Army burying a shitload of pilots, my gung-ho, sometimes called idiot attitude compelled me to volunteer to fly. I spent two tours flying in that shithole of a country for the First Air Calvary." He slid the chopper door open. "I flew this same type of bird in Nam, except back then they always had bullet holes in them. I know this baby inside and out. All I ask is that you follow my orders when you're around my ship. Go ahead climb inside."

I felt an intense adrenaline rush as I stepped in that chopper, maybe from seeing all the helicopter footage from the Vietnam War. After a few days of classroom study, we moved outside to practice tactical exercises: hand signals for landing choppers in tight areas, hooking up sling loads and water bucket cables. Once completed, we gathered at the platform to learn how to jump from the skids, a practice used when there wasn't a suitable place to land the helicopter. When the instructor asked for a volunteer, my hand shot up.

"This is a smokejumper suit," the instructor told me, handing me a heavily padded Kevlar jacket and pants, an outfit nearly as thick as a spacesuit. The word 'smokejumper' rang in my ears as I pulled it on. "This will protect you from the fall. Execute an Allen Roll when you hit the ground. Let your shoulder follow your legs, use the momentum to carry you into the tuck."

'Okay,' I thought, standing on the platform and looking at the pile of sawdust below, 'sure sounds simple enough.' Of course, my first jump ended in a bruising face plant and the laughter of all the trainees.

But just a few days later, every one of us could Allen Roll in our sleep, and we again found ourselves in Dusty's ship, buckled in for our very first ride. Before lifting off, he looked back at us from the pilot's seat with a sinister grin. The turbine whined to a deafening roar, the blades developed their distinctive whopping sound, and the cabin shuddered from the torque as he pulled back on the yoke. From my window, I watched the ground slip away, the landing spot grew smaller, and suddenly the nose pointed down as Dusty dropped us into a canyon. I grabbed the sides of my seat as my body becomes weightless, my stomach in my throat. Everyone around me hollered, and I know I'd just been hooked on this kind of flying for life. I fantasize I'm in Nam, a helicopter gunner. Dusty's flying just above the treetops while I'm filling the jungle with hot lead, shooting at ghosts. He happened to look back, and when he saw my antics, he just shook his head and smiled.

When I returned home, the excitement over my first helicopter ride lingered. I grabbed my wife, swung her around. When her feet touched the floor, she asked, "What's this all about?"

"I wore a smokejumper suit and went up in the helicopter! Our pilot pulled some out of this world G-forces. One moment it felt like I'm floating, the next, I felt my stomach about to come out of my mouth."

Sarah looked at me and said sarcastically, "I wish you could be this excited about other things."

The moment, *my moment*, totally smothered. I whistled up my dog Duke and took him for a hike in the foothills. He wanted to play, so we wrestled in the sand. A formable opponent weighing in at 120 pounds of pure muscle, but I still pinned him. While he struggled, I asked, "Why does she have to be so fucking unsupportive?" He just licked my face.

*****

Two weeks later our training concluded and we took off on our first real mission. An ominous mass of smoke boiled to an altitude where it formed a pyro cumulus cloud, a weather anomaly created only by volcanoes and forest fires. As we closed in, flames whipped off the treetops dancing across entire canyons. Dusty glided us over a ridgeline and we saw a transient firefighter 'city' developing in a big meadow. He made his ground hugging Vietnam approach to a side clearing where numerous helicopters of all sizes sat ready. Once down, we waited by our gear as a steady traffic of choppers swooped in and out ferrying crews back and forth from the fire line.

Our assistant foreman, John, came and pointed toward the camp. "Those big tents are the sleeping area. Go to the supply tent and check out sleeping bags. We'll chow down after that."

My saw mate, Joe, muttered under his breath, "Sleeping area? We didn't come here to sleep!"

The supply tent had stacks of hand tools, chainsaws, drip torches, and fire clothes. We checked out sleeping bags, and found empty cots in a tent half-filled with filthy, snoring firefighters back off the lines. Joe dumped his gear on the cot next to mine and sat down beside me. When I ran the saw, he swamped for me, responsible for pulling brush as I cut it, and acted as my lookout. This made us inseparable. We communicated intuitively, essential to running a screaming chainsaw safely. Joe stood shorter than me, had a thick belly and a messy beard that blended into his long brown hair. When I needed to get a point across, I'd call him, 'Butterball.'

Joe smacked his knee and said, "Shit! Stuck in camp!"

Harold happened to walk by at that moment. He raised his eyebrows and eyeballed Joe long enough to send him a clear message: *No complaining!* Harold told us, "We've been assigned to ground support on this one. We'll be working the helipads starting at 6 a.m., that's all for now. The rest of the evening is yours."

A groan ripped through our crew. Assigned to ground support? Hell, we're initial attack; we've come to fight fire! After Harold left, I said to Joe, "I'm with you, brother. We're Helishots, not heli-slugs! But next time, don't mouth off when I'm sitting next to you, Butterball."

"Kiss ass," he said, jabbing me in the ribs.

After chow, Joe and I wandered out of the dining area to have a look at camp, and quickly found ourselves on a sort of Main Street with logistics tents lining either side: Plans, Resources, Weather, First Aid, Commissary, and Fire Information. Next to the Fire Information tent a plywood board had weather and situation reports and a map of the wildfire tacked to it, the perimeter marked in red, and four divisions marked in black. Again within each division were a number of sectors. Beyond that area, two shower tents had hand written signs: 'HIS' and 'HERS.' Next to 'HERS,' a man sat on a lawn chair in front of a new 2,500-gallon water truck. He wore shorts, a tank top, sandals, and had a book opened on his lap like he'd been enjoying a day at the beach. Not having seen any women on firefighting crews before, I asked him, "What's with the 'HERS'?"

"It's for the support gals, kitchen staff and the like. They need to shower too, you know."

"Then you've found the best spot in camp!" Joe grinned.

The guy shrugged, "Just doing my job. This is my new water truck. Been here from the start and by the time this fire's over, she's going to be paid for. I'm making big bucks just sitting here."

"Just sitting here?" Joe frowned.

"Yup, need to watch the water level," he said pointing to the truck's tank. "Let's just say I'll make more money off this one gobbler than you guys will make all season."

Joe snorted. Just before he stormed away, he looked at the man's sandals in disgust and said, "Hope you don't stub your toe!"

"What's that all about, Butterball?" I said catching up to him.

Joe swung around. "Like he said, he'll make more money just sitting there than we'll make all season, but to rub it in our faces? I think we're in the wrong business, Ralph."

Back at the dining tent, we heard laughter inside. A group of firefighters had gathered around a table and we could see them arm wrestling. Harold, our usually stern foreman, had allowed himself to cut loose and appeared to be the event's grand master. When he caught sight of Joe and me, he grinned and called us over with a cock of his head. The man seated at the table before him looked eager for a challenger. His body resembled that of a pro wrestler. His clothes covered in ash, his forearms looked like bowling pins, and he had an eager, crazed look in his eyes. Harold smiled at me like ordering me to sit and face that monster. I turned on my heels and said, "He's all yours, Butterball. I'm going to bed!"

In the sleeping tent, I took off my boots and slipped into my bag. From my cot, I saw the fire on the mountain. Flames made periodic forays up the canyons, filling the sky with an orange glow. This wasn't typical fire behavior. Most fires quieted down at night from the higher humidity and cooler air. This one, though, made runs with the same intensity as it had during the day. I looked at the blaze with longing, not wanting to be stuck in camp, but where I'd been trained to be—in front of the flames. I reached down, grabbed my hard hat and gazed into Sarah's eyes. Another flame erupted.

Next morning, our crew manned three different helipads: one pad for crew transport and the other two for resupplying spike camps near the fire lines with sling loads of food and gear. Joe and I worked the crew transport pad all day off-loading incoming firefighters, checking manifests, and sliding chopper doors shut on crews going out. Toward the end of our shift, the Heliport manager told us that the next group coming in had worked the fire since its earliest stage: Smokejumpers!

Dusty brought in his ship with his customary attack approach. When he settled on the pad, the side door slid open before I got to it. I saw four of the filthiest, most ash-covered men I'd ever seen, each sitting on a large pack. These guys were the famous smokejumpers everybody talked about. They looked so ragtag and wild, more like hippies or cavemen than professional firefighters. When they hopped out, I grabbed one of their packs and tried to lift it. The thing must have been filled with rocks, I couldn't budge it. Before trying again, one of them nudged me aside saying, "Don't worry about it, kid. I'll get it."

He stood the pack upright inside the chopper, slipped into the shoulder straps, and walked away bent over from the weight. The three others did the same. When they dropped their packs in the staging area, clouds of dust exploded around them.

As Dusty shut the turbine down to refuel, I kept my eye on them. The one who'd nudged me aside had dirty red hair and a matted beard. The words stenciled on the back of his soot-stained fire shirt read, MUCHO DINERO HOTSHOTS, below that, TERRA DEL FUEGO NATIONAL FOREST. Patches or crew names stenciled on their shirts identified most fire crews, and I understood enough Spanish to know his meant, 'Big Money Hotshots from the Land of Fire.' I noticed another smokejumper's shirts had a hand-drawn parachute harness and emergency reserve parachute on it.

When Dusty took off to pick up the rest of their crew, I quietly positioned myself near the smokejumpers to eavesdrop. One paced restlessly, the others lay on the ground with their heads against their packs, telling dirty jokes. I had many questions, but didn't know how to break the ice. Finally, the pacing one noticed me, came over and offered his hand. "I'm Pigpen," he said.

"Ralph Ryan."

He glanced at the crew patch on my shirt. "Valyermo Helishots, huh?"

"Yeah, we formed last year. We share a helicopter with the Tanbark Helishots out of the Angeles."

"I've spent a lot of time on the Angeles," he told me. "I'm originally from the Los Padres. This is my first year smokejumping, and it's the best thing in firefighting. Whatever you've heard about smokejumping—you'd better believe it all. I'm never going back to the fucking district. After jumping out of planes, anything else would feel like a lousy desk job."

Jumping out of planes? I couldn't contain myself and immediately blurted out, "What do I have to do to get in?"

Pigpen gave me a quick once over. "First, you have to get yourself into excellent shape. Better than you ever thought you could. If you can't pass the physical fitness test the first day of training, you're gone. Even just to get to take the test, you'll probably have to apply a couple years running. So, if the chance actually comes your way, you won't want to blow it. My advice? Bust your butt like you never have before, sit-ups, push-ups, and pull-ups, do as many as you can every single day, run your ass off like there's no tomorrow. Other than that, just cross your fingers and keep applying. That's what I did, and here I am. These guys are the greatest; I've never had more fun."

I left Pigpen to guide Dusty down again. Six more smokejumpers exited the ship. I wondered who was in charge. They didn't line out in formation—standard operating procedure for other firefighters—they walked in pairs, or else alone, as though each to his own drumbeat. Pigpen turned and hollered, "Good luck, Ryan! Maybe we'll see you in the sky one day!"

Excitement dominated my night, I couldn't sleep. When I looked around for the smokejumpers the next morning, they'd already left. Before my shift on the helipads, I pulled my assistant foreman, John, aside and told him, "Man, I want to be a smokejumper."

John's face turned serious, a look I knew well, and said, "Those guys are tough, Ryan. If you want that, you'll have to be totally dedicated."

"I can do it. Help me. Put me to the test, and I'll do everything I have to."

He nodded, seemed to understand and tells me, "Let me talk to Harold. If you do your part, I'm sure we'll be happy to help. So, you want to be a jumper, fine by me. You understand that from now on you'll be held to a different standard. You'll have to work harder than everyone else, no more bitching, moaning, or grab ass among the crew. There'll be no slack for you, none at all. You sure you really want that?"

"Whatever it takes, John. Whatever it takes!"

My attitude changed that day. Instead of bitching about being stuck on ground support, I shut up and attacked all my tasks just like I would a fire.

*****

Finally on our fourth day in camp, we received a fire line assignment. Dusty flew us out at first light. He landed on a sand bar in the bed of the Kern River. After he took off, we gather around Harold. He points on his map. "We're here, our sector goes east. We'll secure this area. Keep an eye out for spot fires. Let's go."

We followed the riverbed into a flat, grassy basin that had escaped the flames and came upon a lone range cow that eyed us warily as we passed. The canyon walls narrowed as we moved east. Behind me in formation, Joe's uncharacteristic quietness had me turning to him, "What's on your mind, Butterball? You haven't said a word in at least five seconds."

Joe kicked a rock. "We need to save our money and buy a water truck."

"That's what you're all bottled up about?"

"Damn right! Who wants to bust ass for next to nothing when you can sit in front of the women's shower and collect big bucks?"

"Come on, do you have any idea how much money a water truck costs?"

"It can't be that far out of reach! Besides, one good fire and it's paid for, just like that a-hole said. We're going to be too old for this crap one day, Ry. Then what are we going to do?"

I thought about it: retirement, security, the future, firefighting didn't offer too much in the way of that. Still, I put it out of mind. "I'm not planning for 'one day,' Joe. I'm going to be a smokejumper."

He laughed like a hyena. "A smokejumper? Those guys are crazy! What the hell are you thinking, Ryan?"

"I don't want to sit on my ass and make money," I said giving him a friendly shove. "I want to jump out of planes."

"Sure," he said, shoving me back. "That's easy to say now. But what about when you're standing in the door of a plane and the world below you is in flames? What are you going to do then?"

"Guess I'll wish I'd be sitting on my ass in front of a water truck with you," I said chuckling.

We ended up fording back and forth across the Kern River many times over the next two days as we chased down and contained spot fires. My boots became water logged; the nails broke through the sole and dug into my heels. It became so bad, my socks smelled like compost, and pain throbbed through my foot. I had to walk on my tiptoes. Joe noticed, but kept quiet, John's warning that there would be no more bitching or moaning from me, dominated my mind. I starved my misery by fantasizing about parachuting out of airplanes. To make matters worse, during a meal break, I cooked up my favorite desert by mixing a can of the C-ration jelly with pound cake and heated it up. When the hot jelly hit my incisor, a laser-like pain lanced through my jaw. "Oh great," I quietly cried, "a toothache, just what I need to top it all off."

CHAPTER 3

Where Do We Go From Here?

With new boots and a fixed tooth, I'm ready for the fire season of 1976. I killed time until the first call-up by working on the Pacific Crest Trail and nervously checked the mail for a response to the smokejumper application I'd filed. Finally, the day came; I ripped open the envelope with trembling fingers only to find a few simple sentences rejecting me. I exhaled, felt crushed, but not ready to give up. I decided to pursue my dream with renewed vigor. I increased the already rigorous physical regime I'd been putting myself through by running the six miles to and from work. On weekends, I ran for hours through the San Gabriel foothills with Duke. He became a trusted companion, the first I ever had all to myself, a little ball of fur I saved from the gas chamber. When we'd run in the desert, he'd jump a jackrabbit and take off after it. Sometimes he beat me back home, other times; he'd be gone for days. Being a jock in high school, physical activity dominated my life. I always strived to be the best in whatever I did.

Sarah seemed relieved at the news. I became so upset I didn't want to look at her. If this is what married life is all about, maybe I'd made a mistake!

Harold and John saw my disappointment, too, but they didn't let me mope. Just before fire season began in earnest, Harold pulled me aside and said, "If you really want to be a smokejumper, you'll need to learn more about fire behavior and how to run a crew. From now on, you're going to be the Squad Boss."

The sudden promotion excited me; my learning curve would soon expand. But it also meant I'd have to give up my beloved chainsaw. I loved nothing better than being at the head of the line, wielding my trusty weapon with supreme proficiency and robbing the fire of life.

*****

Coyote Fire, San Bernardino National Forest
July 8, 1976

My lessons began a week later on our first fire, a Class F—between 1000 and 5000 acres—on the San Bernardino National Forest, when I stood back with the bosses and learned how to size up a blaze. As we looked down at our sector from the ridgeline, Harold said, "Determine if you're attacking the fire head-on or an indirect attack. Read the weather, topography, fuel types, fuel density, humidity, temperature. Never take anything for granted. Got that, Ryan?"

I nodded remembering the initial training I'd received years earlier. We studied fire behavior constantly and by 'head-on,' he meant a direct attack, getting as close to the flames as possible. By 'indirect attack,' he's referring to constructing fire line at a distance from the flames. Weather is one of the most important aspects in determining which attack is the most effective and safe, as is the lay of the land, is it steep or level. What types of fuels are burning, are they explosive or slow burning and how thick the fuels are. So many things to consider and I loved it when he sent me ahead of the crew to flag the fire line, or to serve as a lookout. Solitary functions I didn't mind.

We'd been on the fire line for over twelve hours when the Division Boss, an older man with a lantern jaw came through our sector and the incident that followed bolstered my respect for Harold to its highest level.

Harold signaled for me to tag along with him and the Division Boss, the three of us hiked to the top of a spur ridge that gave us a view of our sector. Down the canyon, the fire flared through mixed stands of pinion, oak, and chaparral, explosive fuels. A strong up-slope wind fanned the blaze. Now and again, it made hot runs up the side draws, spewing embers everywhere. I watched Harold and the Division Boss scan the entire area, and after some reflection, the boss pointed down the canyon and said, "I want your crew to cut line all the way to the bottom over there."

Harold raised his eyebrows. He said flatly, "I don't think so."

I couldn't believe he'd just said that to a Division Boss, and by the look on the man's face, he couldn't believe it either. The firefighting hierarchy is as rigid as the military's, the Division Boss being in charge of hundreds. To see Harold refuse his order made me uncomfortable, still I felt sure he knew what he was doing. He took a step closer to the Division Boss and said in the same stern tone he often used on me, "We're not cutting downhill under these conditions; it's already spotting below the main fire. If we commit ourselves into this chimney and the spots flare up, where do we go?"

"It's an order!"

"I'm not doing it. I'm not putting my crew in danger. We could cut line down this ridge line," he pointed to a ridge not threatened by the fire yet, "and burn out as we go. That way, we'll have an escape route."

The Division Boss flexed his jaw, he looked royally pissed. At the same time, it seemed like he chewed over what Harold had said. "Cut down the ridge line," he told us at last. He didn't say another word and hiked back the way he'd come.

Harold didn't gloat, or seem much surprised. He simply said, "Don't ever let what happened to us on the Village Fire go down on your watch, Ralph. You should've learned from it, not many people get to survive a burn-over. Size up your fire and if you feel someone is asking you to put your men in danger, refuse, but you'd better have a good explanation for your decision. And always, always have an alternate plan. "Oh," Harold pointed out to me, "did you notice his name tag showed he's from Georgia? The overhead team is pulling people from states that don't have our type of fires or terrain, so always be aware of that also."

The Village Fire haunted Harold. I knew he felt personally responsible for putting us in danger that night. As he trained me, I understood he wanted to make certain I'd never make a similar mistake.

*****

RALPH RYAN

ABC Lightning, Sierra National Forest
July 17, 1976

Four days after leaving the San Bernardino fire, I'm sitting in the
gunner's seat as Dusty flew us up the backbone of the Sierras.
We'd been assigned to assist in fighting numerous small
lightning fires sparked by a passing storm in the national forest
of the same name. Crossing over the Grapevine Mountains, the
landscape changed abruptly from high desert to magnificent
forests. Timber stretched beyond sight and granite peaks
shimmered in the sun like diamonds.

The ship hovered over a barely visible wisp of smoke and I
saw a small fire burning slowly by the base of a tree. Harold
looked at me and said, "It's your fire, who do you want?"

I had Dusty drop Joe and I off on a ridge top a mile up-
slope. By the time we hiked down, the trees had long shadows as
darkness approached. We broke a light sweat putting the fire out,
and Joe began to shiver in the cool night air. "Guess we need to
start a fire," he laughed as he gathering twigs and rekindled the
fire.

Once our warming fire had a good base of coals, I cut a
little bench at the base of a tree, stuck my can of beef stew in the
embers, and stretched out. With a long sigh of contentment, I
said, "It doesn't get any better than this, huh, Butterball!"

"I beg to differ, what could be better than sitting in front of
a water truck raking in the big bucks?"

"Still grinding on that?"

"Just think about it. Big money, no work, what's better
than that?"

"First of all, it takes money to buy a truck. Money we don't
have."

Joe stood before the fire and warmed his hands. "There's
this thing called a loan, you know."

"A loan? How are you going to pay it off if a fire season
fizzles out? Besides, I want to jump."

"Still stuck on that fantasy? They didn't take you this year,
what makes you think they ever will?"

"A man has to have a goal, keep faith in it, and pursue it to
the end."

"Yeah, yeah," he laughed. "How many years are you going
to keep the faith?"

"Until the end," I told him.

"Good luck with that," he said. "Me? I'm getting a water truck."

He looked at me strangely. I said, "What's that look for?"

He kept staring and blurted out, "What you really need Ry, is to forget about jumping from planes and settle down with that beautiful wife of yours and make some babies."

"Ha, ha," I grumbled sarcastically.

The following days of fighting lightning fires on the Sierras weren't as pleasant as it should've been. Joe had filled my mind with doubt. I knew he meant no harm; he just wanted to cast some reality onto my lofty plan. But could he be right? Might I never hear from the smokejumpers?

*****

Harold and John continued to push and train me. As fire season headed into fall and quieted down, I immersed myself in firefighting manuals. A call came in from the Los Padres National Forest, our sister forest to the north, to assist with a series of small lightning fires. We buckled into the ship. Not long into the flight, the helicopter began to shudder, a violent vibration developed and around the cabin, fear blanched my crewmates' faces. I saw Dusty in the cockpit fighting with the control stick, my hands gripped the edge of my seat with such force I thought I'd break it.

The high-pitched whine of the turbine faded into an eerie silence followed by the dull sound of rotor blades slicing through air without power. I started sweating, my muscles tightened to the point of hurting. Dusty had briefly discussed the concept of auto rotation during our first helicopter training sessions, but said it to be so unlikely that I didn't pay much attention except to note his final comment: 'Under the right circumstances, a pilot can land a powerless helicopter.'

As we glided toward the ground, that didn't give me any comfort. Dusty struggled with the controls like a kid fighting a pinball machine. Voices around me yelled out impact warnings, everybody grabbed onto whatever they could.

The helicopter slammed down, bounced once like a basketball and came to a stop, silence filled the cabin. My strangle hold on the seat relaxed as Dusty yelled out, "Son of a goddamn bitch!"

I looked out the window. Dusty had put us down in a meadow next to a highway. He radioed our support vehicle, practically shouting, "Get out here ASAP! We have a fuel problem. We're off Highway 33."

Waiting by the side of the highway for the support vehicle, we appeared to be a somber bunch. Dusty, on the other hand, walked around, joking and laughing as if our crash landing had been no big deal. I knew he'd seen worse in Vietnam, could sense he wanted to show us how to cope with such a frightening event. He told us, "You have to let it go guys otherwise it will gnaw you to death every time you're in the air." The support vehicle arrived and within an hour, the mechanics said we were safe and ready to fly. Nevertheless, the question that sobered me, '*Am I?*'

It wasn't easy getting back in that helicopter, but once I did, something dawned on me. Adrenaline! That's why I do it. The adrenaline rushes had gotten to the point where I knew I'd become an addict.

*****

Fire season ended shortly after and I spent the winter working in our forest's tree plantations, removing brush, burning slash piles, as well as painting out buildings and building trails on the Saugus Ranger District. I know I talked too much about smokejumping throughout the winter, but I had a mission. Unfortunately, though, Sarah didn't share my vision, and after many comments along the lines of, "When are you going to consider getting a real job and forget this nonsense of jumping out of planes?" I began keeping my thoughts to myself.

By spring, restlessness dominated me. My internal clock reared its ugly head telling me it's time to shuffle on, the result of being a military brat, where permanency wasn't allowed. But to where? My options seemed limited and having someone with me to worry about felt awkward. Every time my dad announced that we'd soon be shipping out, I'd start distancing myself from my friends. I never had the chance to know commitment to someone else. I developed a callused core around my heart.

Would I be able to hang onto Sarah? Would she get fed up and disappear? I'd never faced questions like this before. Though Humboldt State had accepted me for their Forestry Program, I decided to hold off on making a decision until I heard from the smokejumpers. By March of 1977, the suspense drove me crazy. I picked up the phone and dialed their number.

"Sorry, Mr. Ryan," the smokejumper told me. "We've already selected our candidates for the season." This devastated me. I contacted Humboldt State and registered for the fall semester, which allowed me to work one more fire season to earn the money I'd need to move us. I did my best to hide my disappointment from the crew. Even Joe toned down his teasing for a change.

Returning from the field on May 1, Harold met me and said, "The smokejumpers left a message for you to call."

I tried to read his expression, but he just pointed to his phone and left the office. As I dialed the number, my knees went weak, and I slumped into Harold's chair. I identified myself to the guy who answered the phone, he put me on hold. At last, a friendly voice said, "Mr. Ryan? I'm Gramps, operations foreman. I have some good news for you. Six of our new candidates washed out. We're organizing a second new-man training session and if you can be here by May 6th, we'll give you a shot."

I leapt out of Harold's chair. "I'll be there! I'm on my way!" I ran out of Harold's office yelling to everyone, "I'm going to Redding! I'm going to Redding!"

CHAPTER 4

Pogues

Northern California Service Center
Smokejumper Unit, Shasta-Trinity National Forest
May 1977

I rushed into our house excited. "Sarah!" I yelled. "We're going to Redding! The smokejumpers are giving me a chance!"

She looked up from the dishes in shock. *"The smokejumpers?"*

I grabbed her, pulled her close. "Yeah, baby! We have to be in Redding by the 6th!"

She eyed me suspiciously. "I thought they didn't want you?" She pushed me off, had a funny look on her face. "Where are we going to stay? What about our stuff? How can we get all this done in five days?"

My excitement and Sarah's confusion needed leveling out. The first glass of wine took the edge off. By the third, I had the plan all set. "Baby," I begged her, "tomorrow I'll say good-bye to the crew and rent a storage shed. We don't have much stuff. If my brother wants to stay here, that would solve the landlord problem. We'll drive up to Sacramento and you can stay at my parents' while I go through training. If I make it, we'll move up to Redding after the fire season. If I don't, we'll stick to the Humboldt plan." Sarah's eyes widened at the mention of my parents. I quickly added, "You'll have the truck. I'll send money."

She stared at me with her signature 'You've got to be fucking kidding me' look. "Come on," I pleaded. "It's the only way. There's not enough time to find an apartment up there. The training's intense; I'll need to be focused."

"Don't you think you should check with your parents first?" She asked. Then added in a quieter voice, "And maybe with me, too?"

"This is a chance of a lifetime! Of course they'll agree."

With icy words, she said, "Everything's always about you! What about me?"

Now I became pissed. "What about you? You're the one who wanted to get married so you wouldn't have to move to Alabama! Isn't that enough?" I paced the kitchen feeling rage. "We followed our dads all over the world. I never bitched about leaving friends behind, at least not in front of my dad. What's so different now? You knew I fought fire when we met. You know I want to be a smokejumper. Why can't you just be fucking happy for me for a change?"

She shouted, "We're not in the military anymore!"

"Well think again," I shouted back. "This is damn close." The same old fight we always had, how often I'm away, how my plans directed our lives. Well, we had discussed her plans, which centered on children, but she had a rare blood type that would require expensive procedures for her to conceive, I felt ambivalent about it, and we fought often about that, too. Now, she turned on her heels and stormed down the hall. When I heard the bedroom door slam, I grabbed my .22 rifle, went outside, looked up into the sky and pleaded with 'Big Ernie,' the mythical fire god firefighters prayed to in times of need, "Talk to her, will you? With or without her, I'm going to Redding. I hope that it's with her. I want this so bad! What else am I supposed to do?" I heard no answer. I looked at Duke sitting at my feet and said, "Come on! I need to shoot something!"

*****

I said goodbye to my crew the following day. Harold hugged me so tight I thought he'd break my ribs. He was over the moon for me, I'd never seen him so happy, and it filled me with pride. John hugged me, too, saying, "Show them what you've shown us and you'll do just fine, Ryan." The last to say good-bye; my buddy Butterball. Joe and his wife were our friends. We'd barbecued and camped together many times, and had partied together just the night before. He pulled me into a bear hug and said, "Sorry for all the ribbing, Ralph. I knew this day would come. I fought it because we're best friends. We're going to miss you. I'm going to miss you. Be an animal up there, okay? Show those damn jumpers what 7-Charlie is made of."

"I hope you get that water truck, Butterball."

"Me, too!" he laughed.

I'd been through farewells like this many times as a military brat and it never became easy. As I left the Valyermo Work Center for the last time, sadness overcame me at leaving so many friends behind, but at the same moment, the excitement over the unknown trumped my sadness.

*****

Sarah and I hit the road to Sacramento that Friday morning. Her silent treatment drove me crazy. Every time I looked at her or tried to make conversation, she'd clam up. The weekend at my parents' didn't fare well either. Sarah appeared unhappy, though my parents had no problem having her stay with them, they did have a problem with me jumping out of planes. They cornered me at every turn: "Do you have a death wish?" "Are you out of your mind?" "Do you even know what the hell you're doing?" My siblings came over and did that, too.

I had to remind them about our near misses as a family. "What's so different than screeching down the Swiss Alps without brakes, or the fire in Germany, or almost rolling off the Grand Canyon, or the bears in Yellowstone? Talk about danger!"

On Sunday, my dad, Sarah, and I drove the three hours north on I-5 to Redding, home of the California Smokejumpers. As we pulled into the Northern California Service Center, my dream seemed finally at hand. I gave them a quick goodbye, hoisted my gunnysack, took a deep breath, and walked in. Now the journey belonged to me alone, the way I wanted it.

I hoofed past a research center, a softball field, and the smokejumper-training units. The door to a six-story parachute-drying tower was open and thinking the office might be close by, I walked in. Dozens of orange and white parachutes hung from the ceiling as if a squad of Green Berets had just come back from a mission. The smell of nylon strong in the air. A muscular, shirtless man suddenly emerged from between two parachutes. He barked, "Can I help you?"

"I'm here for the new-man training."

"Oh, the next group?" he sneered. "Hope you guys have better luck than the last wimps." He eyed me hard and said, "You know what a wimp is?" Before I said a word, he explained, "It's a Weak Incompetent Malingering Pussy! We'll see how many we have this time, won't we?"

I didn't have any words to say to him. John had warned me before I'd left, 'They'll get in your head any way they can. Don't react and give a hundred percent.' Still, could I really survive in a place this hostile? The guy grinned, said with a chuckle, "I'm just kidding. The office is out that door to the left."

In the office, a lanky man in a Forest Service uniform stood from his desk and greeted me with a handshake. I introduced myself.

"Glad you made it Ryan. I'm Gary, operations foreman. Let's keep this simple: be ready to take the physical fitness test tomorrow at 0800 hour. If you pass, you move on, if you fail, you go home. Since this is the second training group and we're already into fire season, the schedule will be faster than normal. If you pass the PT test, be prepared for long, hot days on the units. Any questions?"

"No sir!"

"Welcome aboard. I'll get someone to show you the barracks."

*****

They put me in a barracks room with a guy named Wally, one of the lucky trainees from the first group who'd made the cut. With short hair and clean shaved, he appeared a rarity among wildland firefighters. In a quiet, soft-spoken voice he said to me, "Don't worry about the hostile attitude. They make it a point to be hard-asses with the 'pogues.' Any one of you could be gone at any time, so they prefer not to develop relationships. Once you become 'bona fide,' you can buy a smokejumper T-shirt and say you're a jumper. But first, you have to complete the unit training, six training jumps, the dreaded seventh jump into timber, and a fire jump. You'd better get yourself ready for tomorrow, Ryan. They'll send you packing if you don't pass the PT test."

I had all night for the enormity of where I'm at settle in. I slipped in and out of restless sleep. The morning would be my day of reckoning.

*****

At 0800 hour, six of us new pogues—a term borrowed from the Navy and used by the Redding Smokejumpers as a mocking name for trainees—stood nervously in the operations building. Veteran jumpers milled around in shorts and running shoes, all in top physical condition, chiseled, physically intimidating. After roll call, the instructor said to us, "Let's do this."

We followed him to an exercise yard beside the barracks. "This is how it's going to work," he explained. "For the pull-ups, your chin must be above the bar to count, and you must totally extend your arms before each pull. Your chest must touch the instructors' fist on the ground for the push-ups to count, and your sit-ups must pass 45 degrees and finish flat. We'll start with push-ups." We lined out in front of our trainers as they positioned their fists on the ground. "You have five minutes to do 25, starting now," the instructor shouted. I looked directly into a hard set of beady eyes as I quickly counted off each push-up. I did 30, just for measure. The other five pogues made it, too. We paced around a minute, and the instructor shouted, "Sit-ups! Grab a spot. Ready, go!"

I did 60, adding a few extra. I hopped to my feet thinking, 'This ain't so bad.' After all, I'd been practicing 100 at a time.

"Pull-ups!" We hustled to the bars. I quickly pumped out the required seven, another easy test for me. I watched as one of my pogue brothers struggled with his last one. "Pull! Pull!" I and the other trainees shouted as he barely stretched his chin above the bar. We all patted him on the back and I felt a bond developing amongst us.

The instructor broke us up. "You have five minutes to get ready for the run."

We jogged to the tarmac, where a group of veterans eyed us and laughed about placing bets, I felt like we were sheep headed to the slaughter. I stretched while trying to calm the churning in my stomach. I had no idea where the 1.5-mile course went, and when some of the veterans lined up on the starting mark, I knew the time had arrived. The instructor shouted, "On your mark! Get set! Go!"

One of the vets took off like a jackrabbit. I didn't know whether to pace myself or try to keep up with him, maybe that's what he wanted us to do. I didn't practice against a clock while training and decided to keep with the pack. At the halfway point, a jumper with a stopwatch yelled out our times. 'I'm doing fine.' The jackrabbit vet had disappeared long ago and when I crossed the finish line with the others, well under the 11-minute limit. Even before we could catch our breath, the instructor shouted, "Better than the last wimps! Get into your firefighting clothes and meet me in the training room ASAP!"

In the training room, the instructor finally introduced himself. "I'm Mark; I'll be one of your trainers. Since the first group washed out and we're running out of time, we're going to cram a lot into your little brains over the next four weeks. The faster you get the training down, the better." He paused, looked us over intently before continuing, "In order to become a California Smokejumper, you'll need to show us you can do all the standard airplane exits, as well as identify parachute malfunctions and react to them properly. You'll have to execute landing rolls, which we call PLF's. You'll learn parachute theory and how to maneuver safely and efficiently. In the event you hang up in a tree, you'll demonstrate the letdown procedure, as well as the ability to climb trees to retrieve chutes, cargo, and injured jumpers. We'll teach you all of this on the training units."

Another jumper poked his head into the room and said, "We're ready, Mark."

Mark told us, "Before you hit the units, you're going on a little hike." He grinned, and said, "For three miles." His grin widened, "with 110 pounds on your back." He led us into the warehouse in front of an industrial scale. On the floor around it were jump suits, parachutes, hand tools, chainsaws, and six large packs. Mark nodded at one of the smokejumpers standing there and said, "They're all yours, 'Disco.'"

A stout man with glasses stepped on the scale. He weighed himself, laughed and said, "Shiiiiit." He paced around us, pouring off energy. "Listen up," he shouted. "You're not a real smokejumper until you've done a 'pack-out'. I prefer pack-outs to be long and in places like the Feather River Canyon or Wooly Creek." The veterans around us snickered at the inside joke. Disco went on, "There's nothing like a 10-mile pack-out with 110-pounds on your back, in the rain, up canyons, down canyons, and a blister on your toe. Everything we drop on fires, we bring back. I'm going to show you how to load your packs for comfort, if there is such a thing on a pack-out."

He began with the jump suit. "I put my suit in first with the padding against the back of the pack. This way nothing is poking you when you're carrying it. Next, I stuff in the main parachute, followed by the reserve. I like to put the heavier stuff toward the top so the weight is on my shoulders. The harness, helmet, personal gear bag go in next. I keep water and food on top for easy access. In Montana, Washington, and Idaho, it's not uncommon to pack-out for days."

I grabbed a pack, spent a few minutes arranging my gear in it, and stood it up. It looked four-feet tall. He showed us how to strap the hand tools to the outside of the pack and struggled to lift it on the scale. "Only 98 pounds, pogue," he chuckled and added a stripped down chainsaw. Now, it tipped the scale just over 115 pounds.

With our packs ready, Disco stood his up and sat on the floor with his back to it. "This is the easiest way to get up," he said as he slipped his arms into the shoulder straps, leaned forward onto his hands and knees, and slowly stood up. He secured the waist strap and said, "You pogues ready?"

After we'd all managed to stand with our packs on, he dropped his to the floor. "Sorry," he winked, "like hell if I'm going with you!" Another veteran stepped forward and said, "I'm Rob, I'll be your guide. The course is three miles on flat ground. You have 45 minutes to complete the test, fail and you're out. Let's go before it gets too hot."

Rob hurried off toward the end of the runway and we followed him like a litter of puppies. Even for how much it weighed, my pack felt comfortable, and by the time I broke a sweat, I'd entered a calm mental zone. My only goal, keep up with Rob. I didn't take my eyes off him once, and when he started running, I did too. Before I knew it, I crossed the finish line.

With the pack off, my body felt weightless, if there'd been a basketball hoop in front of me, I bet I could've dunked NBA fashion. When the last pogue crossed the line, a different instructor barked, "Leave the packs and report to the suit-up room!"

The suit-up room had cubicles surrounding a central dressing area; each smokejumper had one to hang his jump suit in and a small locker for personal items. On the floor sat six suits. The instructor barked, "These suits were designed 38 years ago for tree landings and slamming into the ground, and they haven't changed much since." He picked up a pair of pants and smacked the heavy padding. "It's Kevlar, the stuff they use in bullet proof vests. The jacket has a high collar to protect your neck and the helmet is made of hard plastic with a mesh face guard. Suit-up," he yelled, "pants first."

Just as I slipped the pant straps over my shoulder and pulled the zippers up to close them, the instructor came up to me and kicked me in the groin. Of course, I flinched, but a strap of webbing sewn from the foot straps, up either side, and around the crotch stopped his boot from making contact. "As you can see," he chuckled, looking around at the rest of the pogues, "if Ryan here crashes through a tree and straddles a few branches on his way down, for better or worse," he laughed. "He'll still be able to reproduce."

Once in our jackets, he picked up a harness. "This is the H-4. It's made of heavy-duty nylon with eight points of adjustment. This is the link between you and your parachute. Your life depends on it; get it snug on your back."

As we tightened the straps, veterans checked our harnesses, the tension made it difficult to stand up straight. The instructor picked up a coiled rope with a friction device attached to the rope for sliding down during a let-down. They called it a Sky Genie. "See how nice this coil looks? We call it a 'bird's nest.' You'll learn how to coil your 150 foot letdown rope so that when you drop it to the ground from a tree, it will unravel all the way without knotting. The only place that uses a longer rope is the North Cascades base in Washington State, they use 250 foot ropes. If you ever hang up in their monster timber, you'll understand why. The coil goes in a leg pocket, doesn't matter which one. The other leg pocket will hold your hardhat, first aid kit, map case, and radio if you're the fire boss. The draw strings close the top so nothing falls out during your jump." He gave us each a small backpack. "These are your personal gear bags, PG bags from now on. They attach to your harness below your reserve. You can pack whatever you want in them, but I recommend a change of socks, foot powder, Visine, and a toothbrush for starters. You'll figure out your individual needs after you start jumping fires. All right, you each have a locker, stow your gear and meet in the training room in five minutes."

*****

The table in the training room had six stacks of handouts. I grabbed a set and leafed through it in my seat until two men walked in. One sported a plaid shirt and jeans, the other wore fire clothes. The guy in fire clothes pointed to the man in jeans and said, "This is our base manager, Dick Tracy." He started his jumping career in Missoula in 1953, the year I was born. Tracy reminded me of my dad; small framed, always had something going on, and served in the Korean War at the same time. The smell of cigarette smoke swirled off him as he addressed us. "We have a respected program here and a fine group of jumpers. They'll train you well. Welcome aboard men, I'll leave you in their hands."

The guy in the fire clothes is Gary 'Gramps' Johnson, a nickname he'd earned from being the oldest pogue in his class, the one who'd told me over the phone that I'd been accepted. I began to notice that the smokejumpers were strong on nicknames. On the Flat Fire, I met Craig 'Pigpen' Irvine. Here I met Larry 'Disco Duck' Hartgrave. Other names I'd heard the trainers toss around included, Dick 'Hurricane' Tracy, Richard 'Vise' Linebarger, Bob 'Hairhat' Harris, Rob 'Squirrely' Early, Mike 'Buffalo' Neilson, and Dave 'Boy' Nani. I wondered what they'd call me.

Gramps said, deadly serious, "We want you fire ready by the first week of June, less than a month away. It all depends on how fast you absorb the training and how well you work as a team. After today, you'll begin every morning on the training units, every afternoon in the classroom. As I bet you've noticed, we're having an unusually hot spring. We've had a few years of drought up here, this year is no different. You know what that means, a severe fire season's on the way. As soon as you're trained, you'll be on the jump list and fighting fires."

Gramps left and a hard-nosed statue of a man came in and stared us down. He began: "We have a lot to cover, let's get started. Today, you'll learn the fundamentals of exiting an aircraft and the parachute-landing roll. But first, you'll need to know the duties of the spotter." The instructor walked around as he spoke, slapping his hand with a bundle of different colored crepe paper rolls. "The spotter will either be a foreman, squad leader, or a squad leader-in-training. He's in charge of the tactical operations in the plane. He picks the jump spot, determines the exit point with these streamers, and communicates with the pilot during the jumps. After the jumpers are safely on the ground, he'll drop the cargo with the help of an assistant."

The instructor raised his arm and let the streamers unravel. "These are essential to what we do. They're twenty-feet long, ten-inches wide, and at the bottom is a small metal weight. They're orange, yellow, and red so they're easy to spot from the plane. Some engineer designed them to simulate the descent rate of an average jumper. The first set is dropped over the desired landing spot and the plane circles until they land. The spotter notes how far they drift downwind, he'll then give the pilot alignment instructions and release the second set. If they land close to the spot, that'll be the exit point. The goal here is to get you from the plane to the landing spot as precisely as possible. You pogues following me?"

The instructor must've noticed our confused looks. Before any of us could answer, he drew the streamer sequence on the chalkboard. He moved from the board and shouted, "Okay," diverting our attention to him. "Let's assume—and I'll emphasize that this is the only time we're going to assume anything, because in this business if you assume something and you're wrong, you're dead—let's assume the exit point has been established through the streamer process. The spotter will indicate with his fingers how many jumpers he wants in the first stick. A stick can be one jumper or it can be the whole planeload, but normally it's going to be two men." He stopped talking and stared us over. "Whenever you're in a plane and suited up, you will—I repeat—you *will* cover your reserve parachute ripcord handle with a hand at all times. The reason is simple; we're flying over 100 miles-per-hour with no door. This creates a vacuum in the cabin. We crawl around in close quarters; therefore, the chance of a ripcord handle being caught on something is very real. If a reserve deploys in the cabin, it will be sucked out the door within seconds. If this happens to you, you will first attempt to wrap the chute up. If that fails and it starts going out the door, follow it, because if you don't, it will pull you out through whatever part of the plane that gets in your way." He gave us a moment to take

33

that in. "Out at the jump tower, we'll be watching you. If you don't cover that handle, you'll do push-ups until it becomes an automatic response. Are we clear?"

We all nodded.

"Now, the spotter will flash how many jumpers he wants in the first stick. The type of plane you're jumping from will determine the type of exit you'll do. In DC-3s and Caribous, you'll do a standup. For medium sized planes, it's a step. The sit down exit is for smaller planes. I'll explain how to do these on the units. I'm turning this over to Ed 'Fast Eddie' Strong now. He's our resident expert on parachute malfunctions."

Shorter than most of the jumpers and with a thick mustache, Fast Eddie looked like Yosemite Sam. He flashed a smile, the only trainer so far to offer us even the hint of one. "Okay, pogues," he said, "when we're out on the training units and you exit the tower, we'll want you to yell out the jump count. It takes roughly four seconds for a parachute to fully deploy. The count will go as follows: 'Jump one-thousand, jump two-thousand, jump three-thousand, and jump four-thousand.' If your chute isn't open by four-thousand, you'll likely have a malfunction or a slow opening. We'll expect you to look up at your canopy and check; it's the only way to know."

Fast Eddie crouched in front of us and spread his arms out. He said, "Imagine I'm in the door with my hands gripping the sides. I'm looking at the horizon. The spotter will slap me on the left shoulder, that's the signal to exit the plane. I'll push myself from the step with my left foot, while my arms shove me from the door. Once I'm clear and falling, I'll wrap my arms around my reserve chute, keep my legs together, and start the count."

He tucked into the falling position and did the count. After four-thousand, he looked up. "I'm checking the canopy and suspension lines. Believe me; you won't know you have a malfunction unless you actually see it. If you don't look up on the units, you'll do push-ups." He lowered his head. "When you go out the door, you'll be in a state of suspended animation. You won't feel like you're falling. If you have a shitty exit and start spinning from the propeller blast, you won't feel it until your chute opens. The first few times you jump, everything will be a blur, but we'll still expect you to look up to check your canopy. Right guys?"

A chorus of 'Right' made him smile.

"If you look up and see twists in your suspension lines what do you do?" None of us had a clue. He yelled, "You check your canopy! Always check your canopy! Twists in the lines aren't a malfunction, but they can divert your attention from the canopy, where you might have one. If your canopy has safely inflated, you can start untwisting by reaching up and pulling the risers apart while scissor-kicking in the opposite direction." Fast Eddie glanced at the other instructors standing at the side of the room and asked. "Anybody wants to bet at least one of these dumb pogues'll get twisted up just jumping from the tower and forget to check their canopies."

"Count me in!" one of the instructors fired back. "I only bet on sure things."

Fast Eddie went on. "Now, let's get to some real malfunctions. Say you exit the plane and you feel yourself being bounced against the fuselage. For some reason, your parachute didn't deploy. We call this, 'Jumper-In-Tow.' It's serious, especially if you're knocked unconscious. If you *are* conscious, signal it by putting your hands on top of your helmet and get ready for the ride of your life because the spotter will cut your static line and you'll start your free-fall from 1500 feet."

One of my pogues brothers asked sheepishly, "What if we're unconscious?"

Fast Eddie laughed. "Then you won't feel the impact, will you?" He let the comment settle in before saying, "Let's move on. Say you exit, do your count, and look up to see your canopy streaming above you, unable to inflate. This is most likely due to a rigging error. Our riggers are the best in the business and we pack chutes by the book, but it wouldn't hurt to always be on a rigger's good side, if you know what I mean." He grinned, grew serious again. "The only thing you can do to save yourself during a 'Streamer' is to deploy your reserve. Turn your head to the right, drop your left hand to your side, and yank the ripcord with your right hand. The reserve has a spring-loaded pilot chute that will pull it from the container. If the reserve gets caught in the garbage above you, pull it into a bundle, toss it out as far as you can, and pray to Big Ernie it inflates."

Another pogue raised his hand. "I've heard you're supposed to cut-away from the main before pulling the reserve."

"So," Fast Eddie asked leaning toward him, "you have skydiving experience?"

"No sir, a friend of mine does."

"Well, I bet your friend doesn't jump from 1500 feet, now does he? Fifteen-hundred feet is nothing, you don't have time cut away. Even if you did, there wouldn't be enough altitude for the reserve to deploy. We're not skydivers. We're smokejumpers. If you know any other skydiving techniques, forget them. They'll only get you into trouble here.

"Now the 'Inversion' malfunction," Fast Eddie said, "happens during the last stage of deployment. For a split second, the chute will breathe, or invert. It should regain its normal shape, but may continue to invert until it inflates inside out. This isn't a serious malfunction, but you have to remember to steer opposite. To turn left, you'll have to pull the right toggle, to turn right, pull the left."

He checked his wristwatch. "All right, pogues, this last malfunction is my favorite, I experienced it myself not too long ago. You've all heard of the actress, 'Mae West', right?" He mimed a huge set of cans to emphasize his point. "Mae West has been honored by parachutist with a malfunction. If a suspension line crosses the canopy during deployment, the canopy will like a pair of tits when it inflates. That's a 'Mae West.' With this malfunction, the chute is spilling air and your descent rate is dangerously accelerated. First, try to clear the line by yanking on it a few times. If that doesn't work, you'll have to deploy your reserve."

I raised my hand. "What did it feel like when you had your Mae West?"

He grew thoughtful. "To say I wasn't scared would be a lie. But my training kicked in, and the rest came natural. We're preparing you for worst-case scenarios, so you'll be ready for anything. No matter what," he strongly emphasized, "you'll have to have your wits about you up there. All right," he said looking at his watch, "I have one more thing to cover before you get a break. Visualize you're flying under a perfect canopy, but for some reason you're heading straight for another jumper. What do you do?"

A pogue named Bill said quickly, "Turn out of the way?"

"That's right," Eddie said. "If you're headed for a midair collision, each jumper should execute a hard right turn. If it's too late and you see a solid mass of nylon coming at you, spread out your arms and legs, most times, you'll bounce right off. You can also try running over the top of the other jumper's canopy if you're near the top of his chute, there should be enough pressure in it to do that. The bottom line is, be aware of your surroundings, be ready to react, and always be prepared for the unexpected."

*****

Fast Eddie led us outside on the tarmac, where we gathered around the door of the plane. He set up in the door positioning his left leg on the step and his right leg under his butt. He grasped the sides of the door and stared straight ahead. "This is how we'll expect you to look when you're doing the 'step exit' on the training tower tomorrow." He pushed himself from the plane and went into a tuck, his hands crossing over his stomach and his legs pressed tightly together, before he rolled gently on the tarmac.

He hopped up and patted the fuselage. "This is 'Jumper 1'. We use two of these DeHaviland Twin Otters during fire season. They're ideal for short runways, carry a ten-man load, fly at low speeds for jumping, and can fly on only one engine if they have to."

We followed him into the cabin, inside, it's hot with barely enough room to move around in; a flying sardine can. Eddie told us, "There are three cargo boxes on each side of the aisle. Each box contains enough food, water, paper sleeping bags, and hand tools for two men to last two days. One box contains the chainsaw. We sit on them during flight. There are no seats, belts, or barf bags. If you have to puke, do it in your helmet." A couple of us laughed. He said, "I'm not kidding! If you puke on the floor or someone else, it might start a chain reaction. There's nothing worse than smelling someone's lunch on a long flight. Any of you pogues get air sick?" Even though I had in the past, I kept my mouth shut. "Thank God," he said. "Anyway, if it's a long flight, the spotter will ride shotgun in the pilot's cabin. When the jumping starts, it's critical to cover your reserve handle at all times, especially during cargo drops, when you'll find yourselves maneuvering the boxes to the door."

He directed our attention to a metal cable running the length of the cabin. "This is the emergency static line cable. If the spotter orders everyone to hook up due to an emergency, you'll fix your static line snap here and follow his instructions." He grabbed another steel cable anchored vertically beside the door. "This is the main static line cable. When ordered, you'll hook your static line snap to the cable, slide the copper pin through the slot, and bend it over to keep your snap from accidentally opening. The spotter will either be lying on the floor or kneeling depending on which plane you're in so he can stick his head out the door to see forward and under the plane to better see the jump spot. His assistant will be monitoring the static lines. When you're in the door, the spotter will be sticking his head out over your lap to see the exit point, you'll have to lean back to give him room. Above all else, you *will* protect your reserve ripcord handle during this stage of the drop."

He pointed to a storage compartment behind the bulkhead of the tail. "In there we keep drift streamers, radios, map cases, a trauma kit, tree climbing gear, and crosscut saws—which we like to call 'misery whips'. If you jump into a wilderness area where gas operated tools are forbidden, you'll learn why they have that name."

He led us out of the plane and across the tarmac to the parachute loft. Before we went in, he warned, "Bob Kersh is the loft foreman. He's been here from day one and is very particular. The guys who work for him are all at least two-year vets, we call them 'loft rats'. Bottom line is, don't get caught in here unless you're invited."

The loft had a military air about it, but what took me aback was the row of sewing machines that lined one wall of the loft, I laughed inwardly seeing in bold letters, 'Smokejumper/Seamstresses.' It seemed to be a contradiction in terms. I remembered watching my mom making our outfits on her little Singer machine as I went outside to play war. I thought it to be a woman's job, not something a man would show interest in, unless he wanted to be labeled a sissy. I looked past the machines to riggers packing parachutes in silence. A serious-looking older man came up to us. "I'm Dave, the assistant loft foreman. I'm going to give you a breakdown of our chutes." Clean-cut and shaven, he had an air about him that signaled importance and authority. He guided us into a high-ceilinged room, at least fifty-feet tall, and said, "This is the parachute-drying tower." He pointed up. "After every jump, you'll hook your parachutes to these ropes, and hoist them up to air out. Each one is thoroughly inspected after hanging and before being cleared for rigging, a job every one of you will do, especially during your first year."

He lowered a parachute to eye level and began a long lecture filled with phrases like modified version of the military T-10, low-speed rated parachute, parabolic design, elliptical TU alterations, D-bag, and pack tray. His technical gibberish overwhelmed me.

We followed him back into the loft. As we watched a rigger packing a chute, Boy described the opening sequence: "The strange thing about the opening shock is that the parachute and jumper come to a virtual standstill. The air around the chute continues to move, causing the chute to breathe, or invert. This is when malfunctions occur. The British have come up with a remedy to 'Mae West' malfunctions by way of anti-inversion netting. We haven't seen it yet, but it's described as a fish-net type of nylon, about a foot and a half wide, and sewn around the bottom of the canopy. A simple fix, but unfortunately," he said with a grin, "Forest Service politics always seems to slow a good thing down. If we're lucky, we might see the retrofit here next year." Just then, a truck horn sounded, and all activity in the loft stopped. Someone yelled, "Maggot wagon!" "Lunch time," Boy said, "be back in an hour."

I bought a sandwich from the pretty girl running the 'maggot wagon' food cart and went back to the barracks for a break. I relaxed on my bed, reviewing the morning's activities. Wally poked his head in the door. "You all right, Ryan?"

"I have a headache. I didn't know jumping out of planes would be so damn complicated."

"What'd you think?" he asked.

"I thought you just crossed your fingers and yelled 'Geronimo'!"

*****

After lunch, I finally saw Pigpen, the jumper from the Flat Fire. He waited for us in the training room with his broad grin. He'd been the first smokejumper I'd ever spoken to, and if he remembered me or how he'd given me advice on applying to the program two years before, I couldn't tell. He gave us a once over before saying, "I'm going to teach you how to steer a parachute. It's not that complicated, but I'll bet at least one of you gets out the door in a perfect exit, only to freeze up when it comes time to flying the chute."

Pigpen shuffle-stepped in front of us as he simulated using the steering toggles. He then drew a cone on the chalkboard—like an ice cream cone—and asked, "How do you determine how fast the wind is blowing, and from what direction?"

"Where the drift streamers land?" Pogue brother Larry said.

"What if you can't follow the streamers? What if the wind changes?" Pigpen pointed to the cone he'd drawn on the board. "This is the 'wind cone', the area you must remain in during your descent in order to land in the designated jump spot. You have to know how fast you're traveling, to do this, put your heels together and spread your feet into a 45-degree angle. Sight down, you'll see the ground moving, and you'll be able to calculate your speed and direction."

He raised his arms to simulate parachuting. Looking down, he laughed and said, "Shit, I'm going backwards!" He tapped the bottom of the cone on the chalkboard. "This is the jump spot. The radius of the cone is the maximum distance you can travel during your descent if you want to land on the spot." He drew a cone that leaned to one side. "This is what your cone looks like on a windy day. A jumper who wanders near the edge runs the risk of missing the spot. You hear me, pogues?"

We all stared at him blankly.

"I know this is difficult to visualize on a chalkboard, but once you're jumping, you'll get it. Okay, now say you're flying in your wind cone and a helicopter comes and hovers directly below you. What do you do then?" He didn't even wait for us to answer. "You pull out your letdown coil and drop it!"

We all looked at each other in confusion. Pogue Larry said, "We're supposed to take down a helicopter and its crew?"

"What if it's you or them? You want to drop into the blades?"

"You want us to kill them?" Larry asked.

"You want to get all sliced up?" Pigpen snickered. He shook his head and muttered, "Dumb ass pogues. All right, let's finish up with water landings. If you're about to land in still water, keep your legs together and prepare to hold your breath. Our jump suits are buoyant. They'll keep you afloat, hopefully long enough for you to paddle to land. If you land in a river, ride the current until you can grab onto something. The most important thing is to keep the suspension lines from wrapping around your neck. Water landings aren't common in California, but in Alaska, you'll get wet. We'll practice this at the college's swimming pool."

CHAPTER 5

The Units

Smokejumper Training Units
Northern California Service Center
May 1977

The first few nights in the barracks, sleep eluded me, my mind reeled with all the information they'd crammed into our heads. Tree landings, water landings, helicopters hovering below us— not to mention the shouting instructors—the intensity of the training added up to nerves and restlessness. I pretended to be asleep when Wally came in late from hanging out with the bros, smelling of beer and fumbling around the dark. It made me long for the training to be over. I'd been so preoccupied with doing well that I didn't bother to call Sarah. Just as well, I thought. Any negative vibes during this stage of the training wouldn't be productive. I expected nothing but flak from her anyway.

One morning toward the end of the first week, the instructors waited for us on the tarmac with smug faces. One of them yelled, "Line out!" We followed him to the training units and through an obstacle course with low-level platforms for practicing exits and landings. After two cycles through it, he ordered us to suit up as fast as we could, and he ran us up the metal ramp to the top of the jump tower where two instructors waited in a simulated airplane fuselage.

The instructors attached risers—sections of webbing where the suspension lines are attach to—to our harnesses. The one they called Don 'Mr. Atlas' Sterrett looked like a professional body builder; he told us in a soft voice, "I'm going to treat this like a real jump. I'll signal how many jumpers—pogues in your case—I want to hook up with my fingers. When I say, get into the door, you'll assume the first and second man positions. When I ask if you're ready, I'll expect you to say 'Yes!' or nod your head. Keep your eyes on the horizon and brace for an exit. When you get the slap on the shoulder, I expect to see a vigorous exit. Forget you're attached to a cable, whatever you do, don't let the bloodstained dirt below concern you. Just make a leap of faith. Are we clear?" We nodded our heads.

Mr. Atlas signaled with two fingers. Larry took the first man position and I assumed the second behind him. Mr. Atlas slapped Larry on the shoulder, and he disappeared out the door, me right after. As I fell, I felt like a rag doll, my feet came apart, my arms reached for the risers above my head and the world spun around me. Buffalo, a bulldog of a Marine, whaled on me before I hit the dirt. "What the fuck is that, Ryan? My little sister can do better than you wimps can. This is going to be a long week if you keep coming out the door like a pile of dog shit."

The next two pogues looked just as pitiful as we had. When they hit the dirt, Buffalo yelled at me, "What are you staring at? Get your butt back up there!" I watched the next stick exit from the top of the tower and could see why he called us 'rag dolls'. Legs swung in all directions, arms flailed, and bodies spun like tops.

Over and over, they made us jump, and by lunchtime, my head pounded and sweat drenched me. Half of us spent the afternoon in the classroom analyzing our exits and landing rolls, while the others practiced on the 'Mutilator,' a cabled device that raised you high in the air and dropped you to the ground to practice the landing rolls. By the weekend, bruises covered my body. Sarah waited for me in the parking lot when they let us out. She watched me get into the pickup gingerly and said, "Feeling worked over, babe?"

What could I say? "I have muscles aching that I didn't even know I had."

"Doesn't sound like you're having much fun."

"They're trying to weed us out, see what we're really made of."

"I know what you're really made of," she said as she drove. "Your family does, too. It wouldn't bother any of us if you ended this crazy obsession. Especially me!"

I couldn't believe what she'd just said. "Crazy obsession? You think this is a crazy obsession?"

"Who else would drop everything on a moment's notice and travel hundreds of miles to a place where they expect you to jump out of a perfectly good airplane into a raging forest fire? I thought your burn-over made you realize you aren't invincible, Ralph? You're acting a little obsessed about this, don't you think?"

"The burn-over focused me," I explained. "I know what I want to do and I'm passionate about it. I feel like my entire life has been building up to this, like it's my destiny."

"Your destiny! What about our destiny? You haven't even called."

What about our destiny. I'd helped her escape Alabama. That alone had felt like more than enough. Now, 'our destiny' made me uncomfortable. I guess I thought things would just flow along between us, the way they did for so many firefighter couples. I had no idea how to give Sarah the kind of commitment she wanted. "Let's drive up to Lake Shasta," I said, sick with the thought of going to my parents' and suffering this same kind of grilling. "There's a nice restaurant overlooking the lake." Sarah nodded and drove us up the freeway in silence.

Three years of drought had left the lake nearly empty, as empty as I felt about 'our destiny'. The view from the restaurant didn't resemble any of the romantic pictures they had on the walls, a parched, red bank descended from the tree line hundreds of feet to a muddy, dying creek below. Nothing pretty to look at there just the angry girl sitting across from me. As we ate dinner, I made a spontaneous suggestion: "Forget my parents. Let's get a hotel for the weekend, check out Redding, take a hike on Mount Shasta. Maybe we could look into the rental market, too."

She instantly perked up and said, "I'd love that, Ralph."

The next day, we drove up to Bunny Flat, the staging area for mountain climbers high on Mt. Shasta, and hiked to Horse Flat, another staging area. We found a secluded stand of Alpine firs and leisurely ate lunch, sharing a bottle of wine. We stretched out on a blanket and listened to the birds chirping happily in the trees as the crisp mountain air bathed over us. A lone cirrus cloud stretched from the peak of the mountain as if caught on it. Relaxing together had eluded us since training and I relished the serenity of being with my girl. I felt so relaxed and at easy that I wanted to talk, something I didn't do enough of. I cuddled up to her and said, "I know this is hard on you, babe, but it'll get better once the training is over. Bear with me, if you can. I know this sounds strange, but I feel like my whole life has been pushing me toward this. Moving all the time has left me in a void. I never had anyone to get close to, only things, and now that we're a couple, I'm kind of overwhelmed."

She caressed my head. "I know what you mean, honey. I often wondered growing up, if I'd ever be able to settle down myself. We're both traveling new ground now and I'm sorry if I'm being emotional. But jumping out of planes is just plain crazy!"

"Want to know how it all started?" I said after some thought.

She whispered, "I'm all ears."

"We were stationed in Ramstein, Germany. My friends and I played war in the forest all the time, and when we watched TV, the only shows the Armed Forces Network aired consisted of "Combat," "Have Gun Will Travel," The Rifleman," and so on. Dad would let me wear his helmet while I cradled my plastic machinegun and cheered our soldiers on. I realized during those times that I wanted to be a Green Beret. The desire never left me until I learned about smokejumping, then that's all I wanted to do."

The look on her face spoke of pity. "I had no idea it went that deep. Damn military! I guess being a girl insulated me from it."

I noticed how beautiful she looked with the mountain behind her. A revelation came to me. "You know, whenever we're in the woods, we get along the best. Remember all the times we went camping on the Angeles?"

She giggled nervously. "How about the times we snuck into the Devils Punchbowl on full moon nights? I never clung onto someone like I did on those nights."

"That's because you were scared to death," I laughed. "To tell you the truth, the hair on my neck always stood on end down there. I loved the way you clung to me." Sarah cuddled into me, kissed me, and we made love on the mountain until exhausted. As the sun began to set, a cold breeze chilled us. "We'd better get going before it gets dark," I said, not wanting to let her go. "How about we get a room in Mt. Shasta, and tomorrow drive to the other volcano in the area."

"Another volcano?"

"Mt. Lassen. It isn't that far."

We climbed to the top of Mt. Lassen, found a secluded spot, and made love on a second volcano in as many days. I relished the accomplishment. "You know babe, we christened the last volcano in the Cascade Mountain Range, and the first volcano in the Sierra Mountain Range. This is worth a lot of salt points."

She cocked her head at me in bewilderment. "Salt points?"

I laughed. "It's a way of measuring feats in the jumper world."

When she said, "Oh," the subject immediately died.

*****

I barely made it to roll call on time the next morning. Sarah drove back to Sacramento and I began the second week of training with a smile on my face. Three days into the week, the six of us pogues executed the exits, landings, and tree letdown procedures well enough to move on. Thursday morning, we boarded a bus with a group of veterans. They wouldn't tell us the destination or what lie ahead for us. We drove west out of town and passed a glittering lake full to the tree line. After seeing the depleted Shasta Lake, I asked, "Why is this lake full and Shasta empty?"

"This is Whiskeytown Lake," Mr. Atlas leaned over his seat and told me. "It's a National Park and mandated to be full by Memorial Day. Shasta Lake waters the farms and cities of the Sacramento Valley, so the gates have to stay open."

As I looked at the lake, I knew where I'd be spending my spare time. Soon, we began the steep, winding climb up Buckhorn Mountain. Just before the summit, the bus turned onto a dirt logging road, and after a short, bumpy ride, we pulled to a stop in big timber.

The instructors set six boxes in a clearing surrounded on all sides by huge fir and pine trees. Buster 'Bionic Buster' Klein— reported to be a real 'monkey in a tree' by the other vets—opened a box. "This is tree climbing gear. If your cargo hangs up, you have to go get it. The spurs here have two-inch gaffs, long enough to penetrate Redwood bark." Bionic Buster showed us how to secure the spurs to our boots and the harness to our bodies. He took a long, thick rope and explained, "This is the throw rope. It's made of hemp and has a steel cable inside to prevent you from accidentally cutting through it with your hand saw." He picked up a nylon strap with an adjustable buckle. "This is the limb-over belt. When there are too many branches to cut through, you can throw this over a limb and navigate up to it." The final piece of equipment is a folding Fanno saw. He attached it to his harness, walked to the base of a large pine, and swung his throw rope around the trunk. Pulling with one arm and pushing with the other arm, he flipped the rope in a smooth rhythm as he spiked up the tree. When he reached large live branches, he quickly showed us how to do a limb-over, and came down.

"Each of you will have an instructor. Grab a box and pick a tree."

I grabbed a box and headed for a tall fir. Harold had already taught me how to use climbers, so I strapped the spurs and harness on quickly, and before my instructor knew, I had the throw rope around the tree, and scaled it like a veteran. I cut the lower dead branches with the Fanno saw until I reached the living canopy. The voices below faded away, and all I heard, the wind singing through the needles. I kept climbing until the branches became so small they strained under my weight, and the treetop swayed like a wand in the wind. I inhaled a sweet cocktail of pine and cedar as little birds landed nearby, and the silver peaks of the Trinity Alps sparkled in the distance. I stood at the top of a serene, beautiful world, and didn't have to share it with anyone. Suddenly, a shout broke my reverie, "What the hell are you doing up there, Ryan? Sleeping?"

"On my way down!" I yelled back.

When I touched ground, Bionic Buster came over and told me there'd be plenty of opportunities for guys like me. Requests came in regularly to the jumpers to do hazard reduction in campgrounds, collecting pinecones and foliar samples for research, and construction of osprey platforms. I liked hanging in the trees and Buster guaranteed me that I'd get the opportunity to climb regardless—for parachutes, cargo boxes, and if necessary injured jumpers.

From the trees, we headed to Shasta College's pool for water landing training. To my detriment, water and I didn't have a love for one another. I almost drowned in the Merced River while on a family vacation to Yosemite National Park. My brother and I decided to swim in the Merced River, neither of us knowing how cold it would be. My body had gone numb and my brother had pulled me ashore by my hair and saved my life.

Now standing on the Shasta College pool's high diving board and looking down on the element I feared most, the bulky jump suit I had on didn't bring me any comfort at all. When the instructors ordered me to jump, I just stood there staring down. They'd said the suits were buoyant, at least for a little while, but for how long? I wrestled within myself to just do it, but I must've been taking too long. They started yelling at me, so I took a deep breath, closed my eyes, and stepped off, I fell fast and frightened. I went all the way to the bottom of the pool, and before I panicked, I shot to the surface. Air bubbles boiled up through the Kevlar material and I heard a voice say, "Swim over here, Ryan."

I backstroked to the side of the pool, where two instructors in swimming trunks dove and covered me with a parachute. Another voice ordered, "Pull the canopy over your head and watch for suspension lines." Suspension lines caught on everything: the reserve parachute, my harness, the collar of my suit. As I struggled, I felt my suit getting heavier and lower in the water, and I started thrashing like a catfish in a net. Still covered in nylon, I heard, "Don't panic, Ryan! That's how you get in trouble. Focus on clearing those lines. We won't let you drown."

I made myself calm down and slowly worked the canopy and suspension lines over my head. With all the lines and canopy clear, it took two instructors to help me up the ladder and out of the pool. I knew from then on, if I had the choice, I'd take a tree landing over water landings every time.

CHAPTER 6

Hook Up

Birkland's Jump Spot
Pine Grove, California
June 1977

A note on the jump list board in the marshaling area read, 'June 8—*pogues' first jump.*' My pogue brothers and I had breezed through the boot camp part of training in four weeks, two weeks faster than usual, and no one had washed out. We'd wanted it more than the group before us since we'd all been passed over to begin with. The day before our jump, we reviewed all the required protocols from moving around inside the plane, the static line hook-up procedure, exits and rolls, to protecting the reserve parachute handle. "Eyes on the horizon," Fast Eddie said pacing the classroom. "Hands set, feet set, when the slap comes, I want a vigorous push-off. Remember your four-second count, then look up and check the canopy. Right guys?"

"RIGHT!"

All day, the veterans dogged us: "Who's going to sneak away before morning?"

"I'll bet one of you pogues freezes up in the door."

"Who do you think'll land in the trees?" Anxiety set in and I tossed and turned all night reviewing their comments.

Roll call produced six nervous pogues, no one had snuck away. I'm number five on the jump list. Two vets would be on the first stick to show us what exits are supposed to look like, I'd be first out on the third stick. The ground vehicles headed for Pine Grove, ten miles north of the airport, with video equipment, while our final briefing took place before suiting up.

Veterans circled us like vultures, devious looks in their eyes. With our suits and harnesses on, they moved in to help with securing our parachutes—our very lives. They joked, "Oh no, Disco Duck packed this chute!"

Another said, "Man, he was hung over that morning. Hope he didn't pack a malfunction into it!"

"Hey, remember the pogue that freaked out in mid-air and flew so far from the spot we had to send a truck after him?"

Blocking them out, I concentrated on the sound of the risers mating with the capewells—two clicks that guaranteed everything locked in place. This mating system just didn't seem foolproof enough to me, I'd been having waking nightmares of my parachute opening and the capewells popping loose, sending me into free fall all the way to the ground.

"Hey, what's this?" a veteran said loudly as he helped my pogue brother Bill. I look over to see him pulling parachute material from Bill's deployment bag. "Oh shit," the vet said and quickly stuck the material in his pocket. Bill tried to turn his head to see what they were talking about when Mr. Atlas, the spotter, and his assistant, Fast Eddie, came out of the office and the prank-playing vets scattered.

"Okay," Mr. Atlas shouted. "Line out in reverse order. Time for the final check." After inspecting me, he slapped me on the shoulder and said, "Load up, Ryan." I reached the steps of the Twin Otter, my guts in knots. A voice from the group of veterans assembled on the tarmac to send us off shouted, "Don't come back in the plane, you pogues!"

I took my seat on a cargo box next to Bill and let out a deep breath. Sweat beaded on my forehead. Is it from the cabin heat? With the plane loaded, the pilot fired up the engines. The cabin instantly filled with a rancid, eye-burning rush of jet fuel fumes. I noticed the veterans putting their Nomex gloves over their noses and mouths. I followed suit and listened to the high pitch wine of the engines as they gained speed. The plane began to rock from the torque of the propellers. 'This is it,' I thought. 'No turning back now. I have to show Harold, John, and Joe that I have the balls to jump out of a perfectly good airplane.' The pre-flight check seemed to last forever. When we finally taxied down the runway, I focused my thoughts on the exit procedure.

The veterans by the door joked with each other as the plane lifted off. My pogue brothers and I seemed frozen in place. I became fixated on the dust swirling around the cabin. Sun-lit particles danced in the cabin before being sucked out the door. In short order, the plane banked over an open meadow where a large orange X appeared in the middle. Bodies moved around it like ants as we circled once and lined up to drop the drift streamers.

The first set settled into the oaks, Mr. Atlas gave the pilot instructions; the plane banked and lined up for a second streamer drop. I tried to watch them fall, but there were too many jumpers in the plane to get a look out the window. Mr. Atlas flashed two fingers and the veterans hooked up their static line snaps and settled into position. He stuck his head out the door, pulled it back in, and gave radio instructions to the pilot. The plane made a correction and Mr. Atlas yelled, "We're on final! Are you ready?"

The jumpers nodded. He forcefully slapped the first one on the shoulder and the vets disappeared out the door. He said, "Jumpers away," into the headset, and the plane banked around for the next stick.

Mr. Atlas flashed two fingers again. Pogues Charlie and Larry hooked up and assumed their positions. Mr. Atlas slapped Charlie so forceful it appeared to knock him out the door. Larry hesitated before finding the step and lost some power on the push off. Mr. Atlas's head followed him out and when he pulled back in, he yelled, "He's twisted up!"

From where I sat, I saw Larry wildly scissor kicking to stop spinning while he tried to pull his risers apart. While that happened, Mr. Atlas flashed two fingers, signaling Bill and me to hook up. I set my left foot onto the step and crouched back. Mr. Atlas yelled, "We're on final! The wind's out of the north with a hundred yards of drift. Stay upwind until your final approach. Give me a good clean exit, guys. You ready?"

We nodded. He stuck his head out the door a last time. My heart raced as I forced short breaths out of my mouth. Before I synchronized my breathing, a hard slap hit my shoulder. I pushed myself out into a brave new world. The faces of my bros disappeared as the sky opened up around me. My legs drifted upward, suddenly, everything became a violent blur. The next thing I knew, my feet swung below me. I looked up to a giant orange and white mass opening above me: the canopy. Just after that, a serene, ghostly silence enveloped me as I quickly found the steering toggles and parachuted through the air, I found my jump partner after a quarter turn.

"Turn left," bellowed an instructor through a megaphone below. I turned left. "Turn right! Do a 360!"

After we'd done all that, Bill and I flew our parachutes toward the X. I never felt so free, riding the wind and sharing the sky with the birds. My parachute responded to my every thought through the toggles. It surpassed everything I imagined it to be.

Falling at fourteen-feet-per-second, the earth came up quickly. After my feet touched, I tried to roll, but only managed a half roll; everything became a blur again until my helmet hit the ground. I'd made it down safe! A vet screaming over me cut my victory yell short. "You call that a PLF, Ryan? If I see that horseshit again, you're outta here."

On the bus ride back to base, the veterans filled our ears with rebukes as we beamed and smiled. The critique in the training room hammered us, complete with embarrassing video and accompanying scorn. That night, the thought of three practice jumps we'd do the following day had me too excited to sleep.

*****

When "Time to suit up!" rang across the tarmac after roll call, I sprinted to the dressing room. Vets helped us chute up without any of the intimidation we endured the day before. I figured since we'd completed our first jump without incident, they began to accept us as one of their own.

On this jump, I would be second out on the first stick. After two quick streamer drops, the spotter flashed his fingers. Pogue brother Mike and I hooked up. I positioned myself behind him and though my nerves rattled, I felt a little more at ease than the day before. One of the Kroger twins spotted again—I still couldn't distinguish Mark from Bill—he shouted, "We're on final! Are you ready?" He slapped Mike on the shoulder, he disappeared in a second. I leaned back and catapulted myself into space. The sudden jolt of the opening shock had me swinging. I looked up and actually checked my canopy for malfunctions.

Mike flew below and ahead of me. I sighted down between my feet, determined my forward speed, steered more aggressively than on my first jump, and managed to land much closer to the elusive X. My PLF had also been better, and on the bus back to base, I saw satisfaction in the eyes of our instructors. A quick, positive critique in the classroom boosted our spirits before we suited up for the day's second jump, I'd be first out ahead of John on the third stick.

Back in the Twin Otter, the second pogue class of 1977 chatted over the noise of the slipstream and gazed out the windows like wily veterans. John leaned to me and shouted, "It's a dream come true, isn't it?" I grinned knowing only a month earlier, we'd all been rejected, resigned to the fact that becoming smokejumpers wasn't going to happen for us. Yet here we were, flying to our third jump.

When the Kroger twin pulled out a set of streamers, I tightened my leg straps and focused. The first two sticks went out perfectly. He ordered, "Hook up." I secured my static line snap. As I looked down at the vast world below me, I'm not scared anymore, just nervous about my parachute opening correctly. I took a deep breath, and when the slap came, I vigorously bailed out. Four seconds and one violent jolt later, I looked up to see a large malfunction-free canopy unfurled above me, always the loveliest of sights.

I turned left, the jump spot came into view, and my hands froze on the toggles. John was below me, frantically scissor kicking. His suspension lines twisted from his risers to half way to the canopy. I heard an instructor shouting through his megaphone, "You have a malfunction! Pull your reserve!" Then more urgently, "Pull your reserve! Pull your reserve!"

John dropped fast. I saw he had a 'Mae West'—a line over his canopy. Shouts rang out everywhere as he lost altitude, finally a small piece of white nylon fluttered out from his reserve pack at last, but much too late. He hit the ground and lay motionless as support staff swarmed over him.

I touched down without even attempting a PLF and struggled out of my jump suit, totally overcome with horror. Part of me went with him in the ambulance as it pulled away in a cloud of dust. On the ride back to base a silent shock filled the bus. When an instructor said we're still on for our forth jump, my jaw dropped. After what had just happened? Back in the plane all we learned about his condition, he was alive. As I prepared to jump, fear washed over me, similar to the fear I felt during the burn-over on the Village Fire. The last jump of the day went off without incident, thank God!

*****

At the hospital, John's room felt cold and smelled of chemicals. Seeing him trussed up on a sterile bed gave me the creeps. Needles stuck in his veins and a traction device kept him from moving. His eyes were glazed over, but after a moment, he recognized us and whispered, "I'm sorry I let you guys down."

"You didn't let us down," Bill told him. "All we care about is you, brother."

"From what the doctors say, I'm not going to be jumping, or firefighting, or doing anything that requires a good back anymore."

He started crying, a broken man, and I grabbed his hand. "Don't worry about that now, just concentrate on getting better. Whatever we can do to help, we're here for you."

We visited John almost every day until his release. Though he'd be in the group photo for 1977, the comparison appeared small for his busted back. The image of him hitting the ground will never leave my memory and the only lesson learned from all the precautions and training jumpers go through is that it's a dangerous occupation with few guarantees.

*****

Every jump I'd made so far had some element of fear. I began to think that jumping out of planes is supposed to be filled with stress and anxiety, until my sixth qualifying jump. I'm waiting my turn by the door as Pigpen hooked up to jump. He looked at me with a Cheshire cat smile and I figured he's up to no good. When the slap came, he flew out the door spreading his arms and legs out in what's call a spread-eagle exit commonly used in skydiving. After he disappeared, the spotter shook his head in disapproval.

'What the hell', I thought. 'I want to feel what he did.' When I received the slap, I jumped mimicking his exit. I fell looking down on an earth that seemed to be in a state of suspended animation, like it might feel falling from outer space, lost in a moment of raw sensual stimulation. For four awesome seconds, I felt totally free. The wind bathed over me like flying down a steep hill with my shirt off as a kid. My chute popped open to another new experience. I'm not rigid in my harness as I'd been on the other jumps, surprisingly relaxed without angst. I find my jump partner and swing in behind him flying the sky like Top Guns. I'd strapped my trusty instamatic camera to my wrist and pushed it up my sleeve prior to jumping, and seeing I had time to capture the moment, I took a couple shots of my jump partner from a bird's eye view. I savored every second of that ride knowing the pucker factor would return on the last qualifying jump.

On June 15, our final jump into the tall timber of Trinity Mountain had us pogues on edge. A place better known as, Pogue Camp. They wanted us to purposely land in a tree, a concept I had mixed feelings about, but the instructors strongly suggested we do so, for if we didn't, the vets on the load would, and we'd have to climb for their chutes. They wanted us to experience a tree landing under somewhat controlled conditions. The pucker factor hit me hard as I tried to hit a tree, but I scraped by it at the last moment. My penalty resulted in climbing to the top of a monster pine for an instructors chute. After clearing the chutes from the trees, we settled in for four days of field work.

While we pogues lived off crummy C-rations, the veterans had fresh food, beer, and whisky. While they slept in tents, we slept on the ground in paper sleeping bags. We couldn't enter their camp without expressed permission and had to listen to their endless fun late into the evenings. In the mornings, we awoke to chainsaws screaming by our heads. They herded us out of camp for daylong exercises of compass and map reading, climbing, and the awful chore of cutting down huge snags with crosscut saws—the fabled 'misery whips.' Talk about pure misery, pushing and pulling those teeth through rock hard dead wood while struggling to find a rhythm with my partner.

After our last day of slaving away with the misery whips, the veterans said they had a treat for us. Quite a few jumpers not associated with the training drove in on the last night. Wally told me it's a traditional thing, thrown to humiliate us, but how, I wondered.

That evening, they invited us into their camp. They offered us fresh food, beer, and whisky. I took it at face value that they finally wanted to get to know us as human beings, and we partied with them. At one point late in the evening, I looked around and noticed all my pogue brothers gone. Knowing something wasn't right, I excused myself, and the vets called after me, "Come on Ryan keep drinking! What are you, a light weight maggot? Can't hold your liquor, pogue?" I turned to accept the challenge when one of my bros whispered from his paper sleeping bag, "Don't do it, Ralph. They're setting you up!"

In the morning, I learned why and to keep with tradition, I will not reveal what happened next. When we returned to base, our names were interspersed amongst the veterans' on the list. Now we only needed a fire jump to become real smokejumpers.

Excitement filled every word when I called Sarah to share the news, omitting the malfunction part of course, but she ho-hummed about it, not coming close to matching my exuberance. I felt relieved after hanging up the phone.

CHAPTER 7

Bona Fide

Ruby Fire, Shasta-Trinity National Forest
July 1, 1977

At every smokejumper base in the country, the jump list consists of a large board with magnetic nametags on it. At the beginning of each fire season, jumpers pull numbers out of a hat to determine their position on the list. As they go out on fires, their names are moved to the side and the remaining names move up. How soon a jumper rotates back to the top depends on the number of fire requests. Waiting for a call can be boring. To keep people busy, assignments were handed out on a daily basis: sharpening tools, fixing chainsaws, packing tree climbing and cargo boxes, working in the parachute loft, or ground maintenance. I happened to be doing ground maintenance when at the end of June, a low-pressure system rolled through setting off a spectacular lightning show to the west and north of Redding. As I watched it from the barracks, Wally said, "Those flashes are the same as money in our pockets. We'll be jumping in the morning."

Reports filtering down from the dispatch center that wildfires were popping up everywhere. Our call to duty, an air horn—one blast put the Air Service Unit's lead planes on standby, two blasts had jumpers suiting up, three blasts signaled the Redding Inter-Regional Hotshots to prepare for a fire assignment.

Two blasts signaled the start of our fire season. I held the eighteenth spot on the jump list when our Twin Otter lifted off ferrying ten jumpers to fires on the Shasta-Trinity National Forest. Gramps told the rest of us, "More requests are coming in. When the plane gets back, load it as quickly as possible." The Otter returned, we restocked it, and I readied myself for two outstanding requests. The first seven were to jump the first fire, the remaining three of us on the second. We dropped the seven, and headed for my 'bona fide' fire jump.

When the smoke became visible, Fast Eddie adjusted the jump order by signaling Disco Duck ahead of me. If pogues were on board, the spotter usually preferred having an experienced jumper as the fire boss. We grouped by the door as the plane made a low pass. A lone Ponderosa pine spewed smoke out of ruptured cavities in its trunk and a small ground fire crept upslope from it. The hillside surrounding it looked like green carpet. Fast Eddie picked a jump spot close to the snag as the plane climbed to jump altitude. The first set of streamers indicated a slight breeze out of the north, the second landed near our target. Disco would jump solo, then me and Tim 'Sorry Dog' Huntington. As we circled for Disco's final approach, I scanned the surrounding terrain. To the north, the granite spires of Castle Crags State Park rose out of the landscape like giant teeth taking a bite out of the sky and beyond, Mt. Shasta gleamed in the sunlight. The serenity of the view became shorted lived when Fast Eddie yelled, "We're on final!"

The plane slowed to jump speed; around 110 miles-per-hour. Fast Eddie stuck his head out the door. He yelled commands in his radio and the plane made a quick correction. He pulled his head in, cocked his arm, and slapped Disco hard on the shoulder. He disappeared with a yell. We circled until his chute settled onto the carpet, and then it hit me, I'm next. My mind reeled with apprehension, but the adrenalin coursing through my veins took over and I realized this is the moment I'd been working toward all my life. Fast Eddie signaled me to get in the door. I positioned myself. The prop blast whistled through my face mask as I looked down, the only thing between me and the ground. When Ed yelled, "We're on final," my breathing accelerated, my muscles tensed and fear popped in. I fought it off by reverting to our training; eyes on the horizon, vigorous push off, feet together, hands across chest. I braced for the slap and when it came, I took the leap of faith and stepped into the sky. The world swung around, my feet came up and a sharp jolt had me dangling in pure serenity. The plane noise faded and the wind whistling through my mask calmed me. I floated down a proud 'bona fide' California Smokejumper.

What looked like carpet from the plane happened to be a dense layer of four-foot tall Manzanita? I crashed through the branches and thumped on my ass to a stop, completely swallowed by brush.

"You all right, Ryan?" Disco yelled from somewhere.

"I'm okay!"

"Dog? You all right?"

"I'm good, too!"

I popped my capewells, releasing my chute from my harness. Rigid branches scraped my helmet as I pushed my head above the Manzanita. I saw my parachute all tangled up and wondered how am I going to get it out of the brush without tearing it to shreds? Disco yelled, "Don't worry about the chutes, we'll get them after the fires out. Heads up, boys! Cargo's coming in." I looked up to see two boxes falling from the plane, cargo chutes popping open above them. They too land in the brush.

I stripped out of my jump suit and forced my way through the Manzanita. By the time I reached Disco, my forearms were raw with cuts. Dog arrived shortly and Disco tells us, "We're not packing a chainsaw through this shit. Sorry guys, I radioed for the misery whip."

Gathering the cargo from the manzanita proved a difficult task. All the shroud lines were tangled in the branches, the boxes buried beneath. We forced our way to the boxes and unpacked only the hand tools and water, and attacked the ground fire while Disco sized up the burning snag. Wildland firefighters call the thick branches on a dead tree like this, 'widow makers.' If one breaks loose and hits you, your wife would surely become a widow. Disco looked up at the tree and said, "I don't like this shit one bit. Listen up, we're going to take turns manning the crosscut saw, the third man will be the lookout. We'll tie a cord to one sawyer. If a widow maker breaks loose, the lookout will yell and yank on the cord. If you feel the yank, tell your partner and hug the tree. Don't look up or step away less you want to get clobbered."

The prospect of spending hours at the base of a burning tree pulling on a misery whip with widow makers falling around us seemed more dangerous than jumping out of a plane. Disco ordered, "Let's get to work. We need to get this puppy on the ground by nightfall." The 87 teeth on the crosscut squealed across dead wood like fingernails on a blackboard. The vibration caused an endless cascade of burning material accented by incessant yells and tugs on the cord. We became tree huggers as fiery branches and slabs of bark swooshed down exploding all around us.

Sweat poured off me, it took most of the afternoon just to make the undercut. As the sun dipped behind the spires of Castle Crags, we hear the wood cracking from our back cut. Dog and I scramble away just in time to watch the falling snag trail a brilliant arch of orange embers before exploding like a bomb onto the ground. When the dust and embers cleared, Disco ordered, "Let's get this monster lined, and set up camp. We'll spend the night mopping up."

*****

Dog and I lug the remaining contents of the cargo boxes from the Manzanita field to the flattest spot we could find, and dug benches on the slope for our sleeping bags. I build a warming fire and then hunger had me rifling through the C-rations. I found spaghetti and meatballs, and knew the bottle of Tabasco I'd packed in my PG bag would complement an otherwise drab meal. Disco and Dog placed their cans in the cinders beside mine.

After eating, I watched Disco cycle through a series of energy spurts. He'd be sitting by the warming fire looking completely relaxed one moment, and suddenly jump up like he'd been stung by a bee, and stomp around the fire like a paranoid duck. This went on for hours, and thinking it might have something to do with his nickname, I had to ask him, "Larry, why do they call you 'Disco Duck'?"

He snorted so loud, I heard it echo off the Crags. "Personally?" he said, "I don't remember much about that night. I'd been out with the alcohol squad, so there's no way to know for sure what's true and what isn't. Anyway, the next morning they start calling me 'Disco Duck'. They said my moves on the dance

60

floor had been a spectacle none of them ever saw before from a human. Apparently, I resembled what they thought to be a drunken duck dancing his heart out to disco music."

I laughed as hard as he did, and asked, "What's with all the other nicknames?"

"Let's put it this way," he said, "'Gramps' grabbed 'Boy' and headed into the woods to find 'Cave Man' to talk about his exits. When they got there, 'Mr. Atlas' is trying to show 'Blow Fly' how to steer a parachute. 'Chuckles' is laughing at the adventures of 'Wally-the-Wad,' while 'Ratso' is running around 'Buffalo,' who becomes irritated and flings him into 'Hairhat,' causing 'Squirrely' to fall into 'Pigpen,' injuring himself. The 'Space Cadet' is visiting 'Vise,' getting 'Perky,' and in the process stumbles into 'Slimy Slate,' causing 'Bionic Buster' to order everyone back to work."

Dog and I laughed. I came to realize there's nowhere else in the world I'd rather be than with these smokejumpers, telling stories under the stars, and finally being one of them.

*****

In the morning, I woke to the sound of Disco grubbing around the fire with his Pulaski. He yelled, "This puppy is cold. I'm calling it out." He came back to camp and laid out our exit strategy. "Burn the cargo boxes and the paper sleeping bags. It's going to be a bitch packing through this brush, so the lighter the packs the better." He looked at the map and pointed to where the ridge slipped into a large canyon. "There's a trail down there that leads to a road. I called the district, said we'll be there by two o'clock. Let's burn what we can and pack up our gear."

I made my way to my parachute draped in the Manzanita, a hardwood shrub that grows close together, has rigid branches, and can get as big as a small tree. How in the hell am I going to get it out of this mess? Bob Kersh, the loft foreman, warned us during our loft orientation: 'Take extra care in retrieving your chutes. I don't want to see any of them coming back all ripped up, because if I do, you'll be in the tower inspecting chutes all summer.'

With that in mind, I surveyed the thirty suspension lines reaching twenty-five feet out over brush in a fan pattern and began to meticulously pull the suspension lines together. Being careful wasn't working well and frustration set in. The lines hooked on the spindly branches and wouldn't let go. I dug into the brush to free them, only to pull my arms out covered with bloody scratches. After spending too much time getting nowhere, I began to yank the lines out, branches and all, looking around paranoid for fear someone might be watching. As I moved toward the canopy, I stuffed the lines in my fire shirt to protect them. By the time I reached the canopy, I looked like a pregnant guppy. Freeing the nylon from the Manzanita felt like pulling weeds with tweezers. I tried to be mindful, but as the sun beat down on me, my concern diminished. After what seemed like hours, a large bundle of nylon lay on a small patch of dirt inside the maze. I hacked a path through the brush to the clearing with my Pulaski so the nylon wouldn't get snagged and re-entered. Minutes later, I staggered out with the bundle in my arms. I threw the chute on the ground cursing it, and returned to the thicket for my jump suit. With this ordeal done, I stripped out of my sweat soaked fire shirt and filled my pack. I made my way to the cargo area where we divided the remains between us, and packed for the hike out.

Disco checked the fire one last time. When he came back, he asked, "Do you guys remember what the terrain looked like from the plane?"

"It looked like a frigging' meadow to me," I said, Dog nodded in agreement.

"Okay," Disco said, "important lesson here. When you're in the plane, make mental notes of everything. Look for roads, trails, creeks, and reference points that might help you once you're on the ground." He pointed west. "I remember seeing timber on that spur ridge. I'd rather walk through that than fight this brush. Let's get this over with."

We slipped into our heavy packs and headed west from the Ruby Fire plowing through Manzanita. It became so bad, I walked backwards using the pack as a shield from the slashing branches, and at one point I even considered crawling. Breaking through the Manzanita at last into the open understory of the pines felt like exiting a maze. We reached our pick-up point just before our ride showed up, my back and knees aching. Within an hour, we pulled into the Service Center and promptly hung our parachutes in the drying tower. Hanging the chutes before doing anything else was the law because moisture could destroy the nylon.

The first local jumper to accept me into his circle was Richard 'Vise' Linebarger. His smokejumping career started in 1974 somewhat like mine. He'd been on the Redding Hotshot for two seasons when Dick Tracy called him saying a pogue had washed out and if he wanted to try out, to be there in thirty minutes. He had many words of advice for me, one being that since I lived in the barracks, I should get my jump gear and PG bag in order every time I came back from a fire. Calls came in before and after normal work hours often, and if the first jumpers on the list lived off base and couldn't be contacted, replacements were drawn from the barracks. Now, being a 'bona fide' smokejumper, I should be prepared to suit up at any time.

CHAPTER 8

Disaster

Cone Fire, Plumas National Forest
July 8, 1977

Two air blasts sounded in the morning during my workout. I sprinted to the suit up room. "Where we going?" I asked as I suited in a rush. Buffalo grumbled next to me, "Fucking Feather River! Steep-ass jump country laced with poison oak. Not to mention hot as hell!" The Feather River Canyon on the Plumas National Forest—along with Wooly Creek on the Klamath—had the reputation of being the most dangerous jump terrains in California. The mood in the plane unsettled me. Instead of joking around, the vets remained quiet, a disturbing sort of silence.

Half an hour into the flight, a column of smoke loomed above the horizon. As we circled overhead, all eyes strained through the windows. The fire burned in brush and oaks so thick they looked like dog-hair from the air and flames spread out on both sides of the ridge, a ridge that fell sharply thousands of feet to the Feather River. Remembering what Disco had told me about surveying an area, I looked for landmarks. The river carved a steep, narrow canyon with a road snaking along it.

Tracy shouted to our fire boss, Mr. Atlas, "How about the bowl up there?"

"Too far away, we need to get closer!"

Tracy countered, "The oaks over there look small."

They scanned the area intently. "Okay, let's make those smaller oaks the spot," Mr. Atlas said. After three sets of streamers, Tracy finally flashes two fingers. I felt a wave of relief knowing I'd soon be out of that hot sardine can. My stomach churned from the plane's tight orbits and the last thing I wanted to do was puke in front of my bros.

The first stick bailed, we circled to see how they fared. Both canopies landed in the trees. On the second run, I noticed them gone. How had they gotten out of the trees so fast? The second stick landed the same way. Two fingers from Tracy signaled my turn. I lumbered behind my jump partner, received our briefing and before the slap, Tracy said, "Go get-em babe."

My parachute opened cleanly and as I breathed in the cool air, my nausea subsided. Tracy had said the trees were small, but the closer I got, the taller they became. I turned into the wind and braced for whatever Big Ernie had in store for me. My body punctured green canopy and immediately I heard shouts from below, "Don't hang up! The chutes are breaking out of the trees!" Too late for that.

The oaks stood nearly 80 feet tall, not the 40 feet Tracy had thought. My chute caught on something that yanked me to a stop, then I heard branches breaking, and I'm falling fast. I try to glimpse the ground before I hit, but a rubber band jolt leaves me swinging 30 feet above it. Mr. Atlas yells up to me, "Be fucking careful! The tops are breaking! We have two injuries down here already. I don't want another, you hear me?"

When I finally stop swinging, I froze, afraid any movement might break the spindly oak holding my chute. The last jumpers crashed through nearby trees. I carefully looked up to see a slender oak bowing from my weight, only a small part of my parachute snagged on a branch. I blocked everything out, the yelling below, the cursing in the trees around me, and the airplane noise to only focus on the letdown procedure. Doing it from the simulator with a trampoline to land on happened to be one thing; doing it with a rocky cliff below threatening a pair of broken legs, or worse proved to be something else entirely.

I pulled the Sky Genie from my leg pocket, hooked it to the D-rings on my jump pants, and tied my rope to the tight riser, all the while praying the treetop didn't break. I dropped my rope coil and unsnapped my risers. Sweat drips from inside my helmet as I rappelled down, the rope whizzing through my hands. When my feet touched ground, I kept going until lying flat, completely spent from nerves. Vise boomed over me, "You okay? Mr. Atlas wants us to check on the injured."

"I'm okay," I whispered.

"Better thank Big Ernie. Get up, Ryan! We have men down!"

I stripped out of my jump suit in seconds. Vise and I rushed over to Buffalo, his body propped against a tree with a broken ankle. He's cursing up a blue streak from the pain. There wasn't much we could do to help him. Not far away, Charlie lay below a shattered oak, pale, expressionless, and going into shock. "My back," he choked out. "It hurts. My ribs, too."

Mr. Atlas yells into the radio, "We need the Stokes litter, NOW!" He waits a few seconds and says, "Be advised I ordered up an air tanker. No more men in the trees! Drop the next load in the meadow."

"Ten-four," crackled back from the plane.

Mr. Atlas barked at Vise, "We need to get bodies on the fire, its moving fast. You two get to the cargo boxes, grab some tools, and start working the west flank."

Vise and I cut brush at a frenzied pace, trying to anchor the fire so it wouldn't spread to the oaks where our injured were stranded. Suddenly, the air begins to vibrate from the sound of a heavy air tanker entering the canyon, moments later, the red markings of a C-119 roars overhead. It banks wide and lines up for a drop right above us. Vise and I dash for cover as its payload doors open dumping 'slurry'. The thick, red glob brakes apart and rains down on the fire's leading edge, making a perfect drop.

Slurry, also known as 'mud', is a Phos-Chek retardant mixed into a combination of water, thickening agents, chemicals, and red dye intended to slow fires by coating it. Vise and I run back to the fire to take advantage of the slurry's smothering effect. The C-119's next two passes hit the fire's flanks. Soon afterwards, Vise's radio comes to life from a district crew hiking up to help. Rocks shaken loose by the slurry drops were tumbling down on them and they had to back off, leaving us on our own.

Mr. Atlas comes on the radio, "How you guys doing down there?"

"The tanker drop hit the mark," Vise said. "But we could use some more bodies down here."

"I don't have any to give you," Mr. Atlas warned, "I'm going to need at least twelve men to get the injured up to the meadow. Sorry fellas, do the best you can."

Vise looked at me and shrugged, "Guess we're it."

I looked back at him and began to laugh from the scar on his neck. I jabbed him with my elbow, still laughing, "How's your injury doing?" He'd returned from a detail to Boise a couple days earlier and when they landed in Redding, I helped off loading their gear. When I noticed he had a hickey on his neck, I had to ask, "What's your girlfriend gonna say about that?"

Apparently, he'd forgotten about it, and my observation put him in a panic. "What am I going to do?" I remember him saying. "I can't go home looking like this."

"There are plenty of files in the tool room," I joked. "Run a rasp along it; make it bigger, like a tree branch scrapped your neck, instead of some woman's lips!" He v-lined it to the tool room and began filing on his neck. He groaned from the scraping, and when he finished, it looked like he had sustained a painful fire line injury. I taped a bandage over it and slapped him on the back. "Now, you look like a hero in need of attention."

He explained, "I couldn't help it, those Boise girls are really friendly. I'll set you up the next time we're there."

"Thanks," I said sarcastically, "that's all I need, trouble in every port of call."

We paused a minute to watch the second plane drop the jumpers and Stokes litter. As the orange and white canopies floated down against the smoke-stained sky, a new voice blared over the radio, "Helicopter is en-route."

Vise mutters, "That's Boy. When a foreman gets into the mix, you know it's fucking serious."

Two hours later, two jumpers from the second load made their way down the canyon. They reached us panting. One said, "They've got Charlie in the litter and a couple bros are helping Buffalo. Mike has a neck injury, and Perky hurt his shoulder. A third load's on the way." The jumper shook his head. "Boy is all tensed up. There're so many injuries, he said he should've ordered up a hospital tent!"

The sound of rotor blades filled the canyon, followed by the appearance of a B-1 helicopter. It buzzed over us like a mosquito as it headed for the meadow. I looked at Vise, "That chopper's too small. It'll take all day to ferry them out." Vise nods and we cut fire line until the Twin Otter's drone fills the canyon for a third time. Our reinforcements floated down from the sky. So far, this fire's been nothing but bad luck, I prayed to Big Ernie for no more injuries. As fresh bodies made their way down to us, the helicopter whined to life. It banked over us on the way to the hospital in Quincy, returning repeatedly.

A bro from the third load says, "The shit is already hitting the fan back at base. Brass wants to know why so many jumpers are getting busted up." We worked the fire all night and into the morning. We learn Charlie had fractured three vertebrae and a few ribs.

*****

Returning from the fire, the base was in political turmoil. A Forest Service investigator sat across from me in his badged uniform, looking like a prosecuting attorney. His eyes never leave mine as he taped his pencil on the table and grilled me. "Did the spotter brief you prior to jumping?"

"Yes, sir. He told me to land in the smaller trees below the big timber."

"Was there an alternate spot?"

"I believe they mentioned a small meadow toward the top of the ridge."

"You believe?"

"I don't recall exactly, but it seemed to be the case, sir."

"Did the spotter warn you of any hazards on the ground?"

"The spotter told my stick to avoid the canyon, the fire, and the tall timber."

"Do you think the jump spot was safe?"

"I'm a first year jumper. This is all new to me."

The investigator seemed as annoyed with my short answers as I was with his questions. His tone led me to believe he was looking to find blame with someone. "Did the spotter brief you on the wind speed and direction?"

"Yes, sir. The streamers indicated a slight north wind with 100 yards of drift."

"Where did you land?"

"In the trees."

"Did you break out of the trees?"

"No, sir. I made a letdown."

"Would you jump that spot again if directed to?"

Now that's a stupid question, I thought. I'd jump any fire, anytime, anywhere. "Well, sir," I said grinning. "Knowing what I know now, I might, and then again, I might not."

I knew I given another bad answer. He put his pencil down and excused me. From what I'd gathered about the art of spotting there's two schools of thought when jumps go wrong. The first school would say, "I was miss-spotted," a phrase used to shift blame onto the spotter when the jumper screws up flying the parachute. The second school of thought—and the one I belonged to—believe that once you're out the door; you're on your own. The spotter can't fly the parachute for you. You should always be looking for an alternate landing spot on your own.

Being a spotter carries a lot of responsibility. The findings of the investigation centered on the process of selecting landing spots. Because of what had happened, Forest Service brass changed the traditional approach of landing as close to a fire as possible, to finding a safe jump spot no matter how far from the fire it happened to be. Now, if it meant hiking for miles, so be it. Everyone felt it contradicted the smokejumpers philosophy of hitting fires hard and fast, but directives were directives, and we could do nothing about it.

After a lengthy rehabilitation, Charlie returned to work on his home forest, building gates for service roads until he quit the Forest Service in disgust over how the organization had treated him. He received no disability payments, and other issues made him realize how insignificant he was in the eyes of the mighty Service. To top it all off, they billed him for his ambulance ride from Quincy to Redding.

While Buffalo's broken foot healed, he worked in the dispatch office upstairs from our unit. Since the dispatchers controlled who went out on fires—and therefore, who made money—they had a holier-than-thou attitude. Buffalo eventually wore out his welcome upstairs, and ended up in the dispatch office on the Quincy Ranger District, miles from Redding. Nonetheless, he ordered up jumpers whenever he could which created more bad blood between the dispatchers and jumpers. It seemed the dispatchers thought all jumpers to be wild, impulsive, and only worried about making a buck. A rumor surfaced that the North Zone's lead dispatcher told Gramps, "Broken foot or not, put Buffalo to work in the loft. Jumpers can't have their own personal dispatch service sending them to every fire that pops up."

Buffalo ended up rigging parachutes until he healed. His loyalty to us while dispatching on the Plumas drove the spike even deeper into the dispatcher-jumper rift. The dispatchers soon developed a phrase to answer our questions about why we weren't going to fires. "You're on North State Hold," they'd tell us, meaning 'you jumpers aren't going anywhere,' and sure enough, we didn't go anywhere for three weeks due to the feud, meaning we also lost a lot of overtime pay.

CHAPTER 9

All Hell Breaks Loose

Northern California
August 1977

On August 1, 1977, all hell broke loose in Northern California. The forests had become tinderboxes from three years of extreme drought when a series of dry lightning storms passed through. Minutes after morning roll call, the air horn sounded twice. We suited up for a fire on the coastal Six Rivers National Forest. Once we assembled on the tarmac, Vise warned, "Watch out for the timber, boys. The firs on this forest get over 150 feet, easy. You don't want to hang up."

After the Cone Fire, I knew how dangerous dangling from a tree could be. Still, maneuvering my chute through the maze of monster firs of the Six Rivers had my adrenalin spiking. I'd never seen trees so tall, and turning at the last second to avoid them felt like being in a sci-fi movie. We hit the fire hard before a district crew hiked in to relieve us. By late evening we pulled back into the Service Center. Vise reminded me, "Get your gear ready, we're on the first load again in the morning." How ironic it seemed to have been on North State Hold for so long only to be sent out twice in two days. Maybe Big Ernie had gone upstairs and slapped the dispatchers around for us.

At first light, we flew out and jumped a fire on the Plumas. Our attack kept it small and we rushed back to base. The jump list had grown in numbers from the influx of smokejumpers from Redmond, Oregon and McCall, Idaho. The rotation slowed for a few days until another series of dry lightning storms crossed the state, this time hammering the Klamath. I jumped fires named the Medicine #1, #2, and #3.

Planeloads of jumpers flew to the Klamath, Modoc, Shasta-Trinity, and Plumas National Forests. The Lightning Activity Levels, or LAL, were at the highest level of five. A map posted below the weather report recorded the ground strikes as black dots. They formed a dark horseshoe around the upper Sacramento Valley.

After coming back from the Medicine fires, I stowed my jump gear, resupplied my PG bag, and took a six-pack of beer to the top of the parachute-drying tower to settle in for the show. To the north and west of Redding, the night exploded with lightning bolts. They forked indiscriminately across the sky, blinding bolts of electricity rained down on the forests, dancing wildly in place until disappearing back into the clouds. Orange, yellow, purple, and red hues decorated the clouds and the electricity in the air had the hair on my arms standing on end. When I went to bed, the deafening thunder and the constant flashes lit up my room making it impossible to sleep. At 5am, Gramps called the barracks and ordered everyone to get ready. At first light, the drought-ravaged shoreline of Shasta Lake glared at me from the window of the Twin Otter.

On the way to the Klamath, we skirted the Trinity Alps. Granite peaks rose up to the clouds and small alpine lakes dotted the terrain like scattered pieces of mirror. This area had the distinction of being 'good deal' jump country, nothing like the dangerous Feather River Canyon or Wooly Creek. Vise sat next to me and said above the slipstream, "One day I'm going to jump a small fire by one of those pretty lakes and I'm going to find a couple of college girls camped nearby. We're going to have a party that will live forever in smokejumping history."

"Sure you will," I chuckled and soon fell into a fantasy of my own. What if I 'accidentally' fell out of the plane above one of those pristine lakes and found a couple college girls waiting for me? I thought of Sarah and felt guilty. I hadn't returned her calls and knew more backlashes awaited me. It became distracting thinking about her all the time; I needed to concentrate on parachuting and fighting fires. I noticed a couple of my bros were going through divorces and they seemed distracted, unable to concentrate on flying their chutes, or working fires. I didn't need that being a pogue.

We passed over the Alps into the Klamath forest. I counted eight smoke columns. The first fire had flames crowning through the treetops in steep terrain. I figured it would require the whole load and then some, but the spotter only flashed six fingers. After dropping the jumpers and cargo, we fly to the next fire, which wasn't far away. The signal to hook-up had me settling in behind Kroger. The spotter shouted, "We're on final! Not much wind. Give me good exits, guys. Get ready."

Kroger disappeared with the slap. I followed steering behind him to the ridge and landed right next to him. Once the other two jumpers landed, and the cargo settled in, I assembled the chainsaw filling the swamper pack with gas and oil, as Kroger sized up the fire. I noticed by his body language that he doesn't like what he saw. He gathered us together and said, "Let's secure the top and work down the south flank. This thing's nasty, we sure could use more help."

We cleared vegetation from the ridge top making a natural barrier, and I headed down the slope to cut brush. As I neared the bottom of the fire, a pinecone laced with fire bounced past me down the mountain. I froze, yelled back to the crew, "Roll out!"

If there's two words that can stop a firefighter in his tracks, it's "*Roll out*," because by the time you hear it, it's usually too late. Before I could make the split second decision of whether to chase it down or reassess our attack strategy, a large column of smoke boiled up the slope spewing fire. Kroger caught up with me. We both saw trouble coming. Right then, the mountain exploded in fire sending flames searing through the treetops to a deafening roar. Red embers fell everywhere like thousands of firecrackers going off at once.

We ran up the line. The other two jumpers were sprinting as fast as they could ahead of us. I fell behind from lugging the chainsaw. As a blast of hot air hit me, Kroger yelled above the roar, "Drop the goddamned saw!" The thought of giving up my chainsaw never entered my mind. It would've be sacrilegious, an attitude I acquired from my Helishot days', where relinquishing your saw was unthinkable.

"Drop it, Ryan!"

I felt the heat and yelled, "Fuck it," as I dropped the saw and ran for my life. With the fire on my heels, I reached the ridge top, choking from the smoke. Kroger shouted into his radio, "We need an air tanker, NOW!"

Fire raced over the ridge in a hellish display of natural pyrotechnics. This is it, I'm finally going to die a on a wild fire. A few moments later, we heard the sound of radial engines. A B-17! Slurry rained down on us as Kroger yelled, "He's going to lay a slurry line toward the saddle. Get your gear and follow the drops."

We ran the trail of red slime through a gauntlet of flames. I sucked in smoke, the fire's hunger for oxygen pulled it right back out. When I saw the helicopter hovering through the heat, I launched myself at the Helitack crewmember holding his arms out. He hauled us in shouting, "You lucky bastards made it just in time!"

When we lifted off, the mountain was a raging inferno. That little burning pinecone had ignited the whole drainage. Glancing to the horizon, I saw smoke columns choking out the sun.

I pushed my earplugs in deep and retreated to that place where inner calm resides. I shook my head knowing we'd given it our best shot, but we'd broken a few of the 10 Standard Firefighting Orders in the process. The helicopter swooped into the Salmon River canyon to a fire camp. Kroger reported to the plans tent. Apparently, other jumpers had experienced the same troubling fire behavior we had. All over the area, different fires were joining into one huge blaze.

By evening, we had enough jumpers in camp to form a hand crew. We worked the night shift, taking advantage of the lower temperatures and higher humidity. We made good progress, but once the sun rose, and the inversion lifted, the fire blew up again.

The shifts were long and hard. Constant logistical blunders by the overhead team coupled with frustration over our utter lack of progress began to cause anarchy among the troops. Kevin 'Cave Man' Hodgin became so fed up, he said to me the next morning, "This is a cluster fuck. I'm outta here."

'Yeah, right!' I thought, but he slipped into his pack-out bag, walked out of camp to the highway, and stuck his thumb out. I looked at the veterans around me, no one attempted to stop him. Kroger saw my disbelief and sighed, "Cave Man does what he wants to. He's from the old school and doesn't take much bullshit."

I couldn't believe it. My background of strict regimentation wouldn't tolerate this. If I'd done that in front of Harold, I would've been looking for another job. We cut fire line through the night without Cave Man and when we returned to camp in the morning we found quite a stir going on. A parachute was seen floating through the air without anything attached to it and a few firefighters speculated, 'did the jumper fall from his parachute?' We knew different. The convection column from one of the fires had dislodged a parachute from the trees and carried it over the canyon.

Something else happened that morning that became a turning point in our mission. Our crew bus pulled into camp, when the door opened, there sat Cave Man grinning from ear to ear. As he drove us home, he explained, "I told Gramps how screwed up the overhead team ran the fire and that our efforts were a total waste of time. He must've believed me, because here I am, boys. Besides, we're not suited for cluster fucks of this magnitude."

"Thanks for getting us out of there," Kroger said, patting Cave Man on the shoulder. The rest of us echoed the same sentiment. Cave Man stopped at a liquor store where we bought a few hard-earned twelve packs for the long ride home.

*****

That evening, Wally-the-Wad invited me to party with a group of barracks dwellers. We started out at the Italian Cottage for dinner, and moved on to a number of Redding's nightclubs. I started a conversation with Perky—a pogue from the first training session— about a particular nickname of one of his pogue bros. "Perky," I said, leaning toward him, "why do they call Rob, 'The Maggoty Mayor'?"

Perky laughed a long time before saying, "Rob, our elected mayor, journeyed out one day to take pictures of Bald eagles by the lake. He said he wanted to get a good shot and ignored the bugs flying around his head. A few days later, he complained of hearing something crawling inside his head. We tried to convince him a loose screw might be the problem, but he wasn't buying it. He went to the hospital to get checked out, and when they flushed maggots out of his ear, it grossed everyone out, even the doctor. After that, he became known as, The Maggoty Mayor."

Wally-the-Wad was wooing a couple of local beauties at the bar, he waved me over. He'd gotten his nickname while partying at Whiskeytown Lake. One day the bros saw him and a girl at the buoys stuck together like two horny dogs, bobbing in the water to a steady rhythm. It didn't bother them that kids swam all around and it appeared obvious to everyone on the beach what they were doing. Ever since then, he'd been called, 'Wally-the-Wad.'

I went over and he introduced me to Robin and Claudia. Claudia had creamy skin, friendly freckles, and long auburn hair. She said innocently, "Walt here says you guys jump out of airplanes for a living. Is that really true?"

When our eyes met, I froze. Her big green eyes burned into me like hot needles. I fumbled, "Ah, yeah, we jump out of planes to fight fires," as Wally winked at me.

She touched my shoulder. "He also said smokejumpers are always in heat. I don't get it. What's that supposed to mean?"

I looked at Wally blushing. "I think he means to say we're always looking for a fire to jump on."

Claudia nudged her friend. "See, Robin, you're wrong! Men don't go into heat." She whispered to me, "Maybe you can explain what he meant by, 'Smokejumpers are good to the last drop?'"

"Maybe a little later on," I whispered back surprising myself. We drank and danced until last call.

At one point, Wally said, "You get her number yet or what?"

I thought, 'Why would I do that?' I'm married after all, but to appease him, I asked Claudia for her number and to my surprise she not only wrote it on a napkin, but also invited me back to her place to keep the party going. I told her reluctantly, "I need to get back. I'm jumping in the morning." Disappointment showed when I said, "Goodnight." That was the first of many nights out with the barracks group known as, 'The Alcohol Squad.'

*****

I took a long run in the morning to clear my head. Jogging past the air tanker base, three smoke columns rose over 30,000 feet to the north and west of Redding. They formed a phenomenon known as a 'pyro cumulus nimbus cloud.' The smoke reached such a high altitude it created its own weather, along with lightning. The column to the west, a product of all the fires we'd jumped and lost. They eventually burned together and became known as the Hog Fire.

The Northern California Service Center turned into a hub of activity. Crews from all over the United States flew in and slept on the lawns while waiting for assignments. Lightning storms continued. I jumped a small fire on the Shasta-Trinity, which gave me a chance to get to know some of the Oregon and Idaho jumpers. They noted the only good thing about coming to Redding was the night life. As far as jumping fires, our steep, rock studded mountains, poison oak, blistering heat, and intense fire behavior couldn't compare to nice meadow jumps, cool air, and low intensity fires. They promised I'd see a different world of jumping north of the border. Not knowing any different, I looked forward to experiencing their environment.

I rotated to the first load in short order. Two air horn blasts sent me running to the suit up room, and while gearing up, the spotter said, "There's a Type I overhead team on the Hog Fire now. They want us to build three Helispots around the perimeter."

The first location, a small clearing on a ridge top took three jumpers. The second, a wide spur ridge jutting out from the main ridgeline, a perfect helicopter-landing site once cleared. The spotter flashed three fingers then briefed us. "There's 200 yards of drift. The convection is creating erratic winds down low, so be careful and don't get too far out over the canyon. Any questions?"

We shook our heads.

"Get ready."

I watched my jump partner get the slap and I catapulted out behind him. My chute opened, I looked up to see my suspension lines twisted in a tight braid. I scissor kicked until the world stopped spinning, then it spun in the opposite direction. When the last twist finally unwound, my body snapped into the proper alignment, but my head continued to whirl like I'd just stepped off a carousel.

A massive smoke column filled the sky. I felt it pulling me in and steered toward the open canyon, the very place the spotter had warned us not to go. I saw my jump spot slip away when suddenly a strong up-slope wind lifted me pushing me backwards. I tried to look over my shoulder, but couldn't. Without warning, my body oscillated into the ground back first. My breath exploded from me as my helmet hit dirt. When the dust settled and my breathing returned, I focused to see Pigpen looking down on me. I looked up remembering that face being the first smokejumper I'd ever met, and his last words of encouragement on becoming a jumper being, 'Good luck, Ryan.' Now that my dream had come true, he chuckled over me, "You always land so pretty, Ry?"

I cleared my head and chuckled back, "I'm here aren't I?"

The Twin Otter swooped above the treetops. Pigpen yelled, "Cargo coming in," as two white chutes popped open above the clearing. As soon as they touched ground, I ran to the chainsaw box and assembled it as fast as I could. Five hours later, we finished a helipad wide enough to land a big chopper.

Pigpen radioed the fire camp we'd completed the pad. Soon afterwards, the sound of rotor blades echoed up the canyon. A twin turbine helicopter came in and ten firefighters scurried out. Crews and supplies flew in until dark. After three more days of line building, all three helipads interconnected and we stood ready for a massive burnout operation.

The fire command team instructed it would to be a nighttime operation. Hotshot crews would patrol the line to catch spot fires and slop-overs. The purpose of a burnout is to remove the unburned fuel between the main fire and the control line. We'd rely on the fire's convection to pull the flames we set toward it, effectively robbing it of fuel.

The night sky glowed as firefighters patrolled the line. A few spot fires started in the brush outside the line, the hotshots knocked them down quickly. As I patrolled the line, Claudia's green eyes kept flashing before me. I wanted to see them again, but I was married, wasn't I? I missed Sarah, my first attempt at love, but it wasn't working out. I couldn't figure out why, or I knew why and didn't want to admit it. We drifted in and out of closeness. Smokejumping often resulted in divorce. A few bros were going through it and I knew my marriage might be heading that way, too. Many of my bros considered themselves as swinging dicks, doing whatever they could to satisfy their lustful needs between fires without considering the consequences. I became guarded when Vise said sweetly, "So, tell me Ry, when are we going to meet that pretty wife of yours?" He must've seen her picture in my hardhat.

I told him, "In your dreams!"

After another night of back firing and thinking about the mounting dilemma I'd created with Sarah and Claudia, our sector was secure enough to be released back to base. I wanted to see Sarah right away, but couldn't muster the nerve to call her. Guilt had me on edge.

Early September arrived and our college students headed back to school. The overhead kept the Idaho jumpers in case any more thunderstorms crossed the state, but by mid-September, no fires started and they flew home. October brought only practice jumps, and the fire season ended. Rogue jumpers like me—guys with no district to call home for the winter—usually worked six to eight months, made good overtime, and with unemployment had all winter to ski, travel, or do whatever they wanted. As Vise turned in his jump gear, he asked, "What are you going to do now, Ry?"

I'd jumped eight fires, made fifteen practice jumps, and more money than any other season. Jumping had a hook in me and I wanted this lifestyle more than anything else. I selfishly dismissed the problems this would cause with Sarah and my family. As if a man in control of my destiny, I answered, "I'm staying right here. They've offered me extra work and I'm taking it. Bob's putting me in the loft."

Vise looked just like Mr. Brawny, from the paper towels, now he made a face at me. "No way! Bob doesn't let anyone in the loft until their third season."

"Bob's ex-military. He knows I come from a military family. He asked me a couple days ago, I couldn't say no."

"So much for tradition," Vise snorted. "I couldn't even get close to Kersh's loft without getting his evil stare."

I laughed, "You probably didn't laugh at his jokes."

"Yeah, yeah," he jabbed. "Anyway, speaking of tradition, how you pogues doing with the end of the year party?"

If the stories I'd heard about the end of the year party rang true, it'd be a night to remember, if possible. "We're working on it," I promised.

"Good," Vise grinned. "Fast Eddie and I are making our traditional Fog Cutter."

"Fog Cutter?"

"Yeah, Fog Cutter, it'll cut right through you. We mix fifths of whiskey, vodka, rum, gin, and mescal with Seven-Up, and throw in a dash of punch. To top it off, we put in a big chunk of dry ice, hence the name Fog Cutter."

Thinking about my pogue duties for the party, I asked, "Did you get your ballots in yet?"

"Gave them to Maggoty Mayor," he nodded.

Recipients of the awards were voted on by the crew and given out at the party. Some awards trailed year after year, others made just for that season. The 'Jump Hog,' for example, went to whoever made the most jumps. 'Milker of the Year' went to whoever logged the most overtime, or oats. 'Slug of the Year' went to whoever had worked the hardest at doing the least amount of work. 'Ghost of the Year' signified the jumper who'd managed to disappear from their assigned work area on a regular basis. The best thing about the awards, we made them ourselves. The theme being comedy. Slug of the Year featured a slug made of clay with two balding heads that resembled the Kroger brothers, since they'd won it so many times in the past.

Aside from these awards and the awarding of the pogue wings, at every fifty-jump interval, pins with a 50, 100, or 150 in the center of a pair of parachuting wings were awarded. This year, seven jumpers hit the 50 mark, four had reached 100.

I volunteered to make the 'Milker of the Year' award—an idea popped into my head that sent me searching every department store in Redding. The manager of the JC Penney finally agreed to help out and I left the store with the naked bust of a mannequin under my arm. I made a sign, 'Milker of the Year,' attached a baby bottle just below the breasts, and wrapped the award in parachute material.

I debated about inviting Sarah to the party, but after hearing how crazy they could get, I didn't want to have to deal with her possibly not liking the wild side of smokejumpers, so I didn't even mention it to her.

The morning of the party, we pogues met at the Sun Oaks Fitness Club to set up. We rented the whole facility. It featured a swimming pool and Jacuzzi. We draped the ceiling and walls with parachutes, made displays with cargo boxes, and placed JoJo, our full-sized mannequin dressed in a jump suit at the entrance to greet the partygoers. Vise and Eddie showed up to mix their fabled Fog Cutter.

The party began civilly enough with a potluck and conversation. Awarding of the pogue pins and jump pins followed. Standing with my pogue brothers and receiving our wings from Dick Tracy proved to be one of the proudest moments of my life. As I watched the veterans receive their 50 and 100 jump pins, I developed a new level of admiration.

When it came time for the special awards, I held my breath. Bionic Buster had won 'Milker of the Year' and I didn't take into account his religious background. I could handle his reaction; not knowing how his wife would take it had me on edge though. As the nylon came off the bust, laughter and applause rang out in the hall, only from the crew, not the wives—especially not his. Thankfully, the emcee quickly moved on.

After the awards, a crowd gathered around the bowl of Fog Cutter. Not long after, couples with kids quietly slipped out. Memory of what happened next is still vague. I do remember seeing bodies flying into the pool, the Jacuzzi packed with naked people, and a shopping cart full of tennis balls tumble into the pool. Jumpers wrestled on the floor, bottles broke, and the Fog Cutter never seemed to end. It'd been the wildest party I ever attended. How I ended up at the barracks is still a mystery to me.

The next morning, a telephone call came into the office from the club manager. His exact words were, "Jumpers will never rent this facility again! EVER!"

It took a few days to recover, but once back in form I took to working in the parachute loft to become a licensed Federal Aviation Administration Senior Parachute Rigger, hopefully by the end of my second year.

The FAA required a Senior Rigger to be able to pack, maintain, or alter any type of personnel-carrying parachute. Candidates had to show knowledge of the common parachutes, their components and construction, packing and maintenance procedures, and FAA regulations by passing written, practical, and oral tests. It all seemed overwhelming, but my hunger to improve myself drove me.

*****

One night toward the end of November while relaxing in the barracks, Ted, the strangest veteran jumper around, called upon us pogues, "Come on!" he commanded, "you need to break the old record." He hurried us outside like sheep to the edge of the runway. While we crouched in darkness, he whispered, "See those lights stretching down the runway? Last year a pogue made it to the eighth light. One of you needs to make it down to the ninth light."

"And do what?" I asked.

Ted looked at his watch, "There's a red-eye commuter flight leaving in ten minutes. You need to sneak to the ninth light and lay down in the middle of the runway as the plane takes off."

Pogue brother Jerry said, "No fucking way. I'm out of here."

As he left, Ted sneered at him saying, "Fucking wimp-ass pogue." He looked at his watch, "You two have a couple of minutes to get out there, or are you also going to be weak, incompetent, malingering pussy pogues?"

Pogue Larry and I saw the plane taxing toward the main runway. As I considered the challenge, Larry turned to me and said with confidence, "Let's show him we're not fucking wimps." I reluctantly nodded and we sprinted to the ninth light and lay down. The plane's engines revved to full power, it started rolling. I thought about getting up and running, too late. The roar grew louder, I yelled like a maniac as the belly of the speeding plane lifted off so close to us I thought we'd get burned from the exhaust. A second later, Larry and I are running away like hyenas, laughing hysterically, as flashing lights and sirens started up in the distance.

CHAPTER 10

Feast To Famine

Sarah picked me up for a visit. On the drive to my parents', our conversation took the usual turn: "Ralph, why are you doing this?"

"Baby, I made two-grand more than last year!"

"Is a couple grand worth watching your bro slam into the ground?"

"That was a freak accident. We're sewing netting on the chutes this winter. That kind of thing won't happen again."

"Oh, what a relief!" Sarah said sarcastically.

I kicked into defensive. "You forgot that we're military brats, Sarah? That our dads went to wars, that we grew up with this kind of shit. At least no one's shooting at me."

"Why can't you just be a carpenter or a plumber?" she pleaded.

"Destiny," I answered.

"Oh please," she snorted. "It's no more your destiny to jump out of planes than it's mine to sit around waiting for you to get killed."

"So don't!" I shouted. "This is what I'm doing. If you want to do it with me, fine. If not, go to Alabama."

"I don't want to go to Alabama."

"Well," I said before stopping myself, "that's the only reason we're married, isn't it?"

Sarah began to cry. Oh great, I thought. "Baby, I'm sorry. I didn't mean it that way."

She turned up the radio to drown me out, and then turned it down sobbing, "I thought you loved me."

"I do, baby. I really do. This all happened so fast. We got married. I received the chance of a lifetime to chase my dream. Now, I have to jump, can't you understand that?"

"I can't Ry. I'm stuck at your parents'. I'm floating here all empty inside while you're testing your mortality. Can't you understand *that*?"

I knew being at my parents was awkward for her, but I had a plan. "Okay, baby," I said, "how does this sound? I asked around and found a small house for rent. We could move there right now if you want."

"What about our stuff?"

"We'll rent a U-Haul."

She wiped her tears and said, "All right, let's do it."

The house was old, but cozy, built during the construction of Shasta Dam and located off Interstate 5. It seemed the only time we noticed the traffic was when there wasn't any. I moved out of the barracks and we settled in just before the first winter rains. It rained all winter. Experts predicted it would take years of above-average rainfall to fill Shasta Lake, but soon it borded the rim, and Mount Shasta, completely white with snow. I'd never seen anything so lovely.

We had good neighbors, a couple our age, Jeff and Angie. We partied together and Angie helped Sarah get a job as a medical receptionist before I returned to jumping in early April. I received an automatic pay increase, my salary now equaled that of Harold's, which took him two decades to achieve on the district level.

Bionic Buster filled me in on some of the changes that had occurred over the winter, "Bob Kersh retired and Boy is our new loft foreman."

I would miss Bob. Even though his strict approach to detail reminded me of the military, he was a fair man if you followed his rules. He always wore an Army patrol hat and would start a sentence by calling me 'Kid.' He treated me well even though he didn't like long haired jumpers. It was the '70's, long hair was in, but nonetheless he encouraged me to be a loft rat by showing me how to sew and teaching me how to rig parachutes. I respected the man tremendously and knowing that he'd been the last of the original group that formed the California Smokejumper program in 1957, it meant a lot to the bros and the program. His twenty years as loft foreman turned the unit into a strict, seamless operation. He had a playful side also and to hear his belly laugh put a smile on my face. Now Boy, with fifteen-years of loft experience took over with the same sense of leadership, but with a meticulous twist, so much so, he carried a second nickname. 'Cost,' as in 'checker of small things.'

Buster added, "We sewed anti-inversion netting on all the parachutes this winter. No more Mae West malfunctions. I guess we'll have to wait and see if it works."

"Thank God for that," I said, having a flashback of John slamming the ground.

"We're funded for forty jumpers this year. Only three pogues are returning, so we'll have eleven new ones to train. Oh, and Cave Man has a new title after his stunt on the Hog Fire. He's now, "The Morale Officer."

On May 12, twenty of us piled into our bus, Jumper III, and headed to a small blaze on the Shasta-Trinity, making for a good start to the season. But May rolled into June with only one fire jump amongst the crew. If it wasn't for my Senior Parachute Rigger training, I would've gone crazy. Then we had a week of CPR and EMT training. A nurse from the local hospital taught us how to administer the painkiller Demerol via intramuscular application, and Dextran, used for treating shock, through a catheter inserted into a vein.

In the training room, Hairhat sat next to me, so we paired up to follow the nurse's instructions. I hated needles, couldn't stand to watch. Every time our family went overseas, we endured a barrage of shots. Shots for this disease, shots for that disease, so many damn shots at one time I had to put my arm in a sling it became so sore.

I broke into a cold sweat as I stuck the catheter into Hairhat's biggest vein. "Now," the nurse said, "tape it off so it doesn't move and insert the IV." I took a deep breath, wiped the sweat from my forehead, and finished the job. The nurse told Hairhat. "Now, it's your turn."

"This one looks good," Hairhat said as I looked away. I felt the needle digging into my arm and heard him mumbling, "Your skin's tough as leather, Ry. The needle isn't going in." I felt pressure, then searing pain. He muffled, "Shit. I think it went through the vein." He pulled the needle out and the area swelled immediately. The nurse came over and said, "Try again on another vein. I'll watch."

"Come on Hairhat," I growled, "these fucking veins can't get any bigger."

"Sorry Ry, I'll get it this time." He managed to guide the catheter inside my vein and after he secured it, I ripped it out and went outside for some fresh air. I prayed to never have to do that in the field.

We didn't turn a prop for weeks, which gave me ample opportunity to study the FAA manuals for my Riggers License. While doing this, I stumbled across literature about the history of smokejumping. What made me proud to be associated with this group came with the revelation that a Mr. Stuart Roosa left jumping and eventually become Apollo 14's command module pilot. He'd been one of 24 people on the entire planet to journey to the moon and back. He rooked in Cave Junction in 1953. Another smokejumper, Ken Sisler, jumped out of the North Cascades base in 1957, and received the Medal of Honor for his bravery in the Vietnam War, posthumously. Willi Unsoeld, a Cave Junction jumper in 1950, went on to become a legend in the mountain climbing community. In 1963, with climbing partner Tom Hornbein, they became the first individuals to scale Mount Everest via the peak's treacherous West Ridge considered one of the greatest "feats" in mountaineering history. National Geographic regarded it as one of the top five Everest climbs of all time. Unsoeld died in an avalanche on Mount Rainier in 1979. I felt pride being associated with such people.

When I discovered a particular proposal submitted in 1939, to Evan Kelly, the Regional Forester, on the new idea of delivering firefighters by means of parachute, I had to read on. Experiments in dropping dummies from varying altitudes at the Ogden, Utah airport in 1934 had proven successful, as well as the live jumps that followed. Disregarding the positive results, Forester Kelly made this statement:

"I'm willing to take a chance on most any kind of a proposition that promises better action on forest fires, but the best information that I can get from experienced fliers, is that all parachute jumpers are crazy, just a little bit unbalanced,

otherwise they wouldn't be involved in such a hazardous undertaking."

Mr. Kelly temporarily put on hold the use of parachutes as a means of swift attack on wild fires, but after extensive lobbying by parachute proponents, 1940 ushered in the official birth of smokejumping in the United States. Two jump bases were established, one at Seeley Lake, Montana, the other in Winthrop, Washington. The first fire call came in at 2 p.m. on July 12, 1940. Rufus Robinson and Earl Cooley jumped from a Curtis Travelair on a fire located in Idaho's Nez Perce National Forest near the head of Martin Creek. The 1940 fire season saw twelve fire jumps between the two bases with a savings of $30,000 to the Forest Service in suppression costs.

The Japanese bombing of Pearl Harbor the following year saw a flood of volunteers join the military, which stripped the Forest Service of its firefighters. The Army quickly initiated the Airborne Regiments using smokejumpers' knowledge and equipment.

By 1942, only five smokejumpers remained in the United States, and 1943 saw the number drop to three. The smokejumper program was on the brink of extinction. In 1941, the government created the Civilian Public Service Program, or CPS, for conscientious objectors. Phil Stanley, one such objector was aware of the manpower issue and wrote a letter to the Forest Service asking if it needed help with the fledging smokejumper program. The government answered with a resounding yes. Three-hundred conscientious objectors volunteered for training, sixty made the final cut. Two new jump bases were established, eleven of the new recruits went to Cave Junction, Oregon, five to McCall, Idaho, and the rest staffed Seeley Lake and Winthrop. They received no pay, only the required work clothes. Nineteen-forty-three saw thirty-one fires jumped and sixteen hiked-to fires, with savings to the Forest Service of $75,000. Nineteen-forty-four saw the number of smokejumpers increase to 110 with the majority of them being CPS volunteers. By 1945, the number of smokejumpers doubled to 220.

Aside from the issue of conscientious objectors, WWII forced the program to confront another sensitive issue. The Forest Service had a dilemma on their hands when they hired a Wardell 'Knuckles' Davis sight unseen. When he showed up an

African-American, the Forest Service had a problem; they didn't hire African-Americans. As it turned out, however, Knuckles—who happened to be a welterweight Golden Gloves boxing champion—was allowed to compete for a position. So impressed by his determination and skill, the Forest Service accepted him into the group, thus breaking the color barrier.

As the Forest Service integrated, the military did everything it could to segregate the troops. In early 1944, the 555th Parachute Infantry Battalion, referred to as the Triple Nickels, formed from members of the 92nd Buffalo Infantry Division stationed at Camp Mackall, North Carolina. The men of the Triple Nickels were a highly trained reinforcement parachute infantry battalion and ready for combat overseas. Nearing the end of the war, word from the front lines came back indicating that bringing in blacks would cause more trouble than good, so the military barred them from fighting overseas.

The Forest Service needed more jumpers, so the 555th battalion received secret redeployment orders. They sent them to the 9th Service Command in Pendleton, Oregon, and the Army Air Base in Chico, California, where the Forest Service trained them as smokejumpers. They jumped 36 fires. On August 6, 1945, tragedy struck the 555th with the death of Private First Class Malvin L. Brown, a medic who fell while attempting a tree letdown on the Siskiyou National Forest. He became the first recorded smokejumper fatality in the line of duty. After WWII, the Triple Nickels, and all but five conscientious objectors left the program. They have the legacy of saving the United States Smokejumper Program, and are considered 'bros' by every smokejumper past and present.

In 1945, Carlton Naugle of Missoula, wrote, 'The Smokejumper's Anthem,' based on an existing Army Airborne song.

Chorus:
Glory, glory, what a hell of a way to die,
Glory, glory, what a hell of a way to die,
Glory, glory, what a hell of a way to die,
Oh, he ain't gonna jump no more.

'Is everybody ready?' said the spotter looking up,
Our hero meekly answered 'yes' and then they stood him up.

They jumped him out into the blast, his static line unhooked,
Oh, he ain't gonna jump no more.

Chorus

He counted long, he counted loud, he waited for the shock.
He felt the breeze, he felt the clouds, he felt the awful drop.
He thought about the folks back home he'd never see again,
Oh, he ain't gonna jump no more.

Chorus

He hit the ground an awful splat, the blood was spurting high.
He choked and gasped, he tore his chest, he didn't want to die.
The district ranger grabbed the phone and into it, he said:
Oh, he ain't gonna jump no more.

Chorus

A snag went through his stomach and a branch put out his eye.
His leg was broke below the knee and he began to cry.
The buzzards circling overhead came down to hear him roar.
Oh, he ain't gonna jump no more.

Chorus

Blood was on his risers and his brains were on the chute.
His intestines were a-dangling from his heavy jumper's boot.
The packer found him by the trail and buried him right there.
Oh, he ain't gonna jump no more.

Chorus

He knocked upon the Pearly Gates. To him Saint Peter said:
'You don't belong in this fine place, go down below instead.'
They gave him a brand new chute with risers of gold,
And he jumped once more.

*****

I took a break from studying and walked through the loft to the drying tower. A beam of sunlight reflected off the portraits of the California Smokejumper crews since its inception in 1957. Two gold plaques hung under the 1970 crew photo. One read, 'In memory of Steven Grammer, who died in a helicopter crash while fighting the Forks Fire, Angeles National Forest.' The other read, 'In memory of Tom Regennitter, who died while jumping the Oak Fire, Shasta Trinity.' Tom had been a retread jumper—firefighters trained in Redding and sent back to their districts until called upon—from 1968 until his death two years later. Boy, Cave Man, and Murry 'Leather Sack' Taylor were in the plane when Tom made his final jump.

Cave Man described it this way: "We were flying to reinforce the crew on the Oak Fire in the DC-3. Tom was the last of a three-man stick and while his partners exited, he slipped on his static line extension and fell to the floor. Instead of holding back, he pushed himself from the plane. As we circled, he appeared to be unconscious and stayed that way all the way to the ground."

The investigation that followed came up with a possible scenario. There were problems with the parachutes scraping the fuselage during the deployment sequence, so they added a section of static line to get better clearance from the plane before the chute opened. The jumpers held the extension in their hands, and dropped the bundle prior to exiting. As Tom approached the door about to exit, he slipped on his bundle and fell to the floor. Instead of aborting the exit, he pushed himself from the plane, head first. The slipstream caught his static line, which may have pulled more line out of the rubber band stows on the deployment bag brushing his facemask so violently it yanked his head back breaking his neck.

I tried to visualize how something like that could happen, it didn't seem possible with all the checks prior to jumping. Having rigged a few practice chutes, I noticed some of the rubber bands that stowed the line needed replacement from overuse and brittleness. My thoughts centered on the rubber band stows.

I learned about another smokejumper tragedy that happened at a time when the program made big strides. On August 5, 1949, dozens of lightning fires erupted in Montana. A DC-3 with sixteen jumpers flew to a small blaze in Mann Gulch, located at the gates of the Rocky Mountains on Montana's Helena National Forest. All but one, due to sickness, jumped on a steep slope with mixed fuels of firs, pines, bunch and cheat grass. The crew worked in a routine manner until the wind unexpectedly intensified from the river channel and the canyon exploded in flame, sending embers into the unburned portion of the canyon below the crew trapping them in the middle of the inferno.

In a desperate attempt to save his men, foreman Wagner Dodge, lit an escape fire. The concept of using fire to create a safety zone wasn't taught to the younger firefighters. They had no idea what he was doing and instead of following him, they made a run for the ridge top. The fire won the race. Dodge survived in his escape fire. When the smoke cleared, two jumpers were found alive, but severely burned, both died a short time later. Eleven bodies were found toward the top of the ridge. In all, thirteen men had lost their lives in a matter of minutes.

From the investigation that followed, the deaths were deemed an act of God. The tragedy captivated the nation. Hollywood joined in and made the movie, "*Red Skies of Montana.*" Perhaps the ghosts of those men urged author Norman Maclean to pursue the matter four decades later. He spent years researching the incident before writing a narrative of the disaster titled, "*Young Men and Fire.*"

The deaths at Mann Gulch changed how the Forest Service attacked wildland fires. Safety issues moved to the forefront. Training intensified in the areas of fire behavior and weather conditions and more fires were attacked at night. The Inter-Agency Fire Sciences Laboratory formed in Missoula to study fire behavior and improve the overall safety of fighting wildland fires.

While lingering in the operations office digesting the information I'd discovered, a call came in. I heard Gramps say on the line, "We're capable of climbing any tree for any reason. I'll have the climbers contact you as soon as they're selected."

As he hung up the phone, I raised my hand to volunteer for the project, even though I didn't know what it entailed. Mr. Atlas entered the office. Gramps said to him, "Do you want to go on a tree climbing project on Shasta Lake?"

Mr. Atlas nonchalantly answered, "Sure."

Gramps looked at me, then to Mr. Atlas, saying, "Take Ryan, you're going to be climbing into Bald eagle nests for the Wildlife Department to figure out why the birds aren't having chicks. That's all I know."

*****

Mr. Atlas and I arrived at the Forest Service's boat dock at Turntable Bay early the next morning. The thought of climbing into the nest of America's symbol sent shivers down my spine. Before setting out, Phil, the Wildlife Biologist, briefed us. "I'm hoping to get you into two nests today. They're active and the eagles won't like you being there. They may dive at you, so be watchful. When you get into the nest, gather all the shell fragments, feathers, and fish remains you can find."

We loaded the boat with climbing gear and headed up the McCloud arm of the lake. Phil steered the boat into a deep cove and beached it. He pointed to a big pine tree. "The nest is up there. Can you see it?"

I couldn't miss it. It appeared larger and thicker than I imagined, wedged between massive branches a third of the way down the tree. I volunteered to go first and as I strapped on the climbing harness, Phil said, "Eagles prefer to build their nests down from the top, unlike ospreys, which nest on the tops of trees. Eagles mate for life and use the same nest every year."

A mature Ponderosa with huge, twisted branches loomed in front of me. It stood about 50 yards from shore in a dense patch of poison oak. As I fought my way through the oak, I knew there'd be a price to pay later on. I strapped on the spurs, and needed Mr. Atlas's help to get the throw rope around the five-foot diameter trunk. Starting my assent, I stirred up a few columns of ants that relentlessly attacked my arms. I reached the first major limb drenched in sweat. Phil didn't want us to prune the lower branches, so the climbing took longer than expected.

"How's it going up there?" he yelled from the shore.

"Oh, great," I answered, while ants buried their pincers into my skin. Once standing on a sturdy limb, I took a moment to look around. A full lake lapped the shoreline, the limestone crags of Shasta Caverns glistened in the sun, and a light breeze cooled my sweat. High above the tree, an eagle circled and shrieked.

The nest seemed to grow larger as I weaved through the branches up to its base. I gasped at the diameter, at least six-feet across and it encircled the trunk with no way get into it without having to climb in an inverted position just to reach the four-foot thick edge. "Are you able to get in?" Phil yelled. I looked to the shore and saw him gazing up at me with binoculars. I mumbled, "Hell yeah, I'm going to get into this fucking nest," and yelled back, "Just give me a minute!"

I climbed upside down to the edge of the nest, trembling at the thought that nothing would break my fall, if I lost my grip. After a few deep breaths, I pulled myself up forcefully and tumbled into the nest. An eagle screeched in protest. It sounded like a missile when it strafed by me. I rolled over and found the nest to be flat, no depression in the middle, and at least six-feet wide. A mat of dry grass cushioned me from the branches.

"What's in the nest?" Phil yelled.

I looked around to see feathers, fish bones, shell fragments, and in one corner, the decomposing carcass of a chick. I put everything in a plastic bag, the putrid carcass made me gag, and I felt guilty as a grave robber. I began my awkward climb out of the nest, and once on a solid branch, I slid down my rope to the ground. Phil crashed through the brush to meet me. When I handed him the bag, he looked like a kid opening a Christmas present. "Oh god," he said when he saw the chick's remains.

I stripped out of the climbing gear and headed for the lake to wash off the sweat, ants, and poison oak. Back in the boat, Phil looked at Mr. Atlas and asked, "Think we have enough time to do another one?"

"Let's go," Mr. Atlas ordered.

I sat at the bow and enjoyed the cool wind blowing on my face as we sped toward Bridge Bay. Once we arrived, Mr. Atlas's tree looked much easier to climb. I watched from the boat as he quickly entered the nest. I asked Phil, "Could you let us know what you find?"

"I definitely will. After all," he said appreciatively, "if it weren't for you two, there wouldn't be any research."

Back at the base that afternoon, I felt a real sense of accomplishment, not many people could say they'd climbed into an active Bald eagle nest. A few weeks later, Phil left a message with Gramps indicating the samples we'd collected showed traces of DDT, solving the chick's mortality issues. It wasn't a happy finding, but a finding nonetheless.

August came and went with no fire jumps, only a ground pounder to the Tahoe. September flew by with nothing at all. Finally, Big Ernie smiled on me, because I happened to be in the right place at the right time when the Redding Hotshots came up short a body for an assignment to the Los Padres. Their superintendent, Charlie Caldwell—known in firefighting circles as the 'Fire Guru'—asked if I wanted to fill in for his missing 'pickle.' We called them pickles because they dressed in green pants, green shirts, and green hats, and therefore looked like a pickle. We also used the term to intimidate them. His crew had such a fine reputation that fire overhead gave them the most challenging assignments. At the Los Padres fire camp, our assignment involved implementing a major burnout operation using Vary pistols, napalm, drip torches, and a trailer-mounted flame-thrower. We set fire to thousands of acres for an entire week.

I couldn't have been more grateful for the overtime pay because we'd been on track to break the slowest fire season on record. After that, the Hayfork Ranger District requested climbers to harvest Jeffery, Ponderosa, and Sugar pine pinecones, I quickly volunteered. Bionic Buster led the project and after watching him leap through the trees, I thoroughly believed he had monkey blood in him. He could strip a tree bare of pinecones before anyone else had half of theirs done.

With that project completed, I had one more order of business to attend to before the end of the season. My last step in becoming an FAA certified Senior Parachute Rigger. Boy administered the test. Having studied throughout the season, I knew most of the answers without having to think about them. Waiting the few weeks for the results tormented me more than the test. When the results finally came in, I'd passed.

CHAPTER 11

The Last Frontier

Alaska Fire Detail
June 1979

Sarah's new circle of friends saw her situation—being married to a smokejumper—as not working out very well. The summers had me gone all the time, and when I returned, she was busy with work and them. One night while partying with our neighbors, I noticed Sarah uncharacteristically quiet. When our friends left, I had to ask her, "What's wrong, baby?"

Her look froze me. Tears formed in her eyes, and in a shaky voice, she said, "I can't take this anymore. Sometimes I feel we have a chance, but it doesn't last very long. As soon as you go to work, I feel all alone, you don't call, and you don't include me with your so-called, bros. You can live this way if you like, but I can't do it anymore."

My gut churned. Impending doom smothered me like a blanket. I fought with my feelings. Why can't I commit to her? What is wrong with me? The time had come where asking such questions became futile. I saw it in her eyes, it's over. I struggled to find words. Finally, in defeat, I asked, "So, what should we do?" It didn't take long to realize I'd just said the wrong thing.

With tears streaming down her cheeks, she choked out, "I'm moving in with a workmate. Maybe with some time to yourself, you can realize how you screwed this up!"

After we broke the lease on our rental, I moved into a little house across town. It took a while for the initial shock to wear off, but we decided to continue our relationship without the pressures of being married, which worked out better. The issue of Duke came up since she'd bonded with him over the years, so we decided to share him. He's not one to be tied up and instinctively knew where each of us lived, so I had to laugh when friends said they'd seen him trotting down Court Street heading toward Sarah's house. Being brought up in a large family and having roommates when I left home, living alone seemed so foreign. I didn't like it much, too damn quiet. I found myself thinking aloud, debating with myself over my inability to give Sarah what she needed. At times it drove me crazy, I found myself hanging out with the Alcohol Squad to combat my loneliness and fluctuating emotions.

I focused on work, hoping it would bring relief to my internal struggles. It seemed to work because not only did I manage to pass the Senior Riggers test, I also moved in line for the Alaska Fire Detail. Every third year a jumper, if he wanted to, rotated on the detail list, a reward for sticking around. Now my turn came up and every day as I labored in the loft repairing chutes, my mind centered on Alaska *and* Sarah. Now that we parted, I wanted her. It was so damn confusing.

Vise was on the detail in 1977, he briefed me on what to expect, "The sun doesn't really set up there, you can actually watch it circle the horizon. There's no rocks to slam into, no big trees to hang up in, and hitting the tundra is like landing on a pillow. Overtime is abundant and the mess hall is open 24/7. If you get into Fairbanks, there are plenty of great bars. The only problem is the mosquitoes. They'll drive you crazy. You'll have to wear netting and they issue military grade bug dope that can melt plastic. Stay close to the phone, Ryan. They'll call as soon as they can't keep up with their fires. There's no seasonal pattern to rely on."

I couldn't understand how Alaska could have problems with fires. I associated it with deep snow sitting on a solid layer of ice, but in the summer, they had fires, lots of them. The Bureau of Land Management administered the Alaska Smokejumpers, so that would be a change for me also.

The hot topic of conversation in the loft centered on the BLM experimenting with a new parachute system. They'd been testing square parachutes used exclusively by skydivers, also known as Ram Air chutes. It had the aerodynamics of a wing and a forward speed of twenty-five to thirty miles-per-hour. Jumpers who'd used both systems said switching from the traditional round parachutes to the new squares compared to trading in an old pickup for a racecar.

The BLM justified moving to the squares for one main reason: the wind. A round parachute had a wind speed limit of fifteen to twenty miles-per-hour. When wind speeds exceeded that, the round chutes became non-maneuverable, and the jumper usually ended up going in backwards. Many times in Alaska, the wind exceeded the limits, resulting in aborted fire jumps.

While the BLM experimented with the square parachute, the Forest Service modified its traditional round chutes to incorporate different porosity materials, hoping to achieve the same results. The Forest Service saw the square as a radical approach, one they would never consider, because the jumper had to pull a ripcord to deploy the main chute, a procedure the Forest Service managers considered as too risky.

*****

Activity at the base became hectic for so early in the season. Instructors trained a pogue class of twenty in order to keep our number at 45. As training progressed, half the pogue washed out, and a new group of eight signed on, but with a catch. Being too late in the season to start over with such a large group they traveled to Missoula to train. The poor pogues endured a rash of teasing for having to go there due to the rivalry between our bases. We referred to Missoula jumpers as 'Zulies.'

I loved the fast pace in the loft. My rigging technique improved with every chute I packed. At the beginning of June, Vise asked, "Are you ready for the Alaska call."

I was more than ready and answered, "Ready and waiting."

He chuckled. "That's what I thought until I got there. Keep in mind, Ry, when you change latitudes in the jumper world, you'll see a drastic changes in attitude. When you're in Alaska, do as the Alaskans do. Don't compare, don't contradict, and above all else, don't wear your Nomex pants up there. The mosquitoes can poke right through them. Check out a couple pairs of their fire pants. Thick cotton is much better than thin Nomex."

"Anything else?"

"Don't go to the native bars alone. They don't like white men, especially when they're drunk."

On June 5, the call came in, and the next morning, seven of us boarded a small commuter plane for San Francisco, where we transferred to a commercial flight to Anchorage. Excitement made it difficult to relax in the plane. From my window seat, I forced myself to focus on the outside world. Endless mountain ranges dotted with lakes streamed below until the pilot instructed us to buckle up. The final frontier waited: Alaska!

On our descent into Anchorage, I noticed the city had high-rise buildings, a lake cluttered with floatplanes, and upscale housing—none of the shacks or dirt roads I'd expected. Entering the modern terminal, the first thing that grabbed my attention stood fourteen-feet tall, a Grizzly bear standing on its hind legs, looking down on me with outstretched arms. It froze me in place. I'd heard stories of jumpers encountering Grizzlies on fires, and the sight of this monster had me thinking that I'd rather not see a live version of it, especially in the bush. Next, I came upon an eight-foot tall moose. Vise had told me, "You'll see moose in and around Fairbanks, right in the city sometimes. Whatever you do, don't think they're friendly. Get out of their way because they've been known to hurt people."

Then I saw a huge Polar bear towering in a glass case. Its snow-white fur shown with purity, but its eyes, black as night, cut right through me.

We loaded our gear into a small commuter plane for the hop to Fairbanks. Not long after reaching cruising altitude, I looked out the window and saw a mountain that looked to be standing on the clouds. I figured it to be the size of Mt. Shasta—about 12,000 feet—but little did I know it was only the top half of Mt. Denali. At 20,320 feet, it's the highest peak in North America. Mighty Alaska had me hooked already.

A BLM jumper greeted us and helped us load our gear into a crew carrier. He drove through Fairbanks toward Ft. Wainwright, a military base where the BLM jumpers staged their operation. Along the way, he told us, "All our jumpers are on fires. Once we get to the standby shack, you'll get a quick orientation and a meal. There're fires waiting for you on the Seward Peninsula."

At the standby shack, we arranged our jump gear on speed racks—wooden structures that held jump suits for quick suit-ups. Another BLM jumper handed each of us a small machete. "This is a Woodsman's Pal,' he said, "You'll need it to fashion one of our main firefighting tools, the top four-feet of a Spruce tree." He studied our faces before continuing. "If there aren't any Spruce trees around, we have burlap bags in our fire boxes. Fill one with clumps of tundra and beat on the flames. When the burlap disintegrates, grab another and keep on going."

He handed each of us two packages. "This is your mosquito netting. One is for your hardhat and the other is a tent." He passed out small green bottles. "Over-the-counter mosquito repellant doesn't work here; the military's given us their brand of bug dope. If you have reservations about using highly concentrated, toxic chemicals on your skin, I'll guarantee you the mosquitos will change your mind." A smile formed on his face, "We don't do pack-outs here. When your fire's out, radio the district and a helicopter will come get you." His expression suddenly became deadly serious. "No matter what part of the state you jump in, you'll be in bear country. They're coming out of hibernation as we speak, and they're hungry. They can smell you miles away. Do not, and I mean *do not*, put any food in your hootch. If a bear stalks you, get on the radio and call in a helicopter to get you out. Normally, we send you out with one of our jumpers because they carry guns, but as you can see, there aren't any here. Be careful out there, guys."

We wolfed down our meal in the mess hall and hurried back to the standby shack. On the ramp sat five Beech 18-turbo liners, known as Volpar's, a fast, long-range plane that carried a payload of eight jumpers and cargo. Unlike a Twin Otter or DC-3, the Volpar had a step system built onto the fuselage so the door could be closed during flight to reduce drag. We suited up and waddled to one of the Volpar's and within minutes, the plane taxied down the runway. Now isn't this nice? In Redding, the pre-flight checks lasted much longer.

Once airborne, the spotter briefed us. "The Seward Peninsula is 850 miles west. We're cruising at 240 miles-per-hour and should be there in about three and a half hours. Settle in and enjoy the flight."

We followed the mighty Yukon River west. Brown with silt, it snaked across a wide open flat that stretched as far as the eye could see. Countless tributaries spurred off the main course, many of them ending in long sandbars. Lakes of all sizes dotted the flats, and sunlight glinted off the windswept water, making the land shimmer with light.

When the spotter crawled over us from the cockpit it signaled time to get ready. He opened the door and lowered the exit step to a rush of cold arctic air that streamed into the cabin. I'm five in the jump order, but the fire would only get four. The spotter threw a set of streamers and ordered Bionic Buster, and Disco to hook up. When the streamers hit the ground, the spotter quickly briefed them and yelled, "We're on final!"

No second streamer run or more as in California. The slap on Buster's shoulder sent him and Disco out the door and I watched as they turned into the wind for the entire ride, as did the second stick. We dropped the cargo and left the area without even a second look. When I saw my fire, the spotter gave me a radio and map case. We approached this fire exactly as we had the first, one streamer drop upwind. The slap came and I jumped. Cold air and an endless view of tundra greeted me. As soon as my feet hit, I attempted a roll, but ended up sinking into the tussocks. It felt like landing on a giant sponge. I packed my parachute into the waterproof bag they issued, as a hoard of mosquitoes swarmed around me.

Perky, Big D, and I stumbled across to the leading edge of the fire and began stuffing clumps of wet tundra into our burlap bags. Swatting the flames with the bags proved effective, though our progress seemed slow. I decided to use two sacks at once, one in each hand. I slapped the flames like a windmill. Once I settled into the zone and developed a steady rhythm, I forged on relentlessly.

Being fire boss and not knowing the characteristics of Alaskan fires, I pushed my bros hard until I noticed Big D slump down. He looked pale and exhausted; I tossed him a snack bar and turned back to the fire. When the last flames succumbed to the burlap, I fell to the tundra, cold, wet, hungry, and exhausted. The wind blew hard all the time, so we built a break with our cargo boxes, wrapped ourselves in our jump gear, and waited for the chopper I'd radioed in. We sat in silence; the screech of an Arctic tern occasionally interrupted the wind singing through this lonely wilderness. Everything seemed to belong here, except us. I thought of Sarah and how she would've loved to be here.

These types of places bonded us, they made us whole. God, I missed her.

After the helicopter landed, we loaded up and headed to Nome where a Volpar waited to take us back to Fairbanks. Once in Fairbanks, we found ourselves already at the top of the jump list. A BLM jumper drove us to the barracks and assigned us rooms. After a shower and change of clothes, I walked to the mess for a late night meal with Disco. I asked him, "How did your fire go?"

He shook his head, "You know Buster, he had us swatting so long that my arm is still sore. How'd you guys do?"

"Confusing at first. I had no idea how to attack it. It looked too big for the three of us, but after a few hours of swatting, we had it under control. Quiet out there, kind of eerie."

Back at the barracks, I tried to sleep, but the light from the midnight sun made it difficult. I tied a bandana around my eyes just to get darkness. At morning roll call, the box boy—the guy who received fire requests and dispatched jumpers—told us, "There's another front coming in from the Bering Strait." He yelled out the names of the first eight jumpers and said, "Suit up; there's an outstanding request for the Bettles area."

The box boy assigned two Alaskan jumpers to our load who'd returned during the night. We flew over the White Mountains, where the rolling hills of tundra transformed into ridges dotted with mosaic patterns of Black Spruce. The backside of the White Mountains eased into the Yukon Flats, which gave way to the Endicott Mountains, and a sliver of smoke. The spotter opened the door; I found I liked the Alaskan single streamer approach. No endless circling from drop after drop to establish an exit point. Alaska is one big jump spot, the only hazard being the lakes and rivers.

When my turn came, I catapulted out of the Volpar knowing I'd just earned some valuable 'Salt Points' for jumping above the Arctic Circle. As I floated down for my second tundra landing in as many days, a cloud of mosquitoes swarmed around me, they bounced off my helmet and slipped into my facemask. I felt them biting me everywhere they could. After crashing into the spongy ground, I grabbed the military bug dope, slapped it all over my hands and face to keep them at bay.

The fire boss yelled, "Cargo coming in!" The Volpar came in so low I saw the spotter grin as he pushed the boxes out the door. After we gathered the fire packs in one location, the fire boss asked sweetly, "Who wants to be the camp bitch?"

I glanced at Big D. He shrugged his shoulders. None of us out-of-region jumpers dared volunteer. The other Alaskan jumper laughed and said, "Looks like we have a virgin crew. I'll set up camp so they know what to do next time."

The fire boss said, "Right, the rest of you, let's go swat some flames."

Mosquitoes swarmed my helmet netting as we worked the fire. One moment I'd be aware of the netting, the next I wouldn't. I let loose some spit. Right away, I cursed, looking around to see if anyone had witnessed my dumb mistake. The spit gobbed on the netting right in front of my face! If that isn't bad enough, nothing compared to the mosquito attacks we all endured whenever we had to relieve ourselves.

Spruce trees grew nearby, we fashioned effective weapons for swatting the flames by cutting off the lower branches and lopping off the top. What a strange sight, to see highly trained smokejumpers attacking a fire with broom like tools. Hours later, we had the fire circled, and as I walked back to the jump spot, I realized why the boss had asked for a camp bitch. A metal can with water boiling hung from a tripod over a small fire and a tidy pile of firewood sat nearby. Fire boxes formed a welcoming circle around the fire. The camp bitch said, "Water's hot, boys. Food's in the cargo box over by that stand of spruce." He pointed, "Way over there will be the hootch site. Don't take food there. If you do, it will only be an appetizer. You'll be the main course!"

"Did you see a bear?" I asked.

He laughed. "You won't see a bear unless it wants you to. We've been sniffed out long ago." He rummaged through his PG bag and pulled out a large caliber pistol. My bro Perky's eyes lit up. Being a Vietnam Vet who had part of his elbow blown off during the war, guns interested him. In spite of his injury, the overhead didn't given him any special consideration during the PT test, and to see him do all the required pull-ups and push-ups with that gimp elbow amazed me. "Let me see it," Perky told the bitch, who handed it over. Perky sighed, "Ah, a .44 mag."

I felt better knowing we had that gun. "What happens if a bear does come into camp?" I asked.

"Don't run," the Alaskan, said, "if you can outrun a bear, you're in the wrong profession. Make noise instead. If I hear you yelling, I'll come a running."

Disco laughed at me, "You afraid of bears, Ry?"

"Have you ever been chased by a bear, Disco?" I shot back.

"No, I guess I haven't. Have you?"

"As a matter of fact, yeah, on a family vacation to Yellowstone. We stopped for a picnic and one of my brothers and I went into some trees to take a piss. The next thing I know, my brother is hopping past me trying to pull his pants up. I started laughing until I saw two bear cubs chasing him. I ran like hell behind him. He jumped in the car and locked all the doors. The rest of us stuck outside. My dad tried to chase them off until mama bear showed up. We all started banging on the car, my brother finally unlocked the doors at the last second and we dove in. The bears proceeded to eat our picnic lunch right in front of us. So yeah Disco, you can say I'm concerned about bears."

The Alaskan said, "That's why we keep food away from the hootch area, it's too damn dangerous."

The fire boss started laughing. "Remember the fire where that bear ripped into Rick's hootch?"

"Oh, hell, yeah!" his bro laughed.

The fire boss looked at me. "This guy freaked out, yelling and screaming for help and when no one came quick enough he darted out the other side of his hootch and ran right into a tree, breaking his fucking nose."

"What's so funny about that?" I asked.

"He's a seasoned jumper who must've had the scent of food in his hootch!" the boss said. I understood his message and nodded my head.

The wind had calmed down enough to allow thick swarms of mosquitoes to gather around everyone's head. The camp bitch said, "Who wants to play a game?" Without waiting for a reply, he turned to the fire boss and smacked him on the top of his beanie. Beanies were the preferred method of protecting one's head from the skeet's. I wondered what kind of game is this until he held out his glove and started carefully counting the dead mosquitoes. "Huh," he groaned after almost five minutes of counting, "Only sixty-three."

I walked behind Disco, and before he knew it, I smacked him on the head.

"Hey!" he shouted.

"We have to beat sixty-three," I laughed.

I counted fifty before giving up. My bug dope seemed to be wearing off, so I reached into my fire shirt pocket to get the bottle. I pulled out my note pad and pen at the same time—bug dope had leaked onto my pen and the plastic was twisted and deformed! The fire boss noticed saying, "Think about this, guys. We get all kinds of tourists up here thinking they can tame the wilderness. They pack guns, food, and fishing gear, but some don't bring effective repellant. There's a case where this guy rented a cabin on a lake and when it came time for him to be picked up by floatplane, they couldn't find him. They searched the whole area and finally did. He had a bullet hole in his head. The mosquitoes drove him so crazy that he shot himself. He didn't have enough clothes to protect himself, his face so swollen from skeeter bites; they could hardly recognize his features." He grinned at me and said, "If you don't believe me, go ahead and stop using the dope."

I slapped on more dope. Later when I crawled in my hootch, I realized even more how these little vampires could affect one's sanity. I thought I'd anchored my mosquito tent without any getting inside, but while trying to sleep, a couple had and I spent the entire night trying to locate and kill them as they buzzed around my face.

After returning to Fairbanks, I had just enough time to get a little rest before jumping another mosquito-plagued fire, and then another. My first five days in Alaska became a repetition of flying hundreds of miles across the state, jumping a fire, returning to Fairbanks, and getting ready for the next call. Life became a blur until the lightning activity finally slowed, and the jump list became saturated with names.

I killed the sudden down time in the weight room behind the standby shack. After working out, I'd head to the mess and stuff my face. The grub in Alaska couldn't be beat, steak, chops, and chicken, salmon, pretty much anything you could ever want—as much as you wanted. To be able to eat so well after lifting translated into pounds of added muscle.

One evening after hitting the weights, I went to the mess hall and noticed the whole room silent. Now this seemed unusual for jumpers. I found a table with some of my Redding bros and asked, "Why all the gloom and doom?"

Disco said, "A DC-3 from either McCall or Missoula crashed going to Moose Creek. All twelve on board died. That's all we know for now."

I ate in silence. Who had died? How had it happened? The next morning, the box boy filled us in at roll call. "As you've probably heard, we lost a jump ship in Idaho yesterday. N148Z crashed in the Selway River ten miles from the Moose Creek Ranger Station. The flight originated in McCall, flew to Grangeville, and picked up ten young adults to do trail maintenance in the area. During the flight, an engine blew up and fell from the plane. The pilot tried to glide them into the river but hit a tree. Of the twelve on board, ten died. One survivor hiked seven hours to Moose Creek." What could we do but just look at one another? We climbed in and out of planes all the time.

CHAPTER 12

Steve's Journey

Fire #8648
Galena District, Alaska
June 22, 1979

After eleven days with no lightning, the Fairbanks jump list bottlenecked. My spending money dwindled fast from visiting the Howling Dog Saloon, buying beer, and tips I'd left in the strip clubs. Too many jumpers milling around with nothing to do created a problem. Overhead decided to staff the spike bases in McGrath and Galina. McGrath being 285 miles southwest of Fairbanks on the Kuskokwim River in a mountain range of the same name, and Galena, the more desirable location, 300 miles west on the Yukon, a front line military outpost with F-16 fighter planes that patrolled the Bearing Straits.

I went to Galena, the only Redding jumper to go. The rest of the load consisted of two Alaskans, three from McCall, and two Zulies. With clear weather, the pilot treated us to the scenic route. Sunlight danced off the choppy waves of the mighty Yukon River as it lazily meandered toward the Norton Sound in the Bering Sea. Lakes peppered the surrounding flats. The soothing drone of the engines put me into a semi-trance allowing my mind to drift. I watched an endless wilderness unfold below me. Blue-green tussocks stretched into steppes, yielding to majestic snowcapped mountain ranges glowing in a purple hue. I imagined myself as a rugged explorer challenging this wilderness when another thought crossed my mind. I asked the Alaskan sitting next to me, "Why do you jump fires in the middle of nowhere?"

"Haven't you heard of the Cold War?" he asked.

I looked at him curiously, "I know all about the cold war, never heard anything about Alaska fires affecting it!"

"Sure you do," he said.

"No, really," I said with conviction. "I spent my four years of high school behind the "Iron Curtain," in West Berlin. I saw Russian's with machineguns all the time. Anyway, what does the Cold War have to do with fires in Alaska?"

"National security," he said flatly. "The military needs us to prevent smoke from blanketing the state, which could allow the Soviets to invade us under cover of it. We're keeping the sky clear to prevent an invasion by the Commies."

As I said, "Yeah right," the plane made a sudden sweep north. Sleepy eyes opened and all conversation ceased. The Alaskan said, "Guess we're not going to Galena."

Out the pilot's window, I saw a small coil of silver-brown smoke billowing against a turquoise sky. The spotter worked his way from the cockpit through the crowded cabin to the door. He shouted above the drone of the engines, "We're going to a fire! Chute up!" The exit door swung aside, air rushed in to a deafening roar. I heard the spotter yell, "We'll jump the whole load!" There hadn't been lightning in weeks—what's this fire all about, I wondered.

While we put chutes on each other's backs, the spotter dropped streamers, and moments later, the first four bailed out. The rest of us hooked up, and as I sat in the doorway, I gazed down at stands of black spruce that looked like cathedral spires as the fire ripped through them. The spotter yelled, "We're on final! You ready?"

I nodded, felt the slap, and jumped. I swung below my canopy, feeling as free as I always did. I loved flying; I wanted to fly on and on forever, beyond the green steppes and over the purple mountains to the Bearing Sea. The exploding trees beneath me brought me back to reality. I banked right over a large stand of spruce and aimed for a clearing. The tundra softened my landing and thousands of bloodthirsty mosquitoes instantly began their attack. I stripped out of my jump suit frantically slapping on bug dope when I saw movement out of the corner of my eye. A Grizz? My fear evaporated as quickly as it had come. What I saw move looked like a human propped against a spruce tree, the last thing I'd imagined. I hollered, "Guys! Somebody's over here!"

I heard laughter. "Yeah right, Ryan! What have you been smoking?"

The fire boss tromped over and stood next to me. He'd been jumping for ten years and I'd heard his stories of being chased by bears, being snowed on while fighting fires, facing down a bull moose in the bush during mating season, and having to jump from a C-119 cargo plane before it crashed onto a sandbar. I figured he'd seen everything there was to see in Alaska, yet when I pointed to the man against the tree, his jaw dropped in astonishment. "No goddamn way! This can't be!" He radioed the pilot requesting the trauma kit. We cautiously approached the man and as we neared, shivers shot up my spine. Hundreds of mosquitoes fed on his grossly swollen face, his blue eyes looked vacant and hollow. He mumbled a few incomprehensible words to us from puffy, cracked lips. The fire boss nervously eyed the man, then the spreading fire behind us. I sensed his concern and told him, "I'll take care of this, go back to the fire." He hurried back to the flames.

I couldn't stand seeing the mosquitoes eat away at him, but what bothered me more, he had no reaction to them. I dug out my repellant and before slathering any on his skin, I warned him, "This is going to sting." Imagine my shock when he didn't even flinch? The mosquitoes instantly retreated hovering just out of range. I held my canteen to him and he worked at the small stream of water with his swollen tongue. "You hurt?" I asked.

He pointed to his feet. I carefully pulled the sleeping bag off his legs and noticed a rip in one of his boots, a flesh wound visible through the gap. As I slid the boot off, again the man showed no pain. I bandaged a deep cut, grateful it wasn't infected. I offered him a candy bar.

How had he gotten out here? How long had he been sitting against the tree? That he'd started the fire didn't bother me at all. It kept us from a potentially boring time in Galena after all, and by all measures, it had saved his life.

The man gnawed the candy bar while staring numbly at me. I'd never seen such a vacant expression on a person. I rummaged through his backpack looking for identification. I found clothing, a rain poncho, an unopened first aid kit, and a .357 revolver—no food or drinking water anywhere in sight. "How long have you been without food?" I asked.

The candy bar started to revive him. He took a long drink of water, and sheepishly told me, "I think I've been here a couple of days...ran out of food about then...been boiling mosquitoes until my sterno ran out."

"Eating mosquitoes?" My stomach turned. I ran to our cargo boxes, grabbed some freeze-dried meals, and cooked one up. He attacked it like a starving wolf. After he'd eaten, he said his name was Steve, and began telling his story:

"I had a partner and a dog when we started out. Hell, we'd planned this trip for a year, the tip of North America to the tip of South America on foot. A few big name companies sponsored us; we even had a magazine offer to pay for the rights to our story. We planned our route and pre-mailing supplies to places along the way. When we flew into Noatak in May, the spring snowmelt had come early. Instead of using cross-country skis, we had to travel on foot through freezing, calf-high water. We made it to Huslia, our first supply stop way behind schedule. My partner couldn't take it any longer and quit on me."

He shook his head in disgust and stared at the ground. After a long pause, he continued, "That pissed me off, but I wasn't about to quit, so I went on anyway with my dog toward Tanana. Don't know what went wrong. My compass kept swinging in different directions. After a few days of messed up readings, I knew I was lost. I came to a river, couldn't tell which one from the map, so I decided to build a raft and float until I found a village. The current forced the raft into the banks at every turn. Most of my supplies fell in the water. When my dog slipped off and disappeared into the current, I lost all hope."

Tears began rolling from his eyes. "I left the raft and went looking for my dog, but the brush was too thick, that's when I slipped and stabbed my foot on a branch spike. I walked as far as I could until the pain became too intense and I ended up here. I tried to start a fire, but it didn't take. I started this one with my last match."

I shook my head, amazed. I felt sorry for him, but seriously wondered about his judgment. If he hadn't been able to start the fire, he would've certainly died of starvation or ended up in the belly of a bear. I wondered if he'd considered using the gun in his backpack on himself, but couldn't bring myself to ask such an awful question.

We contained the fire by late evening and the boss called in a helicopter to take us to Galena. Inside an hour, the sound of rotor blades echoed toward us. The pilot landed and shut off the engines, letting us to load our gear without the prop wash. While doing so, he adamantly waved his arms around while saying, "There's a Grizz headed this way. I tried to change his course with a few low passes, but he seems dead set on coming here. Let's load up and clear the hell out."

The helicopter lifted us off the tundra and skimmed the treetops. Almost immediately, we looked down on a huge male Grizzly. The sun reflected off his hide, revealing a thick razorback of fur that ran the length of his spine. What a magnificent sight— especially from the safety of the helicopter! Steve wiped his eyes. I think he knew that bear would've finished him off.

We touched down in Galena and a military ambulance took Steve to the infirmary. Later, he returned to our Quonset hut on crutches with one of the ambulance crewmembers carrying three cases of beer. We drank and joked on a bank of the Yukon River until only empty beer cans rattled in the wind. Before he hopped a flight to Fairbanks the next morning, his eyes glazed over as he handed me a slip of paper. "If you're ever in Seattle, I'd be honored if you looked me up, Ryan. You saved my life, you know."

*****

The one-week detail in Galena turned into two due to a lack of lightning fires throughout the state. Confined to a small military outpost presented a real boredom challenge. I read books, watched movies, worked out, and drank. The Fourth of July came and went without any sort of celebration. Finally, news came from Fairbanks that we were rotating back. I rejoiced. Galena was way too small for me. All the out-of-region jumpers soon filtered back to Fairbanks and our time in Alaska ended. Flying home past Mt. Denali, I already looked forward to a return visit.

CHAPTER 13

Home At Last

McCall, Idaho, Smokejumper Base
July 1979

Back in California, it took me awhile to re-acclimate to Redding's dry heat after the chill of Alaska. When Vise had told me, 'When in Alaska, do as the Alaskans do,' I had no idea their way of life would take mine over so quickly. Working in the loft, I began looking for ways to improve our parachute system. That didn't go over well with Boy—a staunch traditionalist—so I curbed my enthusiasm for a while and resumed the Redding way of doing things.

I had to see Sarah. While waiting for demobe from fires in the Alaskan bush, I'd journey out by myself to explore. It wasn't a good idea without a gun, but I ventured out anyway. I always thought about her in the bush and when I stumbled upon flower patches, I'd pick a few and press them in my fire log booklet for her. How they could grow and survive in such a hostile environment seemed to be a miracle of nature. I wanted her to have them as a testament to her nature. She accepted them with delight even though we'd filed our divorce papers. I felt guilty for everything that had gone wrong in our lives; I couldn't apologize enough for being confused about love. We had separate lives now and the one thing that kept us connected was Duke. He loved us both unconditionally, a trait I wished I could've developed.

A major lightning storm had moved across Idaho and Montana and one planeload of Redding jumpers flew to Missoula and another went to Boise. Now, I'm at the top of the list, and I prayed to Big Ernie to get me out of Redding. He answered with a request to McCall, Idaho. Gramps headed our group of ten. He didn't get to leave the office much due to administrative duties and seeing him get a break would be good for all of us and him.

We flew northeast over the high desert plateau to the granite-studded peaks of the Payette National Forest. Through the thunderclouds, I saw a tiny town nestled beside a large lake. After landing, we taxied to the smokejumper ramp and parked next to a beautifully maintained vintage DC-3. The Forest Service owned a few of them and I looked forward to jumping out of a relic like that once again.

Filing out of our Twin Otter, Neal, McCall's base manager, greeted Gramps with a handshake and warm embrace. We tossed our travel bags into a pickup and headed to their operations center, nestled in the pines. A man introduced himself as Thad Duel, the training foreman, and he gave us a quick orientation. "As you can see, most of our jumpers are out on fires. I'm expecting you to be jumping in the morning. Load up in the crew carrier for dinner."

We went to a restaurant named 'Si Buenos,' known for having the best Mexican food in Idaho and upon returning to the barracks, I made my bed and showered, anxious to check out the town. McCall had great reviews from the vets. Soon, a few of us walked through a quiet, nicely maintained residential neighborhood toward the lake. We found the Foresters Club, the sound of live music blaring. To my delight, I knew the group. The Paul Delay Blues Band played loud to a crowded bar.

Our vets said Foresters could be a rowdy place, since it catered to loggers and Forest Service personnel. The two groups didn't get along well, the loggers referring to the government employees as 'Piss Fir Willies.'

I didn't notice any rivalries as we downed pitchers of beer and watched pretty girls shuffled by. Tony, a second year jumper who'd acquired the nickname, 'The Italian Stallion', from being a self-proclaimed lady's man, nodded his head. "Put this one on the map, boys!"

After Foresters, we walked down the main street of town to the Yacht Club, a quieter and more upscale establishment. It featured a deck overlooking the lake, a perfect place to chill with a lady. Next, we continued our recon mission at another McCall icon, Lardos, a dining and drinking establishment with a large bar and high open beam ceiling. "How about it, Ry?" Tony said signaling to at the pool table. Two attractive girls were shooting stick, one especially caught my eye. She wore tight jeans accented by a low cut top revealing smooth tanned skin. The Stallion walked up to them and asked if they wanted to play doubles. One of the girls bluntly replied while towing with her cue stick, "Sure, who do I get?"

Tony took a cue from the wall, stepped up close to her, and said, "I'll shoot first."

With that settled, I approached the one that originally caught my eye. Not only did she have a tight body, her long black hair accented a set of big brown eyes, but her beautiful inviting smile had the butterflies fluttering. I offered my hand saying, Hi, I'm Ry."

She locked onto my eyes while taking my hand gently, "I'm Denise, nice to meet you. That's a different sort of name."

"It's a nickname my bros call me."

She looked at our table, then at me with a confused look. "Those guys are your brothers?" She giggled, "Each from a different mother?"

I laughed, "And father. We're a tight band, smokejumpers."

"Oh, okay. We have smokejumpers here, never met any though. Are you from here?"

"We flew in from California today to help out with the fires."

"California? You're a long way from home."

"I'm hoping to call it a working vacation, my first time here."

"Well, welcome to McCall."

"Thanks, this is a nice town. You live here?"

"Yeah, I'm a local. Work at the market by the Forest Service office. Lived here all my life, have a house south of town." She giggled again, "You any good at pool?"

Tony had the table set. "I'm not bad."

She eyed me up and down and smiled real sexy like. "Let's knock some balls around, shall we."

As we shot pool, Denise kept giving me long looks with her big sparkling eyes. I couldn't help but blush or concentrate on the table. By our third game and a pitcher of beer, she became cozy, bumping into me, grabbing my stick, and winking at me when I made a shot. It was getting late; my bros signaled it time to head back. I said to her, "All the McCall jumpers are out on fires, I'm definitely jumping in the morning. Is there any way to keep this conversation going?"

She looked me over again biting her lower lip. A rumbling shot through me watching her write her number down on a napkin. Handing it to me, she held my hand long enough for it to feel like a kiss. I followed Mr. Atlas and the others out the door, tripping on some steps from looking back at her. She noticed and giggled. Walking back through town, I smacked The Stallion on the shoulder, "How'd you do with Shelly?"

"Already have a date, how about you?"

"Got her number," I said proudly.

I slept well thinking about those big brown eyes and hoped to hook up with her later.

*****

Van Ridge Fire, Nezperce National Forest
July 28, 1979

Sure enough, morning brought a request for a DC-3 load to a fire on the Nezperce National Forest. I'd jumped a DC-3 once before and loved the roominess. I could stand up in it without hitting my head, and the exit procedure, you simply walked out the door.

Flying to the fire, Denise occupied my thoughts. It confused me; I still missed Sarah, even while thinking of another. It had to do with being a military brat where I had to prepare myself for changing states and countries every few years, never expecting to see my friends again. I found a sense of security in Sarah; she'd been my longest friend, a rarity in my life.

The jump spot, a ridge top above the breaks of the Salmon River took over my thoughts. Steep canyon walls fell thousands of feet to the river below. It was a breathtaking view and I knew if I missed the ridge top it would be a long ride down the canyon. At the shoulder slap, I walked out the door, and fell into the slipstream. A gust of wind blew me slightly off the ridgeline and as the ground came closer, I prepared for a side hill landing. I hit hard and didn't try a PLF for fear of rolling down the mountain. Luckily the wind dragged my parachute along keeping me close to the ground. I released the capewells and watched the chute travel a short distance before collapsing. Lying there, I thought of the way Denise bit her lip when she looked at me. I must've enjoyed the memory too long, because a voice yelled down, "You okay, Ryan?"

I stood up. "I'm all right."

After the last cargo box landed, I grabbed the chainsaw and focused. It took three days of continuous line cutting to control the fire. We didn't get much sleep for fear of losing the fire and worked eighteen hour shifts until we contained the fire. When we returned to McCall, I was exhausted, but as soon as I got to a phone, I called Denise. She picked me up at the barracks that night, we had dinner at the Yacht Club, sipping wine on the deck and sharing our thoughts. Denise loved my stories of Alaska. I, in turn, was fascinated with everything about her. At the end of the evening, I reluctantly said, "I should be getting back. I'm on the first load out tomorrow."

She bit her lower lip, it drove me crazy and when she looked into my eyes and said sweetly, "Want to stay at my house tonight?" It floored me. I accepted without hesitation.

Her glances on the way to her house had my blood surging. Rabbits scattered from her front yard as she wheeled into the driveway. Her home was cozy and well-kept. We sipped more wine on a swing on her porch. Light caresses led to long kisses and after we heated up, she led me to the bedroom where we acted like rabbits all night. Sometime later, I woke in a panic, looked at the clock on her nightstand. "Oh shit," I said, scrambling out of bed. "I'm going to be late for roll call!"

She jumped out of bed with me. "Let's go. I'll drive like hell!"

The crew assembled outside the operations office took notice when she skidded to a stop in front of them. I gave her a quick kiss. "I'll call you if I don't jump today." I dashed out of the car. Thad stopped speaking until I took my place. I glanced nervously at Gramps. He just smiled. Thad, on the other hand, managed to finish his lecture by saying, "For those of you who aren't familiar with our procedures, it's not uncommon to be put on hold for being late to roll call. I'll make an exception in this case, since it obviously had something to do with fire! So Ryan, did you put that fire out?" Everybody started ribbing me, but I'm on cloud nine.

I'd been assigned to packing parachutes for the day, and not long into my first, the alarm went off. The Payette National Forest wanted a ten-man load. We piled into the crew vans, made the short ride to the airport, and climbed into our Twin Otter.

Tony sat next to me. He grinned and said, "You don't waste any time, do you?"

"I didn't plan it, it just happened," I blushed.

"Sure," he said, drawing out the word. "Anyway, you look like shit. Get any sleep last night?"

"Nope," I said slapping him on the shoulder. "Fought fire all night. Looks like you slept well, though. What's the matter, Italian Stallion? You jealous?"

He shook his head. "Just because Shelly is making me work for it doesn't mean I'm jealous."

The smell of burning timber ended our conversation. I looked out the window and saw fire crowning through huge trees, a big fire and I knew we'd be spending at least a few days on this one also. "Crap," I said, thinking of Denise.

*****

Cave Creek Fire, Payette National Forest
August 1, 1979

The spotter briefed us, and we jumped. I picked a gap between two big pine trees and steered for it. The wind knocked me around, I had to make radical adjustments just before the trees. Too late! I released the toggles and readied for the crash. Every part of my body tensed as branches snapped and cracked. All of the sudden I came to a stop and looked up at suspension lines and a deflating chute. Suddenly, I fell again breaking through more branches only thicker. The ground rushing toward me, and then my body jerked to another stop. Somehow, I found myself standing on a huge limb. The plane made a low pass, I saw the spotter in the doorway. I gave him the one finger smokejumper salute and he waved one back. After my letdown, Thad stood near-by. He shook his head and said, "What's wrong with you, Ryan? You did a complete summersault through that tree; I thought for sure you'd busted yourself up."

Tony came over laughing. "Too much pussy will do that to you."

I had to say, "At least I'm getting some."

We toiled two days working eighteen-hour shifts to cut a line around the fire, and spent a couple more days mopping it up. It became a miserable routine of working, eating, and getting a few hours of sleep, just to start it all over again in the morning. On the bright side, I'm making a ton of overtime.

Returning to McCall, I showered and slept most of the day before calling Denise. Feeling racked from all the overtime hours I dreamed about a hot tub and mentioned to her that a McCall jumper said the Burgdorf Hot Springs is a good place to treat sore muscles and I needed it. Soft and sweet, she whispered, "You sure you want to go all that way? I have a big bathtub at home."

"With bubbles?"

"With anything you want," she purred.

She picked me up and took me home. I helped her in the kitchen until she kicked me out for grabbing the wrong utensils. Candlelight accented her smooth skin as we gazed at each other while we dined on a delicious pasta dish. The bubble bath felt awesome, her hands rubbing my back almost put me to sleep. Dessert came in many delicious positions and later while cuddling in bed, she sniffed the smoke in my hair, "What made you want to be a firefighter?"

"I knew at the age of nine," I said remembering the very moment, "during a family vacation in Italy."

She snuggled her head on my chest. "You went to Italy? How lucky. I've always wanted to go there."

I stroked her hair and remembered that long ago trip. All us kids packed in the back of the station wagon, another of my father's jaunts across Europe. "Lucky?" I said. Luck on some of our vacations never crossed my mind. I had a constant traveling companion that ruined a lot of the fun: carsickness. "I puked my guts out while crossing the Alps. Once dad settled on the coastal highway, all these fire trucks passed us and I saw flames rising off the chaparral. I watched a man jump out of his car and begin helping the firefighters, so I yelled to my dad, 'Stop, dad, we need to help them!' Mom hushed me, so I climbed over my brothers to the back of the wagon and watched the firefighters. It was the greatest thing because the adrenalin cured my carsickness. Even at the Vatican, the Coliseum, all I thought about was those men and that fire."

Denise felt warm against me. "That's a nice story," she said. "I didn't know they had fires in Italy. What an experience to see all those places."

"We traveled all the time. We lived in France for four years, back to the States for a few, then Ramstein, Germany, back State side, then high school in Berlin, a total yoyo growing up, one foot on the ground, one foot always in a plane. Want to hear when I fought my first fire?"

"I want to hear more about Europe."

I needed to tell the story. "It was during a Boy Scout troop campout in Germany, One morning, a few other scouts and I came upon a huge anthill in the forest. Massive, like six-feet wide, a few feet high. We poked it with stick until the ants came out. Someone yelled, 'Let's burn it!' I had some matches in my pocket, so I lit one and threw it on the hill. The fire grew out of control right away. The brush and grass bone dry, I was such an idiot."

"A Boy Scout starting a fire?" she laughed.

"I don't know why, but while everyone else ran, I pulled off my shirt and swatted at the flames. Pure adrenalin had me beating on it until the last flame smoldered. Then, pure fear took over because my dad, one of the scout leaders, was coming to the camp that afternoon."

"Your dad a scout leader and you a firebug? That's great," she giggled.

"It gets better. After the fire, I spent the rest of the day frantically pulling up grass to cover the burn. Of course, my dad found out all about it, and at the fire circle that night, we received a lecture on playing with matches. It didn't matter though. The very next day, another scout found another anthill and he set fire to it, too!"

"A bunch of fire bug Boy Scouts!"

"We all tried putting that one out, but the breeze whipped it out of control. Scouts screamed, our leaders yelled, we all ran in panic. Two others and I hopped in a creek. The flames leapt over us and kept burning through the forest. Military police finally fished us out. An investigation followed and the family of the scout who'd started the fire was sent back to the States as punishment."

When I checked to see her reaction, she'd already fallen sleeping, clinging to me like paint on canvas. Had I ever been happier in my life? I kissed her cheek and slipped off, too.

*****

I asked for a couple days off to coincide with Denise's schedule. We soaked in the hot springs, lounged on the shore of Payette Lake, explored the Burgdorf ghost town, and explored each other every chance we could.

It came to the point where the McCall jumpers treated me like one of their own. I received invitations to hunt, ski, and raft local rivers. I even had a collection of real estate brochures. My Redding bros kept reminding me that this is a fire detail, not a love quest, and we'd have to leave eventually. I got comfortable with Denise and pushed all those thoughts aside.

*****

Mortar Creek Fire, Challis National Forest
August 15, 1979

At roll call, Thad announced, "The Mortar Creek Fire on the Challis National Forest is causing headaches for the overhead team. We're on notice that they're probably going to request assistance, so expect a call soon."

Oh great, I thought, another gobbler. Fighting a big fire would mean days away again. I called Denise. "Hi babe, it looks like I'm going to be jumping a big fire today."

"Should we put dinner on hold?"

"And dessert, too," I sighed. Sure enough, the horn sounded not long after, and sixteen of us filed into the DC-3 for the ride to the Challis. We flew just above the granite ridgelines of the Sawtooth National Recreation area. The jagged peaks looked like the jaws of a monster taking a bite at the sky. Waiting for us on the other side of the Sawtooth, a hellscape out of *Lord of the Rings*. The Mortar Creek Fire looked like my vision of Mordor. As far as I could see, sporadic columns of smoke smoldered above the land, pouring sparks against the soot-stained sky. We flew over the main body of the fire. Being so large, I wondered what they wanted us to do when I heard Thad talking to a jumper named 'DooDah.' "They want you to build a helispot for reinforcements and secure that ridgeline."

The fire burned in the bottom of a huge canyon making intense runs up the shoots. Thad dropped the drift streamers, and two by two we exited the DC-3. After landing and assembling the cargo, we split up. I joined the line building crew returning to the jump spot for breaks after every shift, the most relaxed fire I'd had all year. I spent more time patrolling the ridgeline than burning out. The nights cooled down fast and the McCall jumpers began talking about their end of year party.

After five days, we completed our assignment, and back at base, the McCall jumpers scheduled their annual group photo, inviting us to join. We gathered on the tarmac in front of the Beech 99 and the DC-3 and became the only group of out-of-region jumpers with the honor of posing for a different base's annual photo.

Excitement built for the end of the year party, billed as a not to miss affair. Gramps bought a new button-down shirt. The McCall jumpers rented the ski resort outside of town, and everyone started worrying about a few small fires on the Nezperce National Forest. Nothing would be worse than to miss the party because of a jump.

Denise wanted to party with us and as the weekend approached, Gramps and I monitored fire activity with crossed fingers since our position on the list put us on the first load. The day of the party, a group of Zulies jumped a small fire on the edge of the Nezperce, but for us the situation continued to look good until the fire alarm sounded. A wave of frustrated bodies cursed upon hearing a Zulie had stuck a Pulaski in his foot and we'd been called up to evacuate him.

*****

Rabbit Point Fire, Nezperce National Forest
August 25, 1979

I seethed in the phone. "Baby, a damn Zulie hurt himself and we have to jump in and rescue the jerk. I'm going to miss the party."

"Oh, Ry, I'm so sorry. I've been thinking about it all day."

"Damn it, me, too. I'll call you when I get back. Have fun for me, will you?"

"Just be safe. I'll have a drink for you."

"Have a few," I wined.

Barely a wisp of smoke showed when we circled, pissing us off even more. We hit the ground to find the injured jumper on his feet and limping around, the icing on the cake! Most of the cargo hung up. I spent the rest of the day climbing after fire packs and parachutes. That night around the warming fire, we eyed the Zulie evilly. I passed my flask around, intentionally skipping him, while we speculated on the party.

We cut a helispot in the morning for the wounded Zulie and ended up back in McCall before noon. Judging from how near-death everyone looked, it became clear we'd missed one hell of a party. September arrived, the fire season in Idaho waned and word from dispatch indicated our stay was about to end, I felt overwhelmed with sadness. The McCall jumpers had become like family, having to say goodbye to Denise tortured me. She'd opened her heart to me, made me feel like I'd found a real home. We traded addresses, and promised to see each other over the winter. I had second thoughts about getting on the plane.

We passed over her house as we flew out of McCall. I looked down and couldn't believe I wouldn't have her in my arms anymore. I had mixed feelings and thought of jumping out of the plane and landing in her yard. But I did what I'd always done; think about what might have been. I spent the rest of the flight feeling regret.

*****

During my absence in Alaska and Idaho, Redding had a number of firsts. Lassen National Park had its first ever smokejumper fire. The bros who parachuted to it thought they'd scored big salt points, but Vise, Barf Bag Bailey, and The General bested them all by jumping on Mt. Lassen itself. Vise added more salt points to his already vast collection by making a practice jump in California in the morning and a fire jump in Idaho in the afternoon.

Late September saw a flurry of lightning activity across the North State. I jumped a fire on the Shasta-Trinity, and as soon as I returned, I flew to one on the dreaded Plumas. By October, fire season slowed down. By my accounting, it had been a good year. I'd jumped eleven fires, scored eight-hundred hours of overtime, and made my fiftieth jump.

CHAPTER 14

Fire Bug On The Loose

Winter settled in and I reminisced about my adventures in Alaska and Idaho a lot. Money wise, I had the best fire season of my career, earning a whopping $11,349 in straight wages and overtime. I never did make that the trip to McCall to see Denise. In the end, it didn't matter. She let me know she'd hooked up with one of the McCall jumpers not long after I left.

To keep in shape and pass time, I took up martial arts and began studying Kenpo Karate. I fell in love with the vigorous workouts and the careful teaching of my instructor, Big Al. The Dojo became my living room five times a week, and I developed a bond with him and my fellow students almost as strong as I had with my jump bros.

That spring, for the first time in California smokejumping history we had no pogues to train. The jumper turnover rate corresponded with how busy the previous fire season had been, and since 1979 had been great, everyone returned for an encore. Another contributing factor involved the Forest Service's decision to close the base in Boise for financial reasons. The displaced jumpers scattered to all the other bases, we accepted three.

With no pogues to train—meaning no one to haze and intimidate—the season started off slow. I spent all my time in the loft, rigging and repairing chutes. Finally, in June, a thunderstorm hit the north state and I jumped a fire on the Shasta-Trinity. A couple weeks later, a second storm rolled through and I jumped another fire on the same forest. Three days after that, a request came in from the Sequoia for a small fire. After we put it out the Sequoia decided to keep us for a larger, troublesome fire where we spent five days on the line. Maybe this season wouldn't turn out so bad after all!

About that time, Northern California began experiencing the demented work of an arsonist. Fires sprung up all over Shasta and Tehama counties, taxing resources to the point that the counties had to call for help. On June 21, twenty of us hopped into Jumper III, our beloved bus, and rode to the Raven Fire near Susanville. We followed a cat line and burned out all night. Meanwhile, the arsonist kept busy starting so many fires we had to call in the McCall jumpers.

On June 28, I jumped the Chinese Trail Fire. The arsonist had been lighting fires from roadsides, and some of them grew rather large. My fire happened to be one of them. Looking down on the fire from the McCall's Beech-99 jump ship had me wishing I'd been back in McCall. Not only being in thick brush and poison oak, I had to contend with an unfamiliar airplane. Smaller than the Twin Otter, the Beech had a six-man capacity. Squirrely had to drop a lot of streamers to get the exit point down because of the wind and all the while I fought off nausea from the g-forces. I didn't care about the spot, I just wanted out of that damn plane.

The Beech required a sit down exit, which we didn't practice from the jump tower. As I sat in the door with Squirrely briefing me, I looked down at cars pulled over and people standing on the road watching us. I'd never jumped for an audience, and didn't like it now.

"We're on final!" Squirrely shouted.

I didn't feel comfortable sitting on the floor of the plane. The slipstream pressed my legs against the fuselage, which I knew would make for an awkward push off. When Squirrely slapped my shoulder, I wasn't ready. I shoved off with both hands and when my chute opened, my suspension lines twisted up, and I spun like a top. I cleared them with barely enough air left to miss the road, the power lines, and googling tourists, who applauded my landing. The six of us secured the bottom of the fire until two CDF dozers and a hand crew arrived.

The arsonist took a break, but lightning activity continued. It took only nine days to rotate into the first load again. On

August 13, two planeloads flew to a 100-plus acre lightning fire on the Shasta-Trinity. The blaze had many fingers burning down draws, making direct attack unsafe. The plan; cut a straight indirect fire line along the bottom and burn out the fingers. After assembling five burners and all the fusees we could get, we burned through the next three nights, resting during the days to give the line builders time to construct line ahead of us. Toward the end of our fourth shift, exhaustion set it, and I sat down for a break. Flames reflecting off the unburned timber made the trees appear to sway back and forth. 'I must be hallucinating,' I thought. Staring at the flames, I heard laughter fading in and out, it was heading my way. A hotshot crew passed by and I heard one say as he looked at me, "Damn jumpers."

What had prompted that? A short while later two jumpers ambled over and I suddenly understood. Bill 'Noodles' Newlun, one of the Boise transfers led the group and when he stopped in front of me, I couldn't help but laugh, too. He had a silver warming jacket on, a big black bow tie, and a ball cap that said, *Aloha Boise*. He smiled and handed me a pen. The inscription read, Best Dressed Smokejumper. Noodles spent his summer vacations from teaching school in the city of Mt. Shasta, to jumping out of planes and we could count on him to produce a watermelon during lunch breaks.

Back in Redding, the base buzzed with life. A news crew from Channel 5 in San Francisco had arrived to film a segment for its nationally syndicated 'Evening Magazine' program. The overhead demanded a quick house cleaning, and during the shoot, I managed to get on film helping Ron 'Ewok' Omont—a jumper nicknamed this because of his short stature, beard, and semblance to the Star Wars characters—suit up for the camera.

Six days after my film début, I flew to the Tahoe on a two-fire request. Glacier carved peaks rose to meet us and small, lush meadows dotted the alpine terrain. The three days there resembled more of a vacation than a firefighting mission. The fires succumbed to our tools quickly allowing me ample time to explore the area. As soon as we returned to Redding, the arsonist started working again sending twenty of us in Jumper III to the foothills. Two days later, I'm back on the bus for another arson fire. A week later, I jumped a lightning fire on the Shasta-Trinity. Two days passed and another arson fire. The arsonist— never caught—kept me making overtime. I certainly couldn't curse him for that!

Webster defines arson as: 'the willful or malicious burning of property.' The idiot running around the valley starting fires definitely fit the description. Steve started the fire in the Alaskan bush with his last match to save his life. Should he be considered an arsonist? I started the anthill fire out of stupidity. Does that make me an arsonist? Well, maybe so, but it wasn't willful or malicious and it never happened again. Regardless of the cause of a fire, fighting them became my addiction especially moving from one to another all over the country, seeing new land, new action, and meeting new people. In firefighting heaven, I wasn't thinking or caring about anything else.

CHAPTER 15

Enduring Spirit

Northern California Service Center
May 11, 1981

By my fifth season as a smokejumper, I'm in the best shape of my life. The dojo had been my home over the winter and I excelled in the techniques and philosophy of Kenpo Karate, which paralleled the physical and mental challenges of jumping. How hard I'd worked in the Dojo became evident in how easily I passed the PT test. I looked forward to a new season.

With eight pogues to train, I couldn't wait to begin the training. I'd never forgotten the rigors of my pogue year and to be on the other side proved entertaining. When the new recruits arrived in early May, I welcomed each one with a hard stare. Shortly after training began, an ABC affiliate from Los Angeles arrived to film a segment for Eye on L.A.

The overhead cautioned us to keep our shirts on, abstain from profanity, and generally be on our best behavior when filming commenced. Suddenly, cameras followed us everywhere. The highlight of the visit came when we took the pogues and the news crew to Birkland's jump spot to observe a jump. The newswoman looked like a model with her long legs, blond hair, and toned body. You couldn't find anyone friendlier than her. With jumpers in the air, a pogue named Mark 'Magnum' Youmans, slithered up to us and introduced him to the girl. As a jumper landed next to us, she turned to him and asked, "Tell me Magnum, as a seasonal firefighter, what do you do in the off season?"

"In the winter," he told her straight faced, "I teach macramé to unemployed Nicaraguan farmers."

I hurried out of microphone range and laughed uncontrollably. It appeared we had a pogue comedian on our hands, and I couldn't wait to see how this guy panned out in training. When the filming finished, the news crew bought us a keg of beer as thanks for our jump stories and partied with us during an after-work softball game. After a few beers, the pretty newswoman found me and said, "You know Ry, in a different life, it'd be kind of kinky to get to know a smokejumper." Then she flashed her wedding ring at me to say good-bye.

*****

A week into training, all eight pogues remained. I'd get my PT done quickly in the mornings to prepare for my parachute manipulation class. On the morning of May 11, I took off on a short run into a stiff wind. Larry Pettibone, the North Zone Air Unit Manager, readied one of the Air Unit's Twin Beech lead planes for a flight down to Chico. I swung around the tarmac and waved to him, as well as George, Roscoe, and Joe. They waved back.

I finished my run and headed for the shower in the warehouse bathroom. As I dressed, I heard a violent explosion, and the building shook. Two thoughts crossed my mind: either the parachute-drying tower had buckled over in the wind, or we just had an earthquake. Either one could leave me covered in rubble, so I darted out of the bathroom and froze to gobs of fire dripped from the ceiling like molten rain. Not knowing what to think, a warehouseman yelled in panic, "The fucking plane crashed!"

I prayed it wasn't ours and ran across to the south end of the building to the Redding Hotshots office. The smell of jet fuel burned my nose, the radiant heat of the streaming flames singed the hair right off my arms. The hotshot's office was empty, and in a matter of seconds, the whole warehouse filled with black, caustic smoke. I hurried back to our end of the building and entered the operations section. Total chaos greeted me. Gramps and Boy ran around yelling for everyone to get out. I dashed for my locker to grab my wallet, but Squirrely grabbed me and pushed me back. In the parking lot, the squad leaders took a head count. I then learned it was our Baron that had crashed. I felt sick, I'd just waved to those guys, and now they're dead!

One of the dispatchers screamed, "Where are the fire engines?"

Perky yelled, "Why are we standing here? That's our building! Let's get as much equipment out as we can!"

When the engines arrived, the base water system couldn't supply enough pressure to fill them. With the strong wind and the combustible nature of everything in the warehouse, a manager made the decision to abort the firefighting effort. We all watched helplessly as the building that housed the warehouse, hotshots, smokejumpers, dispatch center, and the weather station burned from end to end. Propane bottles exploded as fire destroyed the warehouse.

Everyone looked on in complete shock, a waking nightmare so surreal I felt it couldn't be happening, but as the flames pushed us back, it became all too real. I struggled with all sorts of emotions that day. Life as I knew it had fallen into complete uncertainty in a matter of minutes. Four friends had just died; their bodies still on top of the burning building. Being raised on military bases all my life, plane crashes happened a lot. After a crash the base lowered the flag at half-mast, after a while of mourning life returned to normal. It never seemed personal, just a fact of military life, until now.

I made it home still in utter shock. When I tried to sleep, visions of the building engulfed in flames had me tossing around the bed until fits of anxiety forced me out. Pacing the living room, I wondered, would I have a job in the morning? Was the California Smokejumper program dead? Even if I did have a job, would I want it anymore? What kept something like that from happening to my bros or me? And what about the men in the plane? What did it feel like to know you're going to die just before you do? Too many questions with no answers.

*****

Morning came with no sleep. I showed up to work and right away, Dick Tracy took control and began the seemingly impossible task of securing our future. He didn't wait for directives; he got us into the hanger that had housed the Baron and sent word to every jump base in the country that we needed their help. In short order parachutes, jump suits, pack-out bags, and fire packs arrived in an endless succession. The task proved enormous, and even in our sorrow and despair, Tracy didn't allow our grief to stall us, he found the strength and we followed his lead knowing our fallen comrades would've wanted us to move forward. He swung a hammer alongside us while building storage bins and rigging tables. If it weren't for his leadership, I might have had second thoughts in continuing my career there.

CHAPTER 16

All Wrapped Up

Birkland's Jump Spot
May 29, 1981

On the morning of May 29, 1981, eighteen days after the Baron crashed, I'm sitting in the Twin Otter as it taxied past the skeletal remains of our base, wondering again, what had gone through the minds of Larry, George, Roscoe, and Joe just before they crashed. We'd all pulled together to cope with our loss, even though difficult, we got back on track. As we lifted off, I psyched myself up for my second qualifying jump, looking forward to some peaceful canopy time. A cool breeze whistled through the plane and sunlight sparkled off the wing tips. A good day for jumping—but to tell the truth any day was a good day for jumping to me. Dog and I were the final stick, me being the last one out of the plane. When we reached our exit point, I noticed all the previous jumpers had taken a southerly approach to the X in the meadow. Everything seemed routine as I crouched in behind Dog. He took the slap and I followed him out. I had a good exit, my canopy inflated with no twists. As the sound of the plane faded away, I savored the peacefulness of soaring through the sky yet again.

I turned, located Dog, and faced the X. Looking down between my feet I calculated I had plenty of room to play with before setting up for my landing. I made a downwind run over the spot and while doing so, lost sight of Dog. As I turned into the wind to prepare for my last maneuver, there he appeared, below my position heading for the X when suddenly, I saw his canopy make a 180 straight toward me! I yelled out, "Fuck, Dog!" and executed the evasive right turn drilled in my head during training, but it's too late. Dog's canopy grew larger and larger until it wrapped around my body in a bright orange cocoon and the sensation of falling disappeared. Orange, that's all I saw. It seemed like a dream with no anticipation of being turned into mush when the ride ended. The serenity calmed me, too peaceful to end in disaster. Tension evaporated from my body and my mind began wandered down a very short path.

The end of the path greeted me with such intensity that the air in my lungs exploded out of my mouth. I saw a blinding flash of light, then a dark, peaceful feeling. No pain racked my brain. Time didn't exist until far-off voices yanked me back. Vise yelled, "Call a goddamn ambulance!" He whispered, "Ry, open your eyes. Come on, man. Wake up."

My tongue felt strange. I tasted blood. I opened my eyes, and saw somber faces looking down at me. I tried to say something, but the words just wouldn't come. Dennis 'Big D' Golik looked at me and cringed, "His tongue is almost severed."

I didn't want to hear any more. I managed to say, "My back hurts." I faded in and out of consciousness as Big D, and Sven 'The General' Klaseen held a parachute to shade me from the sun. As the ambulance EMTs cut off my jump pants and strapped me to a litter, one of them said, "The road in here is too rough for a back injury. We need a helicopter."

In what seemed like seconds, I heard rotor blades. Eventually, the whirl of the blades went silent and I felt the litter rise, a voice saying, "Easy now," as they slid me into the ship. The pilot cursed, "Goddamn door won't close. The litter's too long." Then, "Fuck it," echoed in the cabin as the door slammed shut, sending a loud sound of plexi-glass cracking throughout the ship. The turbine revved and we lifted into the sky. From where I lay, the rotor blades chopped through the sun creating a strobe effect that put me in a trance.

When the helicopter landed on the roof of Mercy Hospital, medical staffers rushed out and lifted me onto a gurney. In the examining room, I felt a needle go into my arm, a warm sensation traveled all through me, and instantly, I felt giddy and pain free. Nurses removed my jump jacket and put me on an X-ray table. A doctor stitched my tongue back together and I remember being rolled down a hallway and into a room where they stuck more needles in my arm.

After a while, a doctor came in with X-rays. He studied me closely before saying, "You're a lucky man. They told me you had a collision with another parachutist and fell some sixty-feet hitting the ground in a sitting position. Do you remember any of it?"

My mouth felt like cotton, my tongue like an old shoe. I mumbled, "I remember going into his parachute and waking up on my back."

"You're lucky the impact didn't shove your spine into your brain," he said. "I can't see how that didn't happen except for the fact that you're in excellent shape."

He set the X-rays on a light board and pointed things out. "Right here at T-11 and T-12, you have compression fractures of the vertebrae. You don't have any spinal damage, which is a complete miracle."

"When will I be able to jump again?" I mumbled in my doped-up state.

The doctor raised his eyebrows. "The good news is you're alive. You just sustained a serious back injury. The bad news is that you'll likely never jump again."

I closed my eyes, not ready to hear such fucking garbage. I felt more pain from his words than from my injury. After I clammed up, he left the room. My drug-induced sleep didn't relieve me from the agonizing sense of doom. I tossed in and out of a vision:

I'm dragging my gunnysack along the side of a mountain, there's smoke in the air. Nobody is around except Mr. Ogawa, my counselor at Berlin American High School. He once told me he'd had a vision of me standing on a mountain with smoke in the air all around me. The Vietnam War was raging at the time and most of us seniors hadn't made plans for after high school graduation because of the certainty of the draft. I thought he had a vision of me in Vietnam, but he said it wasn't Nam. Now he's here with me on the mountainside, smiling at me and saying, 'I told you it wasn't Nam.'

'Might as well have been,' I reply and kick a burning pinecone down the slope. 'I'm done! KIA, MIA, poof, gone. No more.'

He laughs, 'People usually fail when they are on the verge of success. So give as much care to the end as to the beginning. Then there will be no failure. Keeping to the main road is easy, but people love to be sidetracked.'

His words swirl in my mind as I watch the pinecone spew fire down the mountain. 'My whole life has been a sidetrack.' I yell in frustration. 'I have no main road to follow. No beginnings, only side roads that always seem to lead to pain.'

His dark eyes burn into me. I slump to the forest floor and light a cigarette with a burning twig, avoiding his glare. He walks circles around me as I smoke. 'We are what we think,' he says after I snub the smoke out. 'All that we are arises with our thoughts. With our thoughts, we make the world. Speak or act with an impure mind and trouble will follow you just as the wheel follows the ox that draws the cart. Speak or act with a pure mind and happiness will follow you as your shadow, unshakable. How can the troubled mind understand the way? Your worst enemy cannot harm you as much as your own thoughts, unguarded.' He stops in front of me. I lift my eyes to his and they sparkle as he says, 'But once mastered, no one can help you as much, not even your father or your mother.' Tears are running down my face. How has he gotten in my head?

I'm falling. A hand grabs me, pulls me up in a cloud of dust, and I hear, 'Develop a state of mind like the earth. For on the earth people throw clean and unclean things, piles of garbage, polluted waterways, pus, blood, and the earth is not troubled or repelled or disgusted. And as you grow like the earth, no contacts with pleasure or unpleasant things will lay hold of your mind or stick to it. Be like the water, for people throw all manner of clean and unclean things into the water and it is not troubled or repelled or disgusted. Be as the fire you love so much, which burns all things, clean and unclean. Be as the air, which blows upon them all, and space, which is nowhere established.' Mr. Ogawa's voice trails off into the wind. Now, someone else is calling my name, "Ryan? Ryan? Ryan?"

I open my eyes. Where am I? Still in the bed? Still wrecked with Sid, the main dispatcher at the Service Center, standing over me and gently saying my name. Sid wasn't anyone I expected to see. The jumpers didn't favor him much; they blamed him for all the times our crew ended up on North State Hold. But oddly enough, Sid and I got on well. I squinted at him and mumbled, "You? Guess I must've died and gone to hell."

Sid slapped my foot and laughed. "I heard my favorite jumper tried to mate with another parachute."

I managed a "Ha, ha," before he continued, "Remember when Buffalo broke his ankle, became a hero dispatcher by sending you guys on every smoke that popped up on the Plumas? Well, I can't allow that to happen again. He didn't help your cause one bit. I'll tell you what Ry you'd better get back to jumping as soon as you can."

My voice remained strong as I said, "I'll be back, Sid, and believe me it won't be as your stool pigeon."

He patted my foot again. "I guess the nurses must've been mistaken when they said you yelled my name out in your sleep."

I laughed, "They weren't mistaken. It was the worst nightmare of my life!" Then I quietly said, "Thanks for coming to see me."

Shortly after he left, three pogues came into my room. Being their parachute manipulation instructor and lying on a hospital bed from a major parachute manipulation error embarrassed the hell out of me. I saw Magnum, and remembering his interview with the newswoman, I asked him, "Do you have a waiting list for your macramé classes?"

The mood lightened. "Actually," Magnum said, "when I heard you yell, 'Fuck Dog!' I looked up and took a picture of you in his parachute. Your boots stuck out of his canopy and your body all wrapped up. I'll have to create a more suitable class for you."

"Let this be a lesson to you guys," I lectured. "Even when a jump seems routine, it can end up, well...look at me."

Pogue Norm seemed uncomfortable. His eyes scanned all around the room. When they settled on my jump jacket, he asked, "Want me to take your jacket back?"

"No," I said. "I plan on wearing it again."

An awkward silence followed, like a constant hum that became unbearable. Magnum said at last, "Take care of yourself, okay? We'd better get back."

I knew what that awkward silence meant. I'd had those same thoughts looking down on John and Charlie after they'd broken their backs. I also knew how the Forest Service had abandoned them following their injuries. Alone in the room, confusion filled my thoughts. Mr. Ogawa's words swirled around in my mind, stirring up shit so thick, I couldn't see. This isn't really happening, is it? I'm just having a nightmare. I can't end up like those guys.

I loved jumping, it defined my life. Even though we appeared to be a dysfunctional family at times, I loved my jump bros. I'm not ready to hang up my harness or have it taken from me without a fight. I knew the drugs messed with my mind. They put me in a doubtful mind set. I needed get off the mind-altering drip and start making plans.

The plan I began formulating took a major step forward when Big Al, my karate instructor, paid me a visit. He towered over me, a man built like a linebacker with a Fu Manchu mustache, his voice calm and direct. "I want you to visualize little ninjas patching up your back, Ry-son. While they're doing that, I want you to enter the Dragon."

Big Al taught better than any teacher I ever had. He ran a strict dojo. The first day I walked in his dojo, he said to me, "The martial arts have two realms. We have the Tiger realm, where you will learn power and tenacity, the physical side of the martial arts. The second realm is the Dragon, where you will learn to ride the wind. This is the mental realm and the most important one. As you learn the Tiger, you will be able to deal with any type of physical confrontation. As you learn the Dragon, you will learn to use the power of your mind to avoid confrontations, to be one with the universe where every living thing is sacred and deserves compassion." Before he left, he said, "Use the power of your mind, ride the wind, become the Dragon. We'll be waiting for you in the dojo."

The visits I enjoyed the most came from Niki, the girl I dated at the time, a real wild one. I met her while bungee jumping from bridges over the Pit River. The second our eyes met, I knew I had to meet her. I volunteered to double-check the harness connected to her ankles prior to jumping. Her rough-cut shorts tight on her body, her legs nicely tanned, and her eyes wide open with fear and excitement. She smiled at me as I made one last tug on the rope and I surprised myself by saying, 'don't be scared, it'll be the most fun you've ever have with your clothes on.' She managed a wink while teetering, and said, 'Guess we'll have to wait to take them off,' and jumped. As her scream echoed through the canyon, I knew she's my kind of girl, and from that moment on, we formed a loose bond. She wasn't the type you'd take home to mom, said things like, "Fuck the piss-fur Willie cops, I'm jumping off this bridge and if they have a problem with it, they can shove it." I admired her frankness, loved her petite body, and her dark inviting eyes drove me crazy. She appeared to have some Native American blood in her and we quickly developed a relationship based on carnal pleasures. She'd come into my room, prop a chair against the door, and administer 'oral therapy,' which I found very helpful. I knew I liked her more than she wanted me to, became one day when I hinted at us becoming an item she told me, as if crawling around in my head, pushing the cobwebs aside, "It's just lust, Ry, not real love, and even if it was, it'd be like your fires. You'd put it out, and move on to the next one. Besides, you don't want to get too close to me...I'm trouble."

She knew my wildness complemented hers and maybe she saw trouble with a relationship between two free-spirited souls, or maybe she'd been just as unsuccessful at relationships as I'd been. At any rate, she made me realize I put fires out wherever they cropped up and her and me, only a lustful affair.

My ex-wife, Sarah, showed up, too. It felt awkward, because I still had feelings for her, regardless of how she always said something like this would happen. Guilt ripped at me, I longed for her, but couldn't commit. When I did feel closeness creeping into my life, demons reared their ugly heads and pushed it aside as if I'd been a man unworthy of love. I often wondered what could've happened if I'd told the demons to take a flying fuck. Could I have had that house in the country with kids in the yard and Duke sitting next to me as I rocked on the patio admiring my good fortune while sipping a cold beer, my wife swinging in the hammock? Hell! Why did I always wonder about how things could've been, instead of making them happen? Her being in my hospital room made for another awkward twist. I'd heard through the rumor mill that she'd been dating a jumper, a newer guy, but nobody talked about it. Perhaps there was some poetic justice going on.

CHAPTER 17

The Road Back

Redding, California
1981

I had to get out of the hospital. It depressed me. The walls closed in on me. After a couple days, I began harassing the nurses, pulling out my IV, gingerly walking the ward, and having my bros sneak in beer. I pressured my doctor until he finally gave in and released me to my own methods.

Prior to being discharged, the nurses fitted me with a back brace, gave me a pair of crutches, and pain pills to hold me over until I filled my prescription. The doctor referred me to a back specialist. When the day to leave finally came, a nurse came into the room with a wheel chair. She saw my repugnance and grunted, "Hospital policy." She wheeled me to the entrance with my jump jacket and crutches on my lap and we waited. After quite a while, she grew annoyed and asked, "You did say someone is coming to pick you up, didn't you?"

I had said that, but didn't call anyone. I lived a few blocks away, and intended to walk home. More time passed without anyone showing up, so I suggested she call a cab. When she went inside, I wrapped my jump jacket over my shoulders, grabbed my crutches, and started down the steep hill. I moved slow and cautious, constantly looking over my shoulder expecting to see an army of nurses running after me. I felt tenderness and an uncomfortable aching sensation in my lower back and realized I should've waited for the cab. When I entered my rundown rental, sweat dripped from me.

Fear of the unknown forced me to pop a couple of pain pills, followed by a few swigs of Old Number 7. I lay stoically on the couch, feeling relieved to be in my own space. Or was I? Sleep eluded me, but once the pills took effect, I entered a disturbing world. I heard voices and looked around the room, but couldn't see anyone. Then little Martians came out of the knotty pine ceiling and hovered over me. They laughed, and chanted, "Oh he ain't gonna jump no more!" I swung at them, swore at them, but they just flew around the room mocking me. I wanted to grab my .22 rifle and shoot them when the front door swung open. Niki came in, and the Martians fled back into the ceiling. Now, she hovered over me, waving her arms as she spoke, "Ry, I showed up at the hospital and you weren't there. Why didn't you call me? How did you get home?"

"I walked."

"Jesus Christ!" she said kneeling next to me. "You have a broken back. What the hell is wrong with you?"

"What's wrong with me? I'll tell you what's wrong! I got a fucking broken back and those damn Martians are messing with me. What did I do to deserve this?"

"Martians?" she said, noticing the whisky bottle on my lap. "What the hell are you talking about?"

I started crying. "I'm talking about my worst fucking nightmare. The doctor says I'm done jumping! Now these creepy aliens are saying the same thing. Goddamit, Niki! What can I do?"

Without another word, she snuggled next to me, and placed my hand on her breasts. Her chest rose and fell to a soothing rhythm. Every breath, every heartbeat sent calm up my arm and straight to my heart. I grabbed her, gave into her, and the demons scattered. As I drifted, I saw us together seeking adrenalin rushes from bridges, canoeing the Sacramento River, hiking Mt. Shasta and Mt. Lassen, and most of all, exploring each other in every way possible. The moment I realized this girl had no fear came about on a campout at the ocean. While snuggling in the tent, she said, 'Ry, I can't stand hearing about how awesome it is to jump from a plane anymore. I've done some checking and there's a sky diving school in Corning. I'm going to learn how to jump. They have a package deal where you get the ground training, five static line jumps, and a hop-n-pop solo at 12,000 feet. It's because of your stories that I want to do this, and I'd love to do it you with. You interested?'

I joyously said, 'Hell yeah!'

I'd never seen a woman so excited. She took to jumping like an addict. I remember her adrenalin fueled excitement after her first jump. She ran around waving her arms in the air and shouting, 'What a trip.' I had to calm her down in between jumps. Her enthusiasm carried over to the bedroom making me the happiest guy in the world. I hope I didn't ruin the experience for her by getting busted up.

I woke to the smell of cooking. "Oh," Niki said when she heard me trying to get up. "While you slept, Big Al called. He said he talked to Frank and that you should start your acupuncture treatments as soon as possible." I met Frank Campanili at the dojo, a small-framed, soft-spoken Italian, who threw a nasty punch. He studied acupuncture under a renowned Japanese master for ten years. If anyone could help me, he definitely could.

A couple days later, I crutched into Frank's office for the first of many visits. Within minutes, I'm lying on the table feeling needles twist in my back. He explained, "The healing energy of the body travels through many different meridians such as veins, arteries, muscles, and spiritual channels. The needles in your ears and feet are stimulating the meridians directly connected to your back. They stimulate the flow of healing energy to the points of obstruction. All I'm doing here is opening the energy paths. The burning moxin balls at the end of the needles are sending heat to the damaged areas, which also helps open the meridians to healing energy."

In addition to acupuncture and heat therapy, Frank also practiced electro therapy, often attaching electrodes to different parts of my back and using a timer to send pulses down the needles. Every time before I'd leave his office, he'd tape magnets to either side of my spine and give me Chinese herbs.

On the other hand, whenever I'd go to my back specialist, I'd sit in his waiting room for hours, and when he finally saw me, he'd do a quick exam of my back and asked how my physical therapy had been going. It wasn't nearly enough, and I wanted to fire him, but since workers' compensation oversaw things, I had to play by their rules to continue receiving pay, which barely covered my rent and living expenses.

I let Frank decide when the time had come for me to return to the dojo to begin my physical comeback. After three weeks of intense acupuncture, he gave me the green light. Big Al instituted a regimen where I sparred with the other students without full contact. "Ry-son," he'd lecture me, "you are on a quest that will have no end. As one journey ends, another is started. You must mentally connect with your physical side. When the mind and body work as one, true strength and inner peace will result. Use your inner strength, your Chi, to draw energy from the universe through your subconscious, and your healing will reveal more than you could ever imagine."

Dripping with sweat, I'd say, "I'll try, Sifu, I'll try."

I knew what he meant; I had a spiritual connection to the world long before studying the martial arts. The first TV show I saw after returning to the states from Berlin was, *Kung Fu*. The show so captivated me that when I had to hitchhike back and forth to college, I often asked to be dropped off at the entrance to Edwards Air Force Base. Miles of desert separated me from home. I'd put on my Kwai Chang Caine persona and head out across the desert on foot, focusing in on my meditative state, which allowed me to absorb the natural beauty of the desert. The teachings of Kwai Chang Caine constantly influenced me during my rehabilitation.

*****

My visits to the jump base felt awkward. I knew the overhead had counted me out for good. Given my talk of returning, they must've thought I'd become delusional from too much medication, or just plain crazy.

Jumpers are a band of brothers, a family of diverse characters sharing the same goals while flirting with danger on a daily basis. Now I felt completely alone and longed for support from someone, anyone. I knew it wouldn't come from the overhead, the very people that held the key to my future. At times, I felt abandoned to wander through a maze of doubt and uncertainty without hope. Now, where are my bros in my time of need? Would I be discarded like Charlie and John? Would I become an ex-jumper, just like that? My life developed into a constant struggle just to keep focused, but knowing that the overhead had practically counted me out actually spurred me on. I resorted to the ancient teachings of Lao Tzu (The Way of Life), Tao Te Ching, Chuang-Tzu, and the Tao. This proverb kept me centered: *"The great question is not whether you have failed, but whether you are content with failure."*

The hangar worked out well enough as a temporary home and the pogues completed training on time. We'd become fire ready by early June. The Alaska detailers made the trip north to a busy season, and ten more jumpers soon followed. Tim 'Quig' Quigley jumped a fire at Portage Bay where a group of Grizzlies chased him onto the roof of a cabin. He said he'd never felt so helpless watching the bears waiting him out. He knew they wanted to eat him.

There wasn't much fire activity in California during my convalescence. I managed to make it to the first kegger party of the year at the Anderson River Park, being around my bros helped a lot. No one focused on my injury; they treated me as though I'd been on a vacation. At one point during the party, Gramps pulled me aside and said, "I'm making calls around the district to find a place for you when you're cleared for duty."

I'd been telling him all along that I planned on return to jumping; obviously he didn't hear me or thought it wasn't possible. Now, I teetered. Did he mean to tell me I couldn't come back, or that he thought I wouldn't be able to handle the demands of the job anymore? I felt betrayed, my emotions took over when I said to him, "But I plan on coming back, Gramps."

With his dark penetrating eyes, I couldn't read him at times, especially now since he didn't respond. Maybe he thought I had denial issues, or that I hadn't accepted the fact that few jumpers returned from a broken back. But he also didn't tell me I couldn't return, so I took his silence as a measure of support. Regardless, after the conversation with Gramps, I felt depressed, even alienated. I needed a beer and crutched my way over to the keg where Perky worked the tap. All of a sudden, he blurted out, "Shit!" I followed his eyes to where a car had just pulled into the parking lot. With panic in his voice, he said, "That's the girl I've been dating. She said she wasn't coming, so I invited the Roach Coach girl instead."

The Roach Coach—also known as the Maggot Wagon— became the terms we used for the mobile food van that came to the base every day at noon. Perky freaked out. "I need your help, man!"

"What do you want me to do?"

He handed me a beer. "Take this over to Sylvia and tell her something came up with me."

I started laughing. "Something came up? Like what, your pecker!"

He said "Shit," again. I saw his mind racing. "Tell her it's my ex. Tell her we have some unresolved issues to discuss."

I slapped him on the shoulder, "I'll think of something, Perky. Just steer clear while I handle it."

As it turned out, Sylvia and I had a good time that night, even though I still wanted wild Niki. When she'd moved on, my heart broke. I had a hard time accepting the fact that I couldn't have her, so I started dating Sylvia out of self-pity. I often wondered why women were so complicated. With a tone of experience, Vise often said, "You can't live with them and you can't live without them. The trick is to not let them get a foothold on your heart." I realized that isn't as easy as it sounded because I wore my heart on my sleeve.

✳✳✳✳✳

After weeks of working out in the dojo and getting acupuncture treatments, I felt strong enough to test myself. From my research into Forest Service Regulations, I knew that aside from a written release from my specialist, all I had to do was pass the PT test to regain active status. I had been hammering away at my specialist for weeks, telling him if he wouldn't release me to jumping, I'd find someone who would. On a cautious run eight weeks after my accident, I made the mile and a half run with time to spare, not much, but enough to pass. When I told my family that I planned to resume my jumping career, they shook their heads and questioned my sanity yet again. One week later, I showed up at the base with the doctor's release in hand and dressed in my running shorts, everyone eyeballed me curiously. When I announced, "I'm ready for the PT test," I heard quiet laughter and whispers, but the regulations forced them to give me a shot.

I breezed through the sit-ups, push-ups, and pull-ups. I'd been doing them every day for some time, but the run concerned me. How would the hard pounding on the tarmac affect my back? Would it give out without warning? I nervously paced the tarmac, while the two pace setters did the same. When the timekeeper said, "On your mark," I took in a deep breath. When he said, "Get set," I drained my lungs. When, "Go," sounded, I shook off the butterflies and began the journey of my life. I took it slow at first, feeling out my back. When I didn't notice any discomfort, I picked up the pace. I reveled at the fact that I ran toward something instead of away from something. When I crossed the finish line with time to spare, I felt reborn, with a renewed sense of belonging. I'm back in the family, a bro again. I remembered Big Al's words, 'You must conquer fear by facing it, and eliminate all distractions by getting rid of your belief in them.'

CHAPTER 18

Are You Ready?

Fire Season, 1981

Mr. Atlas shouted through the locker room, his gaze focused on me, "Suit up boys, it's show time." I knew that once the wheels lifted off the tarmac, there'd be no turning back.

As the Twin Otter flew over the jump spot, I glanced down and noticed there isn't an X in the center of the meadow. I looked at Mr. Atlas in confusion. He waged a finger at me and yelled, "You're first out, shoot for the single panel. Your jump partner has the double panels. This is all because of you, Ryan!"

Because of me? Then I remembered the investigation. The Forest Safety Officer had interviewed me shortly after my accident, he'd specifically asked, "Do you people put money on who gets closest to the X?"

I had to lie—of course we did—I didn't want to be the one to ruin a Redding tradition. It all came clear to me as I looked down at the two separate landing markers. My accident had ended an old practice.

Mr. Atlas tossed out a set of streamers. The plane circled and he yelled, "You really ready for this, Ry?" He winked and said, "We're on final! Get ready."

I synchronized my breathing before my leap of faith. Mr. Atlas pulled his head in, and a strong slap quickly followed. I froze with hesitation. Jump, man, jump! I followed my advice and lunged into the sky, a bundle of nerves. I felt the parachute deploy off my back, and the clean opening sent relief through me. I let out a long, cleansing yell. A dozen yells from the ground echoed up to me.

I didn't care about the spot, I cared about my jump partner and keeping my distance from him throughout the entire ride. Feeling comfortable with our separation, my focus turned to the upcoming landing. This would be the crucial moment. I felt vulnerable because of my back, a good PLF, imperative. The ground rushed up in a blur, as soon as my toes hit, I rolled through the points of contact, calf, thigh, shoulder, and remained motionless on my back as I waited for pain. This triggered an instant reaction from the ground crew. Vise ran over yelling, "Fuck, man! Not again!"

I looked up at him and smiled. "All's good. All's good! Man."

Big Ernie had answered my prayers, I'm a smokejumper again!

*****

Two days after my rebirthing jump, the air horn sounded. I suited up for fire request from the North Cascade Smokejumper Base in Washington State, also one with some of the toughest jump country, and a base I'd never been to. We flew up the Cascade Mountain Range, along the way, word filtered back that McCall had also requested a load of our jumpers. Fire season is on! We passed through a valley with mountains towering on either side, and soon landed at the home of the first experimental jumps conducted in 1939.

Gathering in their Quonset hut, we received a short briefing, and traded in our 150-foot letdown ropes for the 250-foot ropes they used. The coastal mountain range of Washington had monster trees, some over 300 feet tall. It wasn't a secret that the North Cascade base held the record for the longest letdown. In 1970, Larry Hyde had to travel 270 feet to reach the ground. Another jumper climbed to him with a second rope just so he could make the final twenty-feet. I didn't envy the record knowing he had to climb back up the tree to retrieve his chute.

Fire requests waited, we suited up and waddled back to the Twin Otter for a ride to the Okanogan National Forest. As the smoke column came into view, my nerves took over. The terrain, steep and rocky, and there weren't many open landing spots.

Max, my jump partner and I discussed a strategy where he would yield to me in case something went wrong in the air. He must've noticed my nervousness. He calmed them by saying, "I'll keep an eye on you, Ry-son. Don't worry about me; just have a safe ride and a good PLF."

It took the spotter multiple streamer drops to nail the exit point. Once satisfied, he yelled to Max and me, "Hook up." I secured my static line snap and got into position. The spotter yelled, "There's 250 yards of drift. Be careful of the up-slope winds. Any questions?"

'Yeah,' I thought, 'can we get this over with?' We nodded, no.

"We're on final!"

I took a deep breath as his hand slapped my shoulder. I pushed my body hard from the step, and the opening shock had me swinging like a weight at the end of a rope. I scanned the sky and found Max. We had good separation and that's all I cared about, until I made a few corrections and heard him yell. I saw him turning away. 'Oh, shit. I just ran him out of the spot.'

After we landed, I asked, "Did I run you out?"

"Kind of," he shrugged.

"I'm sorry. The wind blew me off course."

"I had my eye on you, Ry-son. Don't worry about it."

"I am worried about it Max. I think I'm having some confidence issues up there."

"Kind of to be expected, it'll get better. Just give it some time."

We cut fire line and mopped up past dark. By daybreak, a helicopter came in to ferry us out. I thanked Big Ernie for not making me do a pack-out because my back had ached all night. I had to pop a couple pain pills just to ease the throbbing.

The chopper dropped us off, and within a few hours, I'm back in the door of the Twin Otter for another fire. The scenario repeated itself until I'd jumped five fires in five days. My groove was back, but my back wasn't. The pain and pressure became relentless, but I dared not say anything for risk of being yanked from the list.

The Icicle Ridge Fire required two loads of jumpers. Crowning through the trees, it put up an ominous smoke column.

I rode in the Beech and they planned to do a tandem jump—two planes dropping jumpers from the same exit point in succession—over the center of a massive canyon that fell thousands of feet into a river gorge. Bighorn sheep loved this country with the jagged, towering peaks and steep ridges. If a jumper made a wrong turn, it would result in a very long ride to the bottom. My last experience jumping out of a Beech hadn't been a good one. I didn't like the sit down exits, too awkward pushing away from the plane with my feet pressed against the fuselage. Twisting up over this drainage would be disastrous.

"We're on final!" the spotter shouted.

I grabbed the sides of the door, felt the slap, and slid out. I kept my head down, and my chute popped open, twist free. The wind had shifted during my exit and I was heading in the wrong direction. I quickly scanned for any decent landing spots on the side of the mountain, but all I saw, large granite boulders and a sheer drop off to the canyon bottom. Suddenly, my parachute surged forward on a strong up canyon gust. The mountainside rushed toward me, the drop off on my right and the boulders on my left. I picked the boulders and made a quarter turn for a hillside approach. I couldn't let the wind slam me into the mountain.

I made small corrections to avoid the boulders, a small dirt patch opened up and I reefed down on both toggles as hard as I could. My parachute lost its forward momentum just as my feet scrapped over the top of a boulder and I augured into the dirt. I didn't even attempt a PLF for fear of rolling down the mountain. When the dust settled, I saw a beautiful cloud-studded sky above me. I lay there a moment amazed I didn't smash myself up.

Magnum's voice echoed down the mountain, "Ry, you all right?"

"I'm okay!" After five fire jump in six days, this brief moment of calm needed to be enjoyed. I forced myself up and began stuffing my jump gear in my pack-out bag when I heard rocks bouncing off the shale to the side of me. I looked up and saw Magnum making his way down.

"Just want to see if you needed any help," he said reaching me.

"Have any beer?" I laughed.

Magnum sat on a rock while I finished packing. Every time I looked at him, he had a pained expression on his face. Finally, I asked, "What's on your mind? You look constipated."

"We haven't had much time to talk since, you know, *the day*."

"Not much to talk about, *the day*" I told him.

"How can you take it so lightly, Ry? I saw the entire thing; it still haunts the hell out of me. You know what I want to know? What went through your mind during it all?"

I thought for a moment, then said, "I didn't have much time to think. Once I saw Dog's chute coming, I just reacted."

"And when you were wrapped up?"

I shrugged. "It felt like floating in a quiet, warm cocoon."

He shifting nervously, "Well, it looked fucking horrifying from my perspective." The Otter flew over just above the ridge top. "Cargo pass," Mag said. "Guess we'd better get up there."

As I slipped into my pack-out bag, I asked him, "How come I'm the only one down here?"

"They adjusted the exit point after seeing what happened to you. You sure you don't want me to pack that for you, man?"

"Just keep going, Mag. This is my test."

Up on the ridge, I placed my pack-out bag with the others and out of habit, went straight for the chainsaw box. The fire boss called us together. "We're going to split in half and work each flank until we meet. Let's get this show going."

Magnum grabbed the saw pack and a hand tool. Many of the trees in our path had the tops broken out from snow and instead of leading the crew we followed behind clearing the downed ones. We worked together until the fire boss called him on the radio to head up the line. I worked alone, sawing the trees to clear the line. On a trip back to the pack to refuel my saw, I found the fire had jumped the line and my PG bag burning. I stomped on the bag until it smoldered a rancid plastic smell, but too late to save any of the contents. I didn't care much about the bag itself or my burnt jacket and clothes. I cringed when I saw my prescription bottle a distorted clump of plastic. I pried it open only able to salvage three pills. My back ached at the sight.

I continued to cut line through the night and into the next morning before getting a few hours break, all the while hoping my back cooperated. The loss of the pills put me on edge and just when I relaxed enough to fall asleep the boss roused us up.

It took two days of digging and sawing to finish the fire and when the boss called it out, a helicopter ferried us back to base, where I managed to get a ride to the local department store to resupply. The stares from the customers had me wondering what I must've looked like, so I just smiled at them glad to have fresh cloths and especially toothpaste and a brush. The barracks had a laundry room and while my clothes washed, I plopped down in a soft chair. That's when I felt shooting pains, the throbbing in my back had returned. I jumped up cursing like a sailor.

With clean fire clothes, I figured a nice nap on a real bed would improve my condition, but on the way the barracks, the siren sounded. Missoula wanted ten of us. As we taxied down the runway, we passed the ready shack. The remaining jumpers had gathered on the apron to say goodbye in the usual smokejumper fashion—a line of fish belly white butts saluted us as we lifted off. Everyone in the plane laughed. I loved seeing the lighter side of jumping again.

Despite my pain, excitement took over knowing I'd be jumping out of yet another base not familiar to me. Missoula had emerged as the hub of the United States Smokejumpers with the largest number of jumpers and the most aircraft. Neptune Aviation Services shared the airport with them supplying a fleet of air tankers, WWII anti-submarine bombers converted into retardant ships. I looked forward to touring their facility since an air tanker had saved my butt on the Hog Fire.

As we circled to land, I saw dozens of air tankers, along with Twin Otters, DC-3's, and Beech aircraft. It looked like an air show. We checked in and stowed our gear. The jump list had ten Redding bros on it. Heading to the mess hall, I saw a Missoula jumper who looked familiar—the same Zulie who'd stuck the Pulaski in his foot, causing Gramps and me to miss McCall's end of the year party two years earlier. I still hadn't let go of it and glared at him as we passed.

In the mess hall, I saw Dan Mitchell, a fellow Redding jumper and while I pigged out on steak, mashed potatoes, and veggies, he filled me in. "After you left, a load went to McCall, another to Grangeville, and some wound up in Redmond. My load ended up here. We've been jumping steadily ever since. How's the back holding up, Ry?"

I looked around the mess hall filled with healthy jumpers and decided to lie. "I've had my moments, but everything's been going well enough."

"You might be tested here. There've been a lot of pack-outs. Resources are stretched thin, not many helicopters available. A few of us are going into town tonight for a beer. Go get some sleep. I'll find you before we go."

I didn't sleep long, but enough. When Dan came knocking, I was ready. We hitched a ride from a Zulie to the Montana jumpers' signature bar: Stockman's. They had live music at the bar and gambling in the back, which inspired the catchy logo on the T-shirts, they sold. It read, "Liquor in Front, Poker in the Rear."

With Missoula being a college town, the place had lots of pretty women. Buddy Reid and the Rip Em' Ups blues band rocked on the stage to a full dance floor. Dan must've noticed my discomfort because he kept buying me shots, saying, "This'll take the edge off." It sure did and we closed the bar down. We began the long walk to the airport, pissing on the side of the road and telling jump stories. He kept going on about a fire he'd jumped two years earlier in Idaho. "While setting up to land, the sight of the mangled plane distracted me and when I saw this guy walking around in a daze, I lost sight of the ground and landed hard. I heard the crack and instantly knew I'd just broken my fucking leg. We're on a rescue jump and I ended up having to be rescued along with that guy. From the way the bros talked, the pilot was in shock and burned real bad. They didn't think he would survive. The look of the guy haunts me to this day, worse fucking jump of my life."

We knew about plane crashes and injuries. In spite of it all, we kept coming back.

*****

In the morning, I jumped my first fire out of Missoula in a stand of bug-killed timber on the Bitterroot National Forest. We'd been directed to attack the fire hard and fast, build a helispot, and return to base as quickly as possible. As the last cargo box hit the ground, I fell into my old habit of grabbing the chainsaw. Dan questioned my decision because of my back, but I reassured him that I, indeed, was a little nuts. We built the helispot, joined the rest of our crew, and spent two days sawing through thick downfall to line the fire. Once out, a helicopter picked us up and we touched down in Missoula to a flurry of activity. Jump planes and air tankers rumbled down the runway in an endless succession. I wasted no time in readying my gear for the next fire.

The jump list tossed bros into the woods at a frenzied pace. In no time, Dan and I ended up on the first load again. We made a dash for the mess hall for a quick meal, but as soon as we reached the door, the siren sounded. This seemed to be a pattern for me. Why couldn't I just sit down and enjoy a meal. Our destination, the Hole-in-the-Wall Fire on the Deer Lodge National Forest. While circling the smoke column, a small meadow appeared about a mile away. Instead of risking parachuting into dead timber, the meadow became the jump spot.

After we completed the line around the fire, Dan, the fire boss, concluded it safe enough to leave for the night. I built a hootch on the edge of the meadow with a cargo chute and used my jump suit as a mattress. The first decent sleeping arrangement I'd had all season, and I settled beside the warming fire for a freeze-dried meal. Morning came with an overcast sky and it began to drizzle.

Mop-up went quickly with the high humidity, and when we headed down the creek toward camp. A couple mountain grouse flushed into the trees. One of them sat on a low limb and stared at me. I saw a plump meal and a barrage of rocks soon followed. They whizzed by its head, bounced off the tree, and still, it sat there looking at me. My arm got tired and on my last attempt, the rock smacked the bird in the head sending it to the ground. I danced around my kill like I starred in the *"Lord of the Flies."* I field dressed it and entered camp, the great white hunter. Could there be anything better than fresh meat, a warm fire, and telling stories in good company?

The weather deteriorated throughout the night, soaking my hootch. Over morning coffee, we talked about getting back to Missoula—a helicopter ride wasn't going to happen. As we broke camp, Dan went back to the fire for one last look. Somebody said after him, "Why even bother, it raining all night!"

I knew why he went back. In California, we usually don't get a lot of moisture on fires and to call one out without thoroughly checking it could result in a re-burn—a condition where the fire comes back to life after leaving it. To be a fire boss and have the stigma of allowing a fire to re-burn wasn't looked upon favorably. We had everything packed and waited for his return. An hour passed, then another. Concern set in and we split up to look for him. I searched down-slope from the fire following a different creek thinking he might have gotten confused. I hollered, listened, hollered. Finally, I heard him call. He followed my hoots until he saw me. He looked sheepish from the ordeal.

"Damn it," he muttered, "I wasn't lost. I just took the wrong creek."

"Don't worry, Dan," I grinned. "There's no shame in getting lost."

"I wasn't lost," he insisted. "I just stepped through the hole-in-the-wall for a while." Even if he had embarrassed himself, at least his humor survived. "The district called while out there. There's a road a few miles away. They'll wait there. Let's get out of here."

We packed out through meadows and thick stands of lodge pole pine on relatively flat ground, but my back ached the whole time. We found the vehicles, they drove us to the district office and we dined in Phillipsburg. As we sat down to eat, Dan announced, "I'm picking up the beer tab."

We all knew he hoped to erase his embarrassment from of our minds and just to tease him, we made toast after toast to the fire boss who'd gone through the hole-in-the-wall and made it back the same man. Returning to Missoula, the fire bust had ended and we flew to Redding with a new cache of nylon webbing, parachute hardware, jump suits, and parachutes to restock what we'd lost in the service center fire. We continued upgrading our operation in the hangar until it resembled a functioning unit.

*****

Thunderstorms soon moved into California. Fires popped up all over the high country and we requested help from Missoula, Winthrop, and McCall. I flew to the Tahoe National Forest where Dan and I jumped the Long Two Fire. We had it lined and mopped up by the next morning. We hiked to a trail that led to a road, where a district worker picked us up. While Dan turned in our fire report, I stood by the management door and couldn't help but overhear a lively conversation between the Fire

Management Officer and Dan. Apparently, the FMO looked at our report and didn't like what he saw. He snarled, "Who authorized you to work overtime?"

Dan pulled out the fire request given to him in the plane and said, "I don't see any instructions here where I had to get permission from you for anything. I'm the fire boss, so I made the call."

"We don't do it that way around here."

"We're not from around here. You called us."

"I can't sign off on your overtime, you have to justify it."

Mild-mannered Dan leaned over the desk and in a tone I'd never heard from him, said, "We had the fire out in a safe and timely manner. I'm not changing our time cards." After a stare down, Dan turned and exited the office. I high fived him as we left the building. Dan was clearly upset, "That dude has a hard-on for jumpers. Maybe he tried to be one and washed out, or a jumper stole his girlfriend."

I chuckled, "Probably both."

We waited for the rest of our load to return from their fires and while cooling our heels, we overheard an engine crewmember say, "Fucking jumpers, taking all our fires." With this kind of atmosphere, Dan and I did what any sane jumpers would do; we walked to the Bar of America and drank until they called on us to fly home.

CHAPTER 19

Last Jump From The Gobi

Wilderness Fire #02-315, Fremont National Forest
Cave Junction Jumper Base, Oregon, 1981

Thunderstorms moved into Oregon from the coast promising a flurry of lightning activity. The jump list rotated at a steady clip. I suited up and asked the spotter which base had requested us. "Cave Junction," he answered. I pumped my fist knowing yet another base would christen me. The anticipation compared to slipping on my backpack and hitchhiking through Europe with my buddies. Like a rolling stone, I bounced around all my life only to land in the great Northwest with a parachute above me.

Of all the smokejumper bases, Cave Junction's history resonated in controversy. In 1943, it opened as the home of the Siskiyou Smokejumpers. Cave Junction is a small, rural community nestled in the arid and remote Illinois Valley, surrounded by the Siskiyou Mountain Range. Long ago, a jumper named Mick Swift, nicknamed the area "The Gobi," because the heat and aridness resembled the desert.

Being isolated from U. S. Forest Service bureaucracy, Cave Junction developed a reputation for being wildly independent. Within the town itself, the CJ jumpers sponsored an annual Fourth of July celebration complete with a barbecue, bag races, tug-of-wars, and one of their own—Allen 'Mouse' Owen—skydiving into the festivities dressed as Superman and packing goodies for the kids. They hosted a Family Day during the water-landing phase of their refresher training where the community came out and watched them parachute into a lake. The kids paddled out in rafts to round up the wet jumpers. This kind of community involvement as well as the jumpers' tribal unity caused friction with the Forest Service's management. The pencil pushers couldn't understand how a group of smokejumpers were so close to each other and beloved by the community around them. They worried it would affect discipline.

In the late '70's and early '80's, the US economy fell on hard times and in an attempt to cut costs, the Forest Service scheduled a number of smokejumper bases for closure. Boise, Idaho shut down in 1980 and LaGrande, Oregon in 1982. Both went without a whimper. Cave Junction, on the other hand, put up a fight. The Gobi jumpers thought the Forest Service had targeted them because of their reputation, and they weren't going to go down easy for no bureaucratic pencil pushers. Some of the crew demanded justification for the closure and became vocal in defense of their base. The Forest Service reduced their numbers in response, taking the unheard of measure of blacklisting two of the loudest protestors—Mouse and Troop—from getting other jobs within the Service. Luckily, the Alaska Smokejumpers watched the brouhaha from afar. They employed the same 'take no bullshit' attitude that Cave Junction did, and offered Mouse and Troop jobs in Alaska.

An in-flight fire request diverted us to the Three Sisters Wilderness Area. We dropped four bros there, stopped at the Redmond base to refuel, and took on four jumpers to fill out the load. We arrived at Cave Junction in late afternoon and found the place empty save for two Redmond jumpers. Evening came without a request. The Redmond jumpers hogged the barracks, so Dan and I spent the night in a motel.

The next day, Dan and I watched the Twin Otter lift off with the remaining crew, leaving only a spotter, a pilot, and a Beech 90A on base. We waited the day out as the spotter, nicknamed 'Pup,' and the pilot, Garry Peters, filled us in on the Gobi's impending closure. Pup practically shouted, "Those damn DC suit-n-tie political assholes! How could they axe thirty-eight years of tradition with the swipe of a fucking pen?"

Bitterness hung like a cloud in the parachute loft. Late in the afternoon, Pup casually called on Dan and me. No air horn sounded, no opportunity for an adrenalin rush, only a disgruntled jumper saying, "We have a fire request for you two. It's in the Gearhart Wilderness Area on the Fremont National Forest." I pumped my fist glad to get away from the pissed off spirits that saturated a base in pain.

We suited up and crawled into the small, cramped Beech. Gary quickly lifted off the runway, banking so sharply we slid from one side of the cabin to the other, and turbulence tossed us around the whole 150-mile flight. The wind blew so fierce we couldn't see the smoke until directly over the fire. It looked small enough for the two of us to handle. Pup picked a jump spot and threw out streamers. They carried hundreds of yards downwind from the intended spot, indicating the wind's too strong for our parachutes. Pup yelled, "Shit."

I yelled, "Try it again," not wanting to go back to Cave Junction. He threw another set and they flew off in a different direction just as far as the first.

Pup directed Garry upwind and threw yet another set. All the sharp banking had taken its toll on me and nausea had me tasting my lunch. My head spun, I didn't care anymore about the damn jump spot or the fire. I wanted out of that plane. Pup yelled, "It's too windy! We'll fly around to see if it dies down a little."

Sweat coated my body. It took all my energy to calm my deteriorating condition. When Pup looked at me, I knew he knew. I had the same look when I began puking my guts out every time we crossed the French, Italian, or Swiss Alps. My dad had the same look as Pup's, feeling my pain, but not about to stop. He shook his head in pity and dropped a fourth set of streamers. He cursed again. I crawled up to him and pleaded, "Get me out of this fucking plane...PLEASE!"

He threw up his arms in frustration. "The goddamn streamers are blowing all over the place. I'm going to drop you out over the fire. Hold into the wind. Good luck, now hook up."

I slid my legs out the door in utter relief. Pup slapped my shoulder, and I felt myself spinning as my parachute deployed to the hardest opening shock ever. As I struggled to untwist, meat chunks and potatoes splattered all over my facemask, and down the inside of my jacket.

Dizziness continued, I brushed my lunch from my mask, turned into the wind and looked down. The ground zipped by moving in the wrong direction! I'm going backwards; no forward speed what so ever. I struggled to look over my shoulder, but couldn't see much from the high collar of my jacket. A gauntlet of huge Ponderosa pines coming at me puckered me up. Quick, pump the right toggle! Stop! Pump again! Okay, missed that monster, keep it tight, Ry! Trying to steer backwards to avoid the trees, I lost sight of the ground and nobody heard my breath explode, or saw the flash of light when I slammed in. When my eyes opened, the world still spun around me. My parachute dragged me across the dirt in a cloud of dust. I released the capewells and the chute took off in the wind hundreds of feet until it wrapped around a tree.

I yanked my helmet off, rolled over, and puked the rest of my guts out. Pup's muffled voice vibrated from the radio in my personal gear bag, "You all right? Answer the radio, over."

I dug it out of my pack, "I'm okay," I lied. "How'd Dan do?"

"He's about five-hundred yards uphill from your location. I'll drop the cargo as close to the fire as possible."

"Ten-four. Could you circle the fire so I know where to go?"

"No problem. It looked like one hell of a ride from up here, Ryan."

"Hell of a lot better than being in that damn plane."

I watched the cargo box drift beyond the ridge above me and made a mental note of it before stuffing my gear into my pack-out bag. I knew I'd waste precious time and energy if I lugged my gear uphill, so as my stomach and muscles quivered, I looked for the most distinctive tree there. A large Ponderosa with a top shattered by lightning stood out like a beacon. I knew I would recognize it later. I propped my gear bag against it and tied long pieces of flagging on the lower limbs for locators.

On top of the ridge, I found Dan under another huge Ponderosa unpacking the tree-climbing gear box. I looked up to our cargo box swinging high in the branches. Dan looked at me and shook his head, "You look like a fucking ghost, Ry. I'll climb for the cargo. Go ahead and check the fire."

Still tasting puke I said, "Worse jump I'd ever had, Dan."

He looked baffled and said, "I don't think so. I can remember a lot worse one at Birkland's."

"I may have broken my back on that one, but at least I didn't puke."

He snickered, "I thought I smelled vomit. Yuck!"

Burning in thick needle duff, the fire posed no immediate threat. I found a tree branch and scratched away at a fire line until Dan arrived with hand tools. We cut every shrub within the line and stacked them on a burning stump. The bonfire supplied us with light and warmth through the night.

By morning, only ashes remained making mop-up a breeze. Satisfied that we'd put it out, I left Dan the radio and headed out in the direction of my gear.

I usually paid close attention to the lay of the land from the plane. But this time, I had no sense of direction or distinguishable landmarks to rely on. North, South, East, West, the land looked the same, rolling ridges covered with mature pines and a healthy, reproductive understory. By afternoon, I'd walked through unending terrain with no sign of the broken tree. I zigzagged back across the ridges, with the same result, no pack-out bag. The land began to shimmer under the baking sun. I yelled out to Dan several times only to hear the wind answer.

Four hours went by with no sign of my gear. Dehydrated and pissed off, I slumped to the ground knowing I was lost. Anger drove me to the highest ridge I could find to get a vantage point. Endless ridges rolled into jagged valleys, glowing in a kaleidoscope of green hues. The valleys melted into a large drainage with granite cliffs shooting out on either side. Lingering evergreens grew from the rocks like fingers clutching a prized possession. The beauty of it calmed me down a little.

Hungry, dehydrated, and demoralized, my mind began to wander. Why did I end up here? On top of the world looking down on wilderness, a place that had stolen my heart the very first time I ventured into one. Buckskin snags stood out like beacons in an ocean of green adding a somber color and the reminder that even in death, existence endures. Death, that's it, I thought, death of a smokejumper base, but not death of the spirits that made it. The Gobi jumpers will stand out like snags, a constant reminder of the smokejumper spirit. Did the voices of a rich past guide me here to feel the pain of death? But why me? Had I been unknowingly chosen to be the last jumper out of the Gobi? By all rights, it should've been Mouse or Trooper. Did the spirits know an era had ended? Did they rush into the plane as the wheels lifted off for the last time? Did they summon an angry wind to follow us the whole flight not allowing Dan and me a safe place to land? Did screaming in backwards signifying the enormous step back the Forest Service had taken in closing Cave Junction? Had puking my guts out symbolize the disgust of the Gobi jumpers? Too many parallels flooded my mind, parallels of what was and parallels of what is no more.

I felt their spirits all around me. My first exposure to the spirit world started at a young age from being brought up a Roman Catholic. Being an altar boy, I accepted and prayed to the Holy Spirit. The religions of the world have based their teachings on accepting the spirits of those who created their beliefs. My exposure to the spirit world expanded while in high school. Being an avid reader, I explored the works of Herman Hesse, and especially Carlos Castaneda. Another realm did exist. Castaneda used psychedelic drugs to transcend into the spirit world of the Mexican Indians. Timothy Leary experimented on his students with LSD and psilocybin at that time, too. He coined the phrase, *"Turn on, tune in, drop out."*

The psychedelic generation flourished. Three of my high school bros and I decided to experiment with drugs. We had no problem getting LSD; it could be bought on most street corners in downtown Berlin. We planned a hitchhiking journey to Frankenstein's castle to see what we could discover. There wasn't much of a castle left standing, but it emanated a thick musk from an old dead time. We set up camp inside the ruins, popped our acid and settled in for the night. A full moon glared down with such intensity, it seemed like day. Not long into the night, I saw shadows moving about the ruins and around our camp. The air thick with a musty smell, the ground seemed to come alive. Entities come out, zipping by us. They swooped through the night with long trails that circled the ruins. The back of my neck tingled, my hair stood straight up. A collective fear gripped us so thoroughly that without a word we packed up and scrambled out of there as fast as we could. The spirits followed us until we reached the safety of a village.

I believe that experience left the spirit door wide open for me. I felt spirits coming from the wreaths on the sidewalks of those who'd tried to escape over the Berlin Wall, only to be mercilessly gunned down. I felt the spirits of the East Berlin citizens who watched me from their side of the wall as I threw rocks at the Russian guard towers, cursing them loudly. I knew the oppressed could hear me, but they remained stoic figures, frozen in place, daring not to respond in any obvious way, but I felt their spirits guiding the barrage of rocks. Spirits of the dead, spirits of the living, they're everywhere!

The spirit world that fascinated me the most is that of our Native Americans. They believe that spirits are alive in everything the Great Spirit created on Mother Earth. I'm fond of this quote by Black Elk of the Oglala Sioux:

"Great Spirit! You lived first, and you are older than all need, older than all prayer. All things belong to you—The two-legged, the four-legged, the wings of the air and all green things that live...I am sending you a voice, Great Spirit, my Grandfather, forgetting nothing you have made, the stars of the universe and the grasses of the earth."

A close second to the spirit world of the Native Americans, I experienced a strong connection to the Blues, a form of expression centered on the trials and tribulations of dealing with love, of broken hearts, feelings that have endured all time. I first met the Blues at the impressionable age of ten, while living in Michigan. I had a girlfriend, I thought I felt love, even though I had no real idea of what love meant. She touched me in an innocent way. I defined love based on those feelings. When her dad caught us coming from a pond by our housing project clearly known as being off limits, he towered over me in his uniform scolding me almost to tears. His last words forbid us from ever seeing each other again. My heart ached from this traumatic experience, the feeling of losing what I perceived as love has followed me throughout my life. Maybe as a result of that incident, I've questioned love. As I matured, I questioned women. I don't understand them, didn't do the right things, or say the right things. Even though I tried my best, I always seemed to end up, *Tied to the whipping post.*

*****

The sun dipped behind the peaks and my thoughts returned to my present predicament. Darkness began to fall and I needed to shift gears. With only a book of matches and a pocketknife, things didn't look good. No food or water, and my T-shirt soaked with sweat. Bear scat all over the place concerned me. Suddenly, I felt helpless. I remembered the Hole-in-the-Wall Fire where

Dan got lost. I laughed at the thought. I yelled loud, "I'm over here Dan!" but my voice just echoed.

Angry with myself, I knew what I had to do. I made a pile of twigs and pine needles in a clearing, struck a match, and soon had fire and smoke. When I piled on green boughs, the smoke thickened, rose to the treetops, but the wind flattened it out into nothing. My spirit sank.

The wind eased with the setting sun and the valley below filled with a sound I knew too well. Rotor blades slicing through mountain air echoed up the canyon walls. I jumped up as the last rays of sunlight faded. The chopper came straight toward me like an arrow. I hopped around my fire with joy until it hovered directly above. I noticed it belonged to the Forest Service rappellers, our archrivals.

The spotter threw out a message streamer. I opened the pouch and read the note: 'If you're the lost jumper, raise your right arm.'

The words hit me hard. I gathered what dignity I had left, and with my head bowed in shame, raised my left arm.

The helicopter maneuvered to a larger clearing and a rope unraveled from each side, with rappellers soon following. Once on the ground, three packages flew out the door behind them. The ship turned and disappeared into the canyon. The rappellers looked at me. I looked at them, the saddest stare down of my firefighting career. How do you introduce yourself under such circumstances? Hi, I'm the lost jumper. I want to thank you rotor heads for saving my butt. Instead, I tried to play down the whole thing by shrugging. For a diversion, I said, "That's a nice 212 you're flying. Haven't heard the pitch of those rotors in a while."

It didn't work. The leader said to me in business-like fashion. "We'll spend the night here. In the morning, we'll escort you to the trailhead and you'll be driven to the district office. Your jump partner is still on the fire looking for your gear."

That sounded simple enough. I offered my hand, "Thanks, I'm Ryan." The younger rappeller snickered, "Oh, we know."

So, that's the way it's gonna be, I thought. The young buck reminded me of the Zulie who'd stuck his Pulaski in his foot in Idaho. He went on with his cocky tone, "I was heading out the door for a couple of days off when our boss called me back." After a moment, he ruefully added, "I had to come on this one."

I would've felt bad for them, but they're rappellers. I said, "You think I want to be here with you? It's a tough business, plans change all the time."

As the night wore on, the youngster loosened up. He told me, "I had to laugh when the boss said a report came in from a smokejumper saying his partner is lost in the Gerhardt Wilderness. You're lucky a commercial airliner spotted your smoke column. After I thought about it, I knew I didn't want to miss the chance of a lifetime. Saving a smokejumper? This'll go down as a classic!"

Embarrassed, I said the only thing I could, "At least you're getting some overtime out of it." I imagined what the rumor mill headline would be: Smokejumper hopelessly lost in wilderness area rescued by rotor head rappellers. At last, I swallowed hard and said, "Go easy on me, will you? After all, I was a rotor head like you before being a jumper."

"Maybe you should've stayed with helicopters," he said. "Besides, you guys are nuts. Nothing could make me jump out of a perfectly good airplane. I'm happy sliding down a rope, thank you very much. Anyway, we're glad we could save you. No one's gonna forget a story like this!"

Next morning, we hiked cross-country to a trail that led to a vehicle. The news traveled fast and at the district office I had trouble looking people in the eye. The dispatcher, who happened to be an ex-jumper, lightened the mood saying, "Just shrug it off. I'm sure it's not the first time or the last time someone is going to get lost. Hopefully the next time, though, they won't have to be saved by rappellers."

I met up with Dan at a local diner. "I know what it's like, Ry. I wish I could've found you like you found me in Montana. So, how'd the night go with the rappellers?"

"How do you think? Embarrassing as hell! I had to sit around my signal fire taking shit from rotor heads!"

Dan slapped the table. "Don't take it out on me! I looked for you all over! I didn't want to call the district, believe me, but after a few hours I had to. They said three timber cruisers were heading my way to help with the gear. One of them packed the fire box. Half an hour into the hike, guess what we found?"

I shook my head, "My gear?"

"Yep," he laughed, "right where you left it. Wait now, it gets better. After more than an hour of hiking the ridges, the leader stopped and scratched his head while looking around. I asked if he's lost, he mumbles, 'I'm not sure, we should've reached the road by now.' The guy carrying your gear slumped on the ground all sweaty and red-faced. I couldn't help but laugh watching the other two straining to get him to his feet. We walked for another hour going this way and that until we finally found the road. When the packs came off, the guy carrying your gear bitched the whole ride about his aching back, burning shoulders, and throbbing knees. They have no idea what we go through! God, did I have a good time watching that!"

Waiting for the Otter to pick us up, I had time to think. There'd been many firsts on this odyssey, first time at the Gobi, first time jumping out of a Beech 90A, first time puking my guts out on the way down, and the first time of not having a designated jump spot to shoot for, only a 'good luck' send off from the spotter. I'd never parachuted in backwards like that, and the first time I'd gotten lost. And to top it all off, I'd been the first smokejumper to ever to be rescued by rappellers and maybe the last.

When Dan and I returned to base, the overhead called Dan into the office and grilled him for an explanation. Why they didn't ask me is still a mystery. Dan happened to be facing the door during the inquisition. Disco and I looking in, then Disco livened things up by doing his vulture imitation in Dan's view. He wasn't able to contain his laughter and when the overhead turned to see the cause, Disco and I had already slipped away. That jump concluded my season, a season that resulted in the most overtime in quite a few years even though I spent nine weeks on disability. I looked forward to spending the off-season in the dojo.

CHAPTER 20

Alaska, Take Two

Fire Season 1982

Cave Junction closed this spring. Dan and I held the honor of being the last smokejumpers to parachute onto a fire from the Gobi. We also shared the honor of being the first California jumpers to bail on a fire on the Fremont National Forest, and the Gerhardt Wilderness. We awarded each other generous salt points for that.

Now, with a new season upon us, a major change in personnel took place. Dick Tracy, our beloved base manager, retired after twenty-nine years. We all loved Tracy, he never forgot his jumper roots and truly cared about us, even though most of us had wild streaks that often landed us in trouble and put him on the spot, he still stood by us. Tracy could bring out the best of his men, even the questionable characters with powerful personalities and big egos. He made due with the resources given him and called bullshit on upper management when necessary. Having been manager of the Silver City, New Mexico jump base before coming to Redding, he knew how tricky spotting could be in the wind. His approach, line up on the spot and throw one set of streamers, and before they hit the ground he'd yell, "Hook up." Never too windy to jump for that man, and his favorite last comment before slapping a jumper, "Go get-em babe." He'd been the type of spotter that hated returning to base with jumpers still on board. As Big D put it, "Old Tracy had the lowest DRA average of anyone"—DRA meaning Dry Run Average. He'd been the kind of boss everyone hated to see leave and I'll never forget the man.

Gramps took over and initiated an unpopular change. He added a three-mile pack-out with 110-pound packs to the refresher training, which produced a fair amount of grumbling from the vets. We also acquired a new parachute, the XP-5, which flew faster, turned more quickly, and braked better than the FS-10. I spent countless hours in the loft rigging and getting to know the new chutes.

The first fire request of the season came on May 29, exactly one-year after my accident. The date continued to be cursed, one of the squad leaders on the second load hit the ground so hard he fractured his femur.

The storm gathered strength igniting fires all across the north state. I jumped a small fire on the Shasta Trinity. Lightning continued to pound us through June, and I made a jump on the dreaded Plumas. Back from the Yellow Fire, I went to the bottom of the jump list. I hoped Alaska would soon call, but by late June, no call had come. I rotated to the top of the list and debated if I should go on hold so I wouldn't miss the detail. Many jumpers frowned upon playing the list in this manner, so I decided to stay on and on June 24, the horn sounded.

*****

Stein Fire, Klamath National Forest
June 24, 1982

When I heard Boy say the fire was in the Wooley Creek drainage, I felt uneasy. An experienced vet had put it this way, "If the Wooley Creek's monster old growth firs don't grab your chute right out of the sky, the steep-assed ridges, rattlesnakes, and poison oak will be waiting for you. If you get past them, be prepared for a pack-out that will test every ounce of your strength and endurance."

We flew into Wooley Creek. Mixed stands of mature pines, firs, and hardwoods towered over steep slopes, the ground littered with logs and rocks. A small smoke rose on an ever-changing wind. Boy and I scan the area for a decent jump spot; a small jagged spur ridge protruded from the mountain like a cave man's nose. It terminates sharply into a sheer cliff where a huge fir with fire and smoke streamed from its branches midway up the trunk.

Boy points and yells, "Right there, see that small dirt patch?"

"It's pretty small," I nodded back.

Boy shouted into his microphone. "Make a low pass over the spur ridge." The plane banked in, the dirt patch had rocks all over it. Boy yells, "What do you think?"

There wasn't much to consider. "It looks good," I yelled back.

The first streamer drop showed the upper winds consistent, but once they entered the influence of the spur ridge; they danced around, and ended up drifting down the canyon. The second set maintained a pattern in line with the jump spot. Dave nodded and gave me the map case and a radio, "I'm going to drop you by yourself to see how it goes. Give me a call when you land. The winds are erratic down low, so be careful and watch out for that wash. There's about a hundred-fifty yards of drift. I'll give me five more jumpers. Any questions?"

I said, "No," while positioning myself in the door and looking across the landscape, I saw a layer of dark clouds building over the Marble Mountains.

Boy yells, "On final, are you ready?"

I nodded, he slapped my shoulder, and I bailed. The moment my chute deployed, I steered for the wind line. As I descended, the terrain became more defined. To the north, a thick stand of second growth concealed the ground. To the south, the rockslide looked treacherous. Boulders of all sizes balanced on a layer of shattered shale. I quartered back and forth before setting up for my final approach. I ran with the wind past the spot, and then turned back. My parachute responded nicely, I landed so soft, I had to force myself into a roll knowing Dave's eyes were on me. I pulled out my radio. "Send them down, Dave. The wind isn't a factor. Make sure they keep away from the rockslide, over."

"Ten-four. I'll drop one at a time."

A lone parachute silhouetted against the clouds. I looked up from time to time to check on Gary 'Spud' Sexton's progress, while packing my gear. When I heard, "Shit!" echo through the canyon, I glanced over and saw Spud crashing into an oak tree at the upper edge of the rockslide. Branches broke and nylon ripped. I imagined what Boy must've been thinking seeing one of his new parachutes crashing through the trees. "You all right, man?" I yelled.

From his dangling body, I heard, "Goddamn, son of a bitch!"

The next three parachutes landed fine, except Magnum, the last out. He ended up near Spud with more branches breaking and nylon ripping. After the cargo drops, I gave them an option, "You guys can climb for your chutes now or after the fire is out."

Spud suggested, "How about we cut the trees down instead of climbing them? It'd be much quicker, not to mention safer."

"Fine," I said. "But don't fuck up the saw. We'll need it when you're done."

We cut line around the ground fire, and by the time Spud and Magnum arrived with the saw, we'd cleared escape routes, posted lookouts, and had a plan of attack on the five-foot diameter fir. We took turns sawing at the trunk as embers rain down on us. Sawdust covered us from head to toe, and when I heard a tremendous crack, I immediately shut the saw down and watched the backcut widen. Wood fibers ripped apart to an ominous sound. When our lookout yelled, "Down the hill," we scattered for cover.

The tree began to fall spewing embers in a graceful arc until it impacted the ground throwing dust and branches everywhere. The earth shook. Once the dust settled, we attacked the remaining fire, then gathered at the jump spot for a communal meal as the sun's final rays filtered through the clouds over the Marble Mountain Wilderness. I called the district informing them we had the fire contained, and we'd be ready for the helicopter in the morning, and settled in for the night.

I woke to lightning and rain, became soaked in seconds, and scrambled out of my drenched sleeping bag joining the bros already huddled under the trees. Suddenly, my radio crackled to life. "Dispatch to the Stein Fire, come in."

"Stein Fire, go ahead," I answered knowing it to be bad news.

"I'm sorry to tell you that with near zero visibility, our helicopter isn't going to be able to sling your gear out. There's a trail up the mountain from you. We're sending in pack horses, over." I looked at the gear, the chainsaw, and the wet faces around me, and couldn't say anything. "Stein Fire? Do you copy, over?"

"Yes," I blurted into the radio. "I copy."

"By the way," crackled back, "your foreman wanted me to tell you that the Alaska detail has been called up. Get back as soon as possible!"

Panic shot through me. Spud and Zeitler were also on the detail, and if we don't get back to base ASAP, we'd miss it. I yelled, "Fuck!" then directed the crew, "Let's get the hell out of here!" I began cramming wet gear into my pack-out bag while barking at them, "Let's go, we don't have all day!"

I stood my pack up, slipped my arms through the straps and tried to stand, but couldn't. I got on my hands and knees, and pushed myself up. The pressure on my shoulders made my chest feel like it was going to rip open, but the words Alaska detail pushed me beyond reason.

The others weren't moving fast enough, which irritated me. The chainsaw still lay on the ground. Someone will have to make two trips, and by the look on their faces, that someone was going to be me. I started up the mountain without a word. The ground was steep and slippery and every step forward resulted in sliding back a few. I wanted to go to Alaska so bad, I began crawling when the slope became too sheer to stand. My leg muscles cramped up, my chest felt like it was on fire, and my back throbbed with pain. After two hours of fighting the mountain, I finally reached the cut bank of the trail. I crawled onto flat ground and rolled over. My heart pounded so hard, my body pulsated with every beat.

I yelled down to my bros, "I'm on the trail," hoping it would encourage them, but when I headed down to get the saw, I saw misery in their eyes. Magnum wiped rain from his glasses and snorted "Pay back, huh?"

"Pay back for what?"

"For ripping up the new chutes."

I burst out, "I don't give a damn about the chutes! I don't want to miss the detail!" and hustled down to gather the rest of the gear.

*****

The horses packed our gear to waiting Forest Service vehicles at the trailhead. I insisted they get us to Redding as fast as they could. The two and a half hour drive added to my desperation. When we pulled up to the parachute loft after hours, I ran inside to find ten names moved from the master list to the Alaska detail marker.

Mr. Atlas, the only one there, looked at me and shrugged. I stormed out of the building pissed off and stewed all night. During morning roll call, I couldn't contain myself. I demanded from the squad leader calling roll, "Who the fuck told the district to tell us to get back as soon as possible?" When no one answered, I blurted, "We busted our asses getting off the fire when you knew we wouldn't make it! Thanks a fucking lot!"

Later, after I'd cooled down, Vise said, "They weren't going to delay the detail just because three of you were in the woods."

I punched the wall. "Why did they give us hope? Just to fuck with us? We busted our asses! That pack-out nearly killed me."

"Let it go, Ry, it's over," he said. "You need to choose your battles more wisely. Pissing off the overhead isn't a good idea, you know that."

I did get some satisfaction a little later on when I overheard a conversation between Magnum and Boy in the drying tower. Boy said, "Magnum, I've been around awhile and have seen some pretty bad damage to parachutes, let's take a look." As he billowed the chute open, I heard, "Oh no! Oh no!" That was my cue to get out of the drying tower.

I moped around the loft for weeks keeping a jealous eye on the fire activity in Alaska. As it turned out, the fire season there didn't pan out and they were coming home after only a month. Our base didn't turn a prop for two months after the Stein Fire. I did bag two practice jumps. On the second one, I jumped with a bottle of Champagne in my PG bag. I'd reached my 100th jump and the toast was especially sweet, because I popped the cork right where I'd landed, smack dab in the middle of the panel.

CHAPTER 21

Alaska, Take Three

Fire Season 1983
Winds of Change

Having missed the Alaska detail last year, my name stayed on the list for another shot. I move into the barracks in March anxious for pogue training to start because rumor had it we'd be getting a woman, our first. Two years earlier, the spring of 1981 witnessed a historic change to smokejumping when Deanne Shulman became the first woman smokejumper ever. It wasn't an easy journey for her. In 1979, she washed out of rookie training in McCall from being five-pounds underweight.

When Allen 'Mouse' Owen heard the news, he jumped into action. He'd been through the same type of discrimination twice before. The first incident happened during the Vietnam War. While a lot of young men were looking for ways to avoid going to war, Mouse fought to get into the service, but standing at 4'11", and weighing 110 pounds, the Marines saw him as too small to absorb bullets, so they rejected him. Not willing to accept the outcome, he fought on relentlessly until he secured waivers from both the Senate and House of Representatives in Washington D.C. allowing him to join the Marine Corps. He served three combat tours in Vietnam, attained the rank of staff sergeant, and was featured in Life magazine as the smallest person to ever enlist. After serving his country, he wanted to be a smokejumper, but hit the same brick wall with the Forest Service. Putting his sword aside, he drew his pen again and secured another set of congressional waivers allowing him to become the smallest smokejumper ever. He jumped out of Cave Junction from 1970 through 1980, and *had* to join the Alaska jumpers in 1981 from the ruckus he created over the pending closure of the Cave Junction base. From 1980 through the spring of 1981, he guided Deanne through the political maze making it possible for her to secure another chance at smokejumping. She returned to McCall in July of 1981 and successfully completed rookie training again.

She'd never met Mouse in person and hoped she'd cross paths with him during the season, but that desire never happened. On Sunday, September 6, 1981, at 2pm, Allen 'Mouse' Owen passed away at the North Pole Skydiving Club outside Fairbanks. He'd been participating in relative work competition—contests where four-man teams attempted to form various hook-up patterns from 8000 feet. On his fatal jump, Mouse's team formed five patterns, capturing the weekend record. At 3000 feet, immediately after their parachutes opened, Mouse and another jumper collided causing his parachute to malfunction. Suspension lines entangled his body preventing him from jettisoning his main. At 500 feet, his canopy collapsed completely and he died on impact. As the wind carried Deanne Shulman into Allen Owen's world, it took him to another. He left us as many true heroes do, way too young. He had so much more to offer his bros' and newly found sis' and he'll truly be missed.

*****

Now our turn for a woman came about and the base buzzed with speculation. I'd never worked alongside a woman on fires, so I had no idea of what to expect.

While waiting for pogue training to start, Gramps asked if I wanted to be involved in a Bald Eagle habitat improvement project on the Modoc National Forest. Ranches didn't like eagles because they preyed on young livestock, which in turn caused ranchers to prey on the eagles. The Forest Service decided to give the eagles a break by considering building platforms in trees along the Pit River in hope they'd nest away from the ranches. Of course, I eagerly obliged. Dan also volunteered for the project and we wondered if Gramps knew he'd be sending two jumpers who'd gotten lost off to the high desert.

I've always been a little superstitious, and when I heard the eagle project was in the Devil's Garden Ranger District, I remembered something that had happened the previous winter while burning slash on the Hayfork Ranger District. On the bus back to camp after burning, I noticed a Great Dane trotting on the side of the road, a goat's head in its mouth. An awful tingling sensation shot up my spine and images of hell conjured up. Now, we'd be visiting the Devil's Garden!

The district supplied us with ATV's and turned us loose on the Pit River. We found the ponderosa trees to have the sturdiest branches for platforms and we roped together cut branches to form a rough platform in the hope a passing eagle would see it as a suitable nesting spot. If they liked what they saw, it would be up to them to fill in the rest of the nest. The view of the river from the trees had me thinking they'd love the seclusion and easy hunting grounds. By weeks end, we'd built over one-hundred nesting sites. If even one eagle took to a platform, the project would be a success. The District Ranger showed his appreciation by writing a letter of appreciation to our base manager.

*****

Back at base, eight veterans weren't coming back. It saddened me to learn that Disco Duck had transferred to the BLM jumpers. I loved his slap-stick sense of humor and his unpredictability kept everyone on their toes. Now, with a pogue class to replace them, the spotlight turned on our base. I couldn't understand why a woman would want to become a smokejumper. The pack-outs kicked my butt at times, and I worried if we'd be able to be the uninhibited goops that we became in the woods. Diane 'The Girl' Pryce arrived in top physical shape, had a look that could turn heads, and spoke softly. Above all, her eagerness showed us her determination in being California's first woman jumper. Adding to the mystique of having The Girl as a pogue, Missoula sent their two rookies to Redding to train with ours. Ironically, they sent two women!

The group of veterans that gathered to observe the women taking their PT test grew larger than usual, and for the first time in my career, I noticed the intimidation factor as being non-existent. Quiet whispers replaced loud, obnoxious bets on who'd wash out. After the initial sit-ups, push-ups, and even though the woman struggled with the pull-ups, they all passed. The mile and

172

a half run would be the endurance test and it did wash out one of the Zulies. The Girl finished right alongside the men.

I continued to teach parachute manipulation and decided to apply a few martial art concepts to flying a parachute. I coined it, 'The Zen of Parachute Manipulation.' Teaching the principles of flying a chute is simple, but getting a person to apply these techniques sometimes proved challenging. I stressed to the pogues, "Become one with your parachute. Make it an extension of yourself. Don't look at it as a foreign tool. If you need to make a turn, be the turn. Make your hands an extension of your mind, and your mind a part of the parachute."

Would they get it? I'd have to wait and see. Meanwhile, during the vets' final qualifying jumps, Vise injured his back during an exit and couldn't go on jumping. He retired and started a business with Squirrely designing and manufacturing software. Learning to sew parachutes and all the gear we made gave them a talent and avenue to gainful employment after jumping.

The pogues completed their initial training without issues and began psyching up for the live jumps, to my delight most had the concept for flying a parachute down. While they jumped, I resumed repairing chutes, and working toward my Master Rigger License. Magnum's torn up canopy loomed as my first challenge. Boy still seethed over it, and I cringed at all the damage. To repair chutes one needed patience, lots of it. Cutting out the damaged areas and tacking the new material was a tedious process, not to mention moving the whole parachute off the repair table to the Singer sewing machine to finish. Removing whole sections or gores for repair took months. The processes of constructing a parachute didn't leave simple options for disassembling them and I found myself pulling my hair out over the ordeal.

With my bags packed for Alaska, I monitored the weather every day. One evening while getting ready to go out on the town, the phone rang in the barracks. The Girl yelled out, "Ry, it's for you."

I answered to hear Phil's voice, the wildlife biologist I'd climbed for on Shasta Lake, and the excitement in his voice had me excited also. "I've made quite a few calls to find you. I'm in a bind and need your help. Fish and Game's been monitoring a nesting pair of eagles near Cottonwood, the first sighting of bald eagles in the Sacramento Valley since 1849. They called me for help, now I'm calling you. This is the most incredible find in over a century!"

Being chairman of the California Bald Eagle Working Team, a research program that monitored the endangered raptors, Phil seemed to be in eagle heaven. As he took a breath, I asked, "What do you need me to do?"

"They found the male eagle dead, no known cause at this time, and the mother hasn't been seen in days. We need to get the chick out of the nest before it dies of starvation. I'm hoping I won't need you to climb, I need you for backup in case my bow and arrow idea doesn't work."

Bow and arrow? "Where do you want me?"

"The Reading Island boat ramp off Balls Ferry Road."

"I'll be there as soon as I collect my gear." I ran to the tool room, grabbed a set of climbers, and hopped in my truck. The more I thought about it, the more it excited me. I could save a baby bald eagle! At the boat ramp, I found Phil, his team, and biologists from Fish and Game, but also a crowd from the Shasta Wildlife Rescue Mission, and media people, too.

We hiked a short distance to the nest site. When I sized up the tree, I shuddered. I'd never seen such a big and ugly sycamore before, and to further complicate things, I'd left in such a hurry I forgot to grab my work boots and gloves. I looked down at my tennis shoes and cursed.

With a five-foot diameter at ground level, the trunk shot up thirty-feet without a single branch, the skin felt slippery as silk and the nest sat 100 feet from the ground. While Phil assembled his bow and arrow, I asked, "What are you going to do with that?"

He tied a light rope to the fletching of an arrow and said, "I don't really know. This is my first time trying it."

"You're kidding, right?"

Phil shot arrow after arrow, either missing the branches or losing the rope. After noticing our daylight fading, I strapped the climbers to my tennis shoes and waited for Phil to give up. He did, and as I inched my way up the tree, I struggled with every step. My fingers shredded from not having gloves, and I heard click, click, and click, from the camerawoman below.

When I reached the first main lateral branch, I tied to it and hung for a while to rest my shaking legs. Urgent voices hurried me on. I set a rope over a thick branch, climbed up to the next one, and set another rope. I yelled down, "I can reach the chick. Send up the cage?"

"No," Phil yelled. "I need to get it. Just set the ropes and come down."

I heard the chick chirping, it drove me nuts knowing I could've reached in and been holding a baby eagle in my hands. As I set the last rope, I whispered to it, "Hang tight little chickadee, daddy will be up to get you in the morning." I rappelled down and would've kissed the ground if so many people weren't around. I begged the camerawoman not to publish any pictures of me since I'd screwed up by not bringing all the required equipment.

Phil invited me to the extraction in the morning, but my work schedule didn't allow it. The next afternoon, he called to say the chick had survived. The details of the operation soon appeared in the local newspaper, and I appreciated the acknowledgment for my part in the rescue.

*****

Bucks Fire, Plumas National Forest
May 29, 1983

On May 29, the air horn sounded, the start of the fire season underway with a request from the Plumas. An irony associated with this date had followed me through the years. Two years earlier, I had my accident. Last year, I had my first fire jump causing me to miss the Alaska detail. Superstition told me to go on hold, but I suited up and boarded the plane anyway not wanting the stigma of playing the jump list to my advantage.

With the fire burning hot and fast, Max, the fire boss, wasted no time in radioing the plane, "This fire's going to hell in a hurry. We need another load!"

Five of us worked feverishly to anchor the fire, while the reinforcements parachuted in. Max took a moment to call me over. I didn't like the look on his face. He said, "Ry, bad news from the plane."

I shook my head and yelled, "Not again!"

"After these guys took off, Alaska put in a rush order for the detail. The top ten are already on their way. I'm sorry."

I stomped on a smoldering pinecone, sighed and said, "After missing it two years in a row, it must be karma."

"Why don't you vent by taking Perky, Cave Man, and the pogues up the east flank? We'll meet you at the top."

We tooled up and started cutting line up the east flank. Veteran jumpers expected pogues to go the extra mile throughout their first season in retrieving cargo, cutting fire line, and mopping up. Perky had pushed them to their limit during training, but they still weren't giving him any satisfaction on fires.

The Girl ran the saw like a seasoned veteran. I admired her spunk and found myself attracted to her tight body, nice smile, and wavy hair. Since my relationship with Sylvia, the roach coach girl, had hit the rocks again, Diana and I went for a ride to Shasta Dam in my MG to watch a thunderstorm, but that was it. She mingled with us, but kept herself at arm's length. On breaks, we didn't notice any discomfort from her while we burped, farted, and cursed. She seemed entertained and right at home with our antics since she'd been on a hotshot crew for a few seasons and been exposed to the same type of behavior.

I jumped another fire a few days after the Buck's Fire, and after that, we didn't turn a prop for three weeks. Every day as I read the Alaska fire reports, I gritted my teeth. The whole state seemed on fire. They had 250 of the nation's 350 smokejumpers there, and while the other bases operated on skeleton crews from sending reinforcements, ours base didn't.

One morning while grumbling to myself, a request did come in. Gramps came out of the office and read out the top five names. "Get your stuff in the Baron. You're going to Alaska."

I let out a hoot and ran to gather my gear. As I did, a cold feeling overcame me. The Baron! I couldn't help but think, 'What if this one crashes, too?'

I worried the whole ride, and as we approached San Francisco, my uneasiness only intensified as a solid layer of fog enveloped the plane. From the shotgun seat, I couldn't see past the windshield. My hands gripped the armrests while I listened to the pilot talk with the tower. He must have noticed my nerves because he said, "I've done quite a few instrument landings. We're going to slip in between commercial airliners so the air might get a little rough." The little Baron bounced around from the wind shear as my knuckles turned white. Suddenly, runway lights appeared out of the fog just as the wheels touched down.

The flight to Alaska gave me time to relax. Once at the jumpers stand-by shack in Fairbanks, we found the ramp cluttered with Volpar's, Twin Otters, King Airs, Casas, and a Bandeirante. We stacked our stuff amid clusters of gear from every jump base in the nation. Hundreds of names filled the jump board on scores of fires throughout the state. They placed our names on the list and we hustled upstairs for a briefing.

They issued us Woodsman's Pals, mosquito netting, and military bug dope. After eating, we received work assignments, mine being in the loft. The drying tower had chutes hanging to capacity; they cluttered the floors and tables everywhere. I wanted to see the details of the Ram Air parachute system, and while looking for the loft foreman, I heard someone say from behind me, "Hey, you stinking rotten Dog Egg, you're late."

Only one jumper had such a colorful vocabulary. I turned, "Hey, Liver Lips, how the hell are you?"

Pigpen came up and we hugged briefly. Ever since the mass exodus of Pigpen, the Kroger brothers, and Fast Eddie from Redding to Alaska in 1979, I hadn't seen them, and to witness his smiling face brought back fond memories. "You finally made it, Ry. Heard you missed the detail a couple times by jumping Wooley Creek and the Feather River. What were you thinking?"

"Third time's a charm," I said, happy to be there. "You're looking pleased with yourself these days."

"Living the dream, man. Heard about the crash and the fire at the base. What a nightmare. How are things shaking out at the Nervous Center?"

"We're working out of the Air Unit's hangar while our new facility is being built. It's a rag tag deal for now, but we're functional."

"It shocked us all hearing about the plane crash and your accident, too. I never thought I'd see you again, Ry-son."

"My boundaries were tested, but here I am living the dream again."

He had a sinister tone when he asked, "How's Boy doing as the loft foreskin?" It must've been an inside joke because I didn't get it. He corrected, "I mean foreman."

I laughed. "You know him, he hasn't changed. I try to fly under his radar. Sometimes I manage to, sometimes I don't. I sure miss the good old days. When you guys left, things changed, can't say for the better."

"Don't know what to tell you except his place treats us like royalty."

"Maybe someday I'll wake up and smell the tundra, too. Tell me about this square system you're working on?"

"Come on, I'll give you the run down."

I followed Pigpen into a room where triangle shaped tables had Ram Air chutes spread out on them. He slid his hand over the nylon, saying, "This is the future of smokejumping right here. With these, throwing streamers will become obsolete one day as well as having to say, it's too damn windy to jump."

I touched the nylon. It felt way too slick for the Forest Service to ever consider using, not to mention it required the jumper to pull a ripcord, which they'd never trust us to do. The Alaska jumper's motto: 'Pull to Live and Live to Pull.'

The siren sounded ending our conversation. "I need to get more chutes on the shelves. Could you rig some rounds now? If you're around this evening, head over to the Officer's Club, I'll buy you a drink." The Officer's Club allowed jumpers to get primed before heading into town.

Before I finished rigging my third chute, the siren sounded again, and within minutes, seven jumpers and I flew to the Brooks Range north of Bettles in a King Air. I hit the dry tundra like milk on Rice Krispy's, the tundra beneath my feet crackled just like that.

We couldn't get close enough to use our burlap gunnysacks on the flames, so the Woodman's Pals came out to lop off the tops of spruce trees. With every determined whack of the newly cut spruce bough, embers exploded in all directions. In a matter of minutes my bough burst into flames. When the flames crowned into the tree tops forcing us back, the Alaskan fire boss clicked on his radio and ordered air tankers, as well as another load of jumpers.

Knowing help was on the way, I whacked hard at the flames until a retardant plane came out of nowhere for a trial run. It streaked in so low, I dove onto the tundra. The fire boss yelled, "Live drops coming in."

The high-pitched sound of the lead plane trailed by the throaty rumble of a DC-7 air tanker had mosquitos scattering and me too. To be in the path of an air tanker ready to drop three-thousand gallons of retardant would be the same as standing in a kill zone. The powerful velocity of the retardant could peel the tundra right off the permafrost, annihilating anything in its path.

A huge red glob fell from two bay doors a hundred feet from the ground painting the flames and tundra bright red. The air tanker made two more passes, extending the retardant line. After clearing the area, the roar of a Casa took its place. It flew over our gear pile and four bodies bailed out. Drogue chutes fluttered above the jumpers, and one by one, colorful parachutes popped open. In seconds, jumpers cut across the sky. One chute flew the perimeter of the fire, another headed toward the Brooks Range.

I couldn't believe how fast they separated themselves. Hoots rang out from the dangling bodies and as they lost altitude, they lined up in a landing pattern like airplanes and hit the tundra within feet of each other. Right then, I fantasied about flying a square.

On our third day, the Alaska jumpers became upbeat. I wondered, why so happy? By mid-morning, a plane circled the camp. By noon, I crossed the tussocks back to camp for a meal break. Before reaching camp, I smelled fresh coffee. Reaching camp, I saw a big frying pan with ham and potatoes steaming above the fire. The fire boss noticed my surprise, he grinned and said, "Fresh food drop. Come on, dig in." He pointed to a spot where a chunk of broken tundra covered something. "There's cold beer over there, help yourself." A bottle of whisky made the rounds, too, as did girlie magazines. An Alaskan browsing through one said, "When it comes time for us to let women jump out of our planes, we're going to demand they look like this gal." He held up the centerfold to hoots. "And," he added, "she's gonna bunk with me."

"No way," another Alaskan said. "If she can pass our PT test and rookie training, she belongs to *all* of us."

"Bullshit," said the magazine bearer.

"Pass the bottle will ya?" A third one said. "None of you are getting her 'cause no woman can pass our PT test, let alone the training." Alaska had the toughest training of all the bases and to pass was an accomplishment to be proud of.

One of the McCall guys chimed in, "Don't count on it. We have one, Missoula and Redding got's 'em, too. They're moving north, boys. Better get used to it."

"Look at the rack on this one!" the guy with the mag said. "It's nicer than the one on the moose I shot last winter."

"Man, like you'd know what to do with her rack?"

"Oh, like you would, pencil dick?"

"The closest you'll ever get to a woman is to have a Mae West."

"Don't think so, shit bird, we don't jump stinking rounds anymore."

"Then you're totally out of luck."

"What's lucky about jumping stinking rounds?"

While they goggled over nudie pictures and swigged whisky, a Redmond jumper said, "Hey, I had a girl with a rack like that once."

"Oh yeah? What happened?" an Alaskan asked.

"Being away on fires all summer wasn't her cup of tea. I came home one day and found her with some stud playing house." He took a long swig. "Now, I'm paying the bills, while her new boyfriend is boning her in my house. How's that for being 'racked' by a rack?"

An Alaskan stared me down. "How 'bout you 'Redding? Ever been racked by a rack?"

I couldn't help but laugh. "Hell yeah, I've been racked, rocked, ridden, and rustled by a rack, but I keep going back."

He laughed. "God, there's so many of them in Redding, ain't there?"

I said with a knowing smile, "The City of Tall Trees and Divorcees."

"Okay guys, let's rack this up," the fire boss said. "We have work to do."

I took one last swig before settling into my hootch for a short nap. As sure as the sun never sets above the Arctic Circle, a few hours later, we took a beating to the flames. Two days later, word from Fairbanks ordered us back as soon as possible. There'd been eighty-four new lightning fires since we'd jumped, and we turned the fire over to native Eskimo crews.

As each helicopter load of native's arrived from Bettles, we packed the ship with our jump gear for the return. Each trip took about an hour, and instead of reading or sleeping to kill the boredom, I decided to mingle with the natives. I'd spoken to a native once outside the Savoy Bar in Fairbanks. Our conversation started and ended with him slurring, 'Hey, whitey, wanna fight?'

I approached two natives sitting by a stand of birch trees, their eyes on me the whole time. The older man had long gray hair and dark weathered skin. The younger man had jet-black hair and he smiled when I approached. They stopped talking as if I'd intruded. I motioned to sit with them anyway and the old man nodded his head ever so slightly.

"Where you guys from?" I asked.

The younger man replied. "We're from Huslia, on the Koyukuk River." He pointed behind him to an endless landscape. "Over that way."

He conversed a little with the old man in their native tongue, and asked me, "You?"

"I'm from California." I pointed southeast. "Over that way."

"What are you called?" he asked.

"My friends call me 'Ry,' and you?"

"I'm Kalaallisut and this is my father's brother. He is Angekok, village elder and spiritual teacher."

I nodded to the old man and he nodded back with a wary smile while he whittled on a piece of wood, occasionally lifting his head to glare at me. I asked Kalaallisut, "What do you do besides fighting fires?"

He chuckled, "We hunt and fish."

I should've known better. What else do you do in Alaska besides survive? While I made small talk with the younger one, the old man finished his carving, a perfect image of a wolf's head. He put it in his pocket and walked to a birch tree. He skinned off two small sections of bark, flattened one piece and trimmed it into a circle. In the center of the circle, he cut a hole, then formed a cylinder with the other piece, stuck it in the hole, and suddenly, a small top hat appeared. He looked at me with a smile and said in halting English, "For my grandson."

I asked him, "Can I make one?"

He shrugged. I jumped up, headed for the birch trees and found the biggest one in the stand. I constructed a hat in the same sequence, only this one fit *my* head. When I put it on, they laughed.

The tranquility of the wind rustling through the birch leaves faded with the approach of a helicopter. The fire boss came over to me and said, "Get your gear, you're on this load."

I stood up and offered my hand to my newfound friends, and we shook as the helicopter set down. I put my hat on, secured it from the prop blast with one hand and walked to the ship. I saw the pilot laughing as I entered. My top hat still decorates my house four decades after I'd made it.

We landed on a gravel runway to wait for the Casa. Other jumpers had amassed there from other fires and to my surprise I saw three Redding bros, Spud, Palermo, and Perky, lying by a pile of gear. They quickly told me they'd flown up on a booster crew after my group left.

Spud said, "Nice hat, Ry. Where did you get it?"

"An old Eskimo showed me how to make it while waiting for the helicopter."

I noticed two square heads playing with their new parachutes nearby. "What are they doing?"

"Screwing around," Palermo said. "They've attached the squares to their harnesses and with this wind, it inflates them and they shoot up into the air."

I had a thought. "Hey, let's pull out some cargo chutes and see if the wind will pull us along the gravel." We took two chutes, attached them to cargo boxes, and set them on the runway. With Spud and Palermo sitting on the boxes, Perky and I lifted the chutes, they caught air and away they went sliding along the gravel like jockeys on a race to the finish. While we played, a Twin Otter appeared and made a wide circle over the strip. Perky looked up at it and shook his head as if in deep contemplation. He said, "Before I came on the booster up here, I jumped a fire in the Bee Gum Gorge area outside Platina. It started out entertaining at first because after my stick landed, we heard all kinds of animal noises coming from the brush. All of a sudden this horse and five cows came running past, chased by a dog. We started yelling at the jumpers in the air to warn them, but too late. Cave Man and a horse headed for a collision, but at the last second, the horse veered away and Cave Man landed with his chute draped over the horse's ass. God, we laughed so hard."

The Otter turned on final. Perky looked at it again and became animated. "We had a newbie pilot on board getting checked out. Boy said it happened to be his first live jump mission. When they came around to drop cargo, we noticed it coming in way too low. We couldn't tell if the newbie was trying to land in the meadow, or was about to crash. We scattered hearing the engines revving like crazy. It barely missed us, almost clipped the trees, and disappeared into the gorge. We ran after it expecting to hear an explosion." Perky's eyes lit up, "I've never heard engines screaming like that before! Thank God, Boy radioed us saying they had it under control, that they're coming back to finish the cargo drops."

"So what happened?" I asked.

"The fucking newbie's hand froze on the controls and the check pilot had to wrestle it from him. We heard after they landed in Redding, Boy and Mr. Atlas were about to kill the guy, and probably would've, if Gramps hadn't stepped in. Now, every time I hear an Otter's revving engines, I get a little freaked out."

I shook my head. "Thank Big Ernie it turned out okay. Let it go, Perky, you're in Alaska now, try and relax."

CHAPTER 22

Where Is My Home?

Alaska/California 1984

The routine of moving in and out of apartments during the winter and spending summers in the barracks wore on me. After seven years of jumping, I had nothing to show for myself. I'd managed to chase away the best damn wife a man could ask for and ended up flopping around in a few relationships that went nowhere. I realized I needed something else to focus on. I wasn't getting any younger and wanted a piece of the American dream, a home to call my own. My problem happened to be my status. Being a temporary employee, I discovered banks didn't make loans to people like me, even though I had a healthy savings account.

Permanent positions with the Forest Service seemed impossible to come by. The jumping program relied mainly on seasonal employees, with only a few career spots available. The Redding crew had an average of forty jumpers every year, of those, five being permanent full-time: Base Manager, Loft Foreman, Training/Operations Foreman, and two Squad Leaders. They worked year-round, had health benefits, and retirement accounts. Beneath those positions, seven Career Conditional Appointments existed in two designations. The Squad Leaders secured 18-8 appointments whereby the government guaranteed them 18 pay periods of work and 8 pay periods where they could work if funds became available, which always seemed to be the case. The four non-overhead positions consisted of 13-13 appointments, indicating 13 guaranteed pay periods and 13 if funds were available. These positions also offered medical and retirement benefits, real luxuries for lowly jumpers.

To qualify for a home loan, I had to get out of the temporary pool. Vise had a 13-13 appointment, and when his back injury forced him out of jumping, his job opened up. The overhead didn't fill his position during the fire season, which agitated me since I was the senior temporary in line for the position.

At the time, firefighters employed by the Forest Service didn't have union representation, so motivation, work ethic, knowledge of the program, and fitting the mold became the criteria for advancement. I excelled in the first three areas, but had trouble fitting the mold. I spoke my mind, usually when I shouldn't have. Smokejumping required independence, but in a controlled way. The overhead didn't appreciate me calling bullshit on things.

Fortunately, when it came time to fill the position, the overhead forgave my shortcomings, and awarded me the 13-13 Career Conditional Appointment. Now, I became a bona fide full-time employee with health benefits and a retirement program. I moved into the barracks in March of 1984 with the goal of saving enough money for a healthy down payment on a house.

After two and a half years of working out of the hangar, we finally had our new *home*. They relocated our training units and planted a redwood grove in memory of the plane crash victims. Our beloved softball field, where we drained countless kegs of beer, disappeared forever. The new Northern California Service Center became an efficient, professional hub of smokejumping activity, a place where rules had to be followed. The increasing pressure drove a lot of our vets to Alaska.

By late April, a number of veterans had completed refresher training, but our plane wasn't on contract yet. To get on with practice jumps, Gramps called McCall, who owned their planes, to see if we could use one of theirs. McCall agreed and sent down their brand new, never-jumped-out-of Twin Otter.

The christening of the new Otter became a disaster for Mr. Atlas. On his first practice jump, he broke his ankle, which put him out for the season. In an attempt to cheer him up, Perky made a poster from our photo shoot in front of the new plane. Mr. Atlas held a sign with a big cherry on it, a chunk bitten out. The caption read; '1st Pop 4-28-1984.' The Birkland's jump spot, where I broke my back managed to take another jumper off the list.

Training pogues didn't happen this year due to only one open position. Hairhat escorted the lone pogue to Missoula for training, where the new guy quickly broke his ankle, too, and washed out of the program.

Our plane came on contract just in time for the season's first call. Due to a dry winter, the first load jumped a fast moving fire on the Mendocino. Abrupt wind changes caused the blaze to reverse direction, and despite the crew's efforts to corral it, the fire made a run for the jump spot, eventually burning over it, as well as all the parachutes, jump suits, and cargo.

With news of this, the air horn blasted and within an hour, I'm looking down on the carnage below. Boy directed the pilot to make a low pass over the burned-out spot. Seeing eight brand new parachutes reduced to a pile of melted plastic put a sad face on Boy. He made sure before leaving the area that we cleared a secure area around our gear before attacking the opposite flank of the fire. I'd never seen a fire burn so hot so early in the season and it took us three days to line it. When we returned to Redding, boosters from McCall and Missoula had jumped numerous fires.

Every year, I wondered what misfortune May 29 would bring. As Big Ernie would have it, that day, I jumped the Up Fire on the Klamath without incident. Two weeks later, I boarded a commercial airliner to Alaska. After jumping my first fire on the tundra, I had a few days to regroup. I hung out in the loft, learning as much as I could about the Ram Air system. One day while repairing a deployment bag, I thought about an issue that had troubled me since my first day as a jumper—the Regenitter fatality. The report indicated a possible premature deployment of the static line secured to the d-bag with rubber bands. I focused on the rubber band stowing system when I sensed someone looking over my shoulder. I turned and saw Raudenbush, a third year Alaskan jumper, watching me. Out of the blue, he asked, "How many times have you hung up?"

I laughed. "I've landed in enough big fucking trees to consider moving up here, why do you ask?"

He took a deep breath. "Last year during a booster to Montana, we jumped a spot that had a lot of hardwoods. Most of us hung up in the trees. Being my first tree landing, I freaked out. I remember crashing through the branches until I came to a stop. Then I fell a few more feet and stopped again. I could reach the trunk, but our trainers didn't teach us to tie off to trees, only to parachutes."

He took on a haunted look. "While I hung there, I heard wood cracking, and a scream. I couldn't see who, but I knew someone had broken out of a tree, and it was bad. Someone yelled up at me, 'Get out of the tree, the tops are snapping.' I started my letdown, made it twenty-feet from the ground when my chute broke out. Thank God, I hit the slope just right. If I'd only had a way to tie off to the tree instead of the parachute, none of that would've happened."

He motioned to the sewing machine. *"If only I had a way."* I knew he wanted me to make something that would allow him to tie off to a tree. "Think you could design something?"

My mind had already been working on it and before I lost my train of thought, I told him, "Go get your jump pants."

He scurried out of the loft, returning moments later with his pants. "Man," he pleaded, "I'd do anything not to have a broken back."

Major tree-landing injuries the previous season in Montana, Idaho, and Washington State exceeded the norm. I needed to design a system so a jumper could secure himself to the tree instead of the parachute. I envisioned a small pouch sewn to the inside of the jump pants with ten feet of webbing coiled inside. One end of the webbing would have a locking snap secured to one of the D-rings on the jump pants. The other end would have a snap tacked to the inside of the jump pants for easy access. By breaking the tack on the snap and flinging the webbing around the trunk or branch the jumper could secure it to the other D-ring, thus securing him to the tree. It would be like a lasso in a pocket.

I described my idea to Raudenbush, and we hit the hardware bin. An hour later, I stood by a tree as he deployed the first prototype without a glitch. I planned on perfecting the system when I returned to Redding, even though I knew this do-it-yourself approach to problem solving would likely be seen as out of line.

Raudenbush climbed down and said, "The beer is on me tonight, Ryan."

"At the Howling Dog?" I grinned and asked.

"The Dog it is!"

The Howling Dog Saloon located in the small town of Fox, fifteen miles outside of Fairbanks, is a popular coming out spot for those who'd been snow bound in the bush all winter. Inside, the walls had a collection of natural wood pieces that resembled body parts in varying degrees of erotic excitement. Out back, a well-used sand volleyball court invited the inebriated to imagine them on a beach somewhere. Being the bar of choice for jumpers, the crew closed it down every chance they could. That night happened to be no exception.

Toward the end of the evening after playing volleyball, I went inside and found a group of jumpers riveted on Hairhat. He tugged on his beard while saying, "So I'm heading back to the jump spot to get supplies and had to cross this shale field. I'm stumbling through the rocks, I get this feeling I'm being watched. I'd move a little, stop, and look all around. Suddenly, I saw movement, a fucking mountain lion starring me right in the eyes from six feet away." He shook his head, took a swig of beer, "It scared me shitless. The back of my neck tingled. I picked up a rock and started back peddling toward the fire, but the cat followed me. I'm being stalked! I hollered to my bros, but the chainsaw drowned me out. Finally, they saw me and the cat. Everybody began yelling until it took off. It scared the crap out of everyone. We had the biggest warming fire I'd ever seen, and nobody slept that night. Man, those eyes! I'll never forget those pitiless eyes boring into me."

I couldn't help myself. I grinned and said, "It probably didn't want to eat you because he'd be spitting hairballs out all day!"

"Ha, ha, Ryan! You're so fucking funny." He carefully scanned the room. When he looked back at me, he whispered, "Talk about hair. Last year, Disco and I were here when this lady came in. She had a beard that rivaled mine, and that's no bullshit. Disco was so drunk he couldn't stop staring at her. He says to me, 'My God, look at that woman's beard!' I said, 'If you like it so much, go over there and ask her to dance.' He had that crazy look he gets and slurred, 'I think I will!' He danced with her all night. The locals call her, 'The Bearded Lady.'"

The next morning, severely hung over, I sat on the ready room floor buckled over trying to clear my head.

"Roll Call."

"Ryan." No answer. "RYAN!" I shook my head for clarity, "I'm here."

The box boy stared down on me. "You plan on being here with us, or do you need to go off the list for a while?"

I grumbled, "I'm here. I'm good." I planned on sneaking to the barracks for more sleep when the siren sounded. My head swirled while suiting up and continued to swirl during the streamer drops. A McCall jumper stood behind the first one out, I watched them exit. The McCall guy didn't set up for a step exit. Instead, he pulled himself up using the overhead rail and in one fluid motion swung himself out the plane. I'd never seen that kind of exit before.

While hooking up for my stick, I looked at Perky, gave him a wink, and said, "Watch this." My jump partner got the slap and bailed out. I pulled up, swung myself out the door like the McCall jumper had and suddenly everything went to shit. Clouds spun around me as suspension lines brushed past my helmet. The ground came into view, then disappeared back into the clouds. My parachute popped open and through my dizziness, I saw quite a few nasty twists in my lines. What the hell had I done wrong? I landed on the tundra to a hoard of mosquitoes trying to get to me. As I stripped out of my jumpsuit, Perky landed nearby and as he unsuited, said, "What the fuck was that?"

I shrugged, "Guess something went wrong."

"No shit something went wrong!" he laughed. "You went out the door horizontal and from there, I saw you do a complete backward summersault while your chute opened. You really messed that one up. You're lucky you didn't get hurt and you're damn lucky Boy isn't here to see it. You'd be in some deep shit, Ry." I didn't care about Boy. While beating on the flames, I tried to figure out what I'd done wrong.

We returned to Fairbanks by early evening. I teamed up with Tony 'Wildman' Loughton, John 'Hollywood' Barker, Joe 'Slow Jo' Wilkins, and Gordon 'Gordo' Woodhead in the Officer's Club to get primed for another night on the town. After a few beers we walked into town. Being close to the Fourth of July firecracker stands could be found everywhere. We bought a couple six-packs and loaded up for battle with Roman Candles, bottle rockets, M-80s, and Lady Fingers. We worked our way back to the base along the railroad tracks, attacking each other with fireworks. Back at base, we found a small party going on at the stand-by shack, so Hollywood started firing bottle rockets at beer cans on the ground. When he became bored with that, he began firing rockets at the beer cans in people's hands. I saw a rocket whistle from him, it spewed flames in a v-line toward us and before anyone could react, it stuck in the can of the guy next to me. We laughed hysterically, and the guy with the dripping can shouted, "You're damn lucky this isn't the last beer!"

Another quick fire jump followed and then a series of days with nothing to do after work. One afternoon, Wildman, Spud, Slow Jo, The Girl, and I were drinking beer on the banks of the Chena River behind the barracks when an Alaska jumper joined us. He had a bandage on his forearm. In Alaska, injuries didn't occur often, so I asked him, "What happened?"

"It's a new tattoo," he said pulling off the gauze to reveal a parachute with wings. "That's really cool," Wildman said. A few beers after the Alaskan left, we started talking about getting tattoos ourselves.

Slow Jo looked at Wildman and said, "I dare you to get one."

"If I get one, you have to get one, too," Wildman answered.

"If I get one, you have to get one," I said to The Girl.

The Girl looked at Spud and said, "I'm not scared to get one."

"Well, I'm not either," Spud answered back.

"Okay," I said, "It's settled. We'll all get one."

The conversation turned to what type of tattoo we'd get. Spud said, "I like the parachute and wings."

I wanted something with a martial arts theme, like a dragon, tiger, or the Yin Yang symbol. Wildman said, "No way, I think it should be jumper related."

The Girl offered, "A rose?"

Slow Jo laughed, "I'm not the rose type!" He stared at me. "How about the design on your T-shirt?" I had a Redding shirt with a simple design of a parachute, the suspension lines anchored at the base by a set of wings.

"We could put a tree in the middle like our pogue pins," Spud said.

"All righty," Wildman demanded. "Let's go. I bet the tattoo shop is still open."

We took a leisurely pace into Fairbanks, and entered the Harley Davidson store—which also featured a tattoo shop—with a twelve-pack. A man came out from a back room. He had long, braided hair, a graying goatee, and tattoos all over his arms. "How can I help you?" he boomed at us.

"We want tattoos," Wildman said.

He looked us over, and his gaze stopped on The Girl. *"All of you?"*

"All of us," she demanded.

"Okay, what flavor are we looking at?"

Slow Jo pointed to my shirt. "That, but with a tree in the middle."

The tattoo artist began sketching, and within a minute, he held up a design with a tree at the base of a parachute, and wings on either side of the chute. "Something like this?" he asked.

We all liked it. "Perfect, that's it," Spud said.

He went to the back room and began fiddling with equipment. He called us in to where an old barber's chair sat. He pulled up a stool with his ink-applying tool, a crude, homemade device with two electrical wires spliced in a few places and bailing wire secured it to a dirty wooden handle. "Who's first?" he said.

I wanted to witness the procedure first and nonchalantly backed away from the chair. Wildman said, "I'm ready."

The tattoo guy turned on the needle, an awful buzzing filled the room.

"Is it okay for us to drink while we wait?" I asked.

The guy laughed. "As long as I get some, too."

By the time Spud and Wildman had their tattoos, the beer was gone. Slow Jo and I went for more, leaving The Girl behind to go next. While paying for the beer, I noticed I'd been burning through my money. I didn't have a credit card, so on the way back from the liquor store, I told Slow Jo, "I don't know if I can afford a tattoo. I'm saving for a down payment on a house, and besides, I don't have enough cash."

Slow Jo stopped in mid-stride. "If you don't get one, I won't either."

Funny he should say that, I thought. Being a quiet, clean-cut, slow-moving country boy who always had a fishing pole and a rifle in his pickup and a red ring around his neck, Slow Jo seemed the most unlikely person to get a tattoo. He pulled out his wallet, sifted through the bills, and handed me forty bucks. "Forget it. We're doing it. Consider it a loan."

How could I back out now? We returned to the Girl still sitting in the chair. A woman who'd been coming in and out of the shop sat next to us in the waiting room. A tall, good looking gal with a bubbly personality. All of a sudden, she says, "Do you guys want to see my tattoo?" I look at Slow Jo; he nods and looks at her. She stands up and unbuttons her pants. Pride beamed from her as she slid her jeans down far enough to expose a mouse leaving her nest. Slow Jo shook his head in approval, "That's very nice, Ma'am. Did it hurt?"

"Only the tail part," she giggled as she pulled her pants back up.

The Girl came out from the ink room and the artist said, "Whose next?"

Slow Jo took the seat. When he came out, I went in and within an hour I'd been branded for life.

Fire activity slowed to a crawl and within a couple of days, all out-of-region jumpers went home. The rumor that some of the crew had gotten tattoos reached Redding before we arrived. Eager jumpers greeted us, and as soon as they learned who'd been inked, their curiosity turned to surprise. "The Girl?" Boy said, as if she'd broken some unwritten rule. Others said, "Slow Jo?" as if he, too, had broken some good old boy law. We all gathered on the tarmac and proudly flashed our tattoos for a picture.

CHAPTER 23

The Red Zone

While in Alaska, fire activity in California kept the bros busy. We returned to boosters from Redmond and Missoula waiting to jump. They flew home just as a weather system entered the state missing the action. I headed to a fire on the Tahoe, relishing the irony of it in the plane: I'm fresh off a fire where we'd been treated to whisky, now I'm going to the Whisky Fire. I loved Tahoe fires. They're usually small, burn slowly in brush patches surrounded by granite rocks and alpine fir. We contained the fire quickly and had the rest of the night to enjoy ourselves.

Still carrying the Alaskan mind-set, I hiked a ways out of camp, briefly considering the consequences of what I was about to do. I pulled a brick of rockets I'd smuggled back from Alaska out of my PG bag. Finding a suitable spot, I lit the fuse. The night exploded in an array of color accenting the star-studded sky. I reveled at the display before walking back to camp. The glare I got from Dog, the fire boss, let me know the incident would come up later. To my detriment, I had difficulty shedding the free-spirited attitude of Alaska.

I scored two more jumps through the month of August before fire activity came to a sudden stop. Injuries had mounted throughout the year to the point where Gramps made a plea to Alaska for extra bodies, and a few volunteers came south. At that time, Cave Man left jumping for a job on the Six Rivers National Forest. He'd started jumping in 1967, one of the old school jumpers. His stubborn way of doing things frustrated the overhead, but they kept him around anyway. I still marvel at his classic hitchhiking departure from the Hog Fire. Cave Man's approach to fighting fires centered on his theory of, 'Let's pull back and torch the pig,' meaning, let's cut the easiest fire line possible and burn out. Oddly enough, this attitude caught on due to the ever-increasing fuel loads on the forest floors from decades of aggressive firefighting.

Cave Man had a reputation for other things, too. When he packed parachutes, he didn't worry about aesthetics. Everyone referred to his parachutes as 'guppy chutes,' since they were more rounded than the standard flat. His response to the criticism, 'Hell, they open, don't they?' I also enjoyed watching him jump. When slapped, he didn't push off vigorously from the plane; he went out the door like a pile of laundry. His lazy approach worked for him. Seeing another unique character leave the organization had me wondering how long I'd last.

*****

This time of year illegal marijuana growing on Forest Service land created safety issues not only for the public, but for us as well. Being close to harvest time, the Campaign Against Marijuana Planting (CAMP) law enforcement agency made it their priority to aggressively locate and eradicate any pot they could find. Common knowledge dictated that in certain areas the growers placed booby-traps around their crops, such as barbed wire, trip lines, fish hooks dangling from line at face level, and in one instance, it's said, they strung a cable across a canyon to take down low flying helicopters. When fire requests came in from forests that had such problems, our maps showed a red border around them. If a fire started in the marijuana Red Zone, we didn't jump it, period.

With late August being slow, I had time to complete most of the Federal Aviation Administration Master Parachute Rigger Certification's practical requirements prior to taking the written and oral tests. The hands on requirements consisted of eight categories:

1. Operation of all sewing machines including the heavy canvas 97-10, which is used in the construction of parachute harnesses.

2. Parachute suspension line replacements.
3. Replacement of complete sections or gores of a parachute.
4. Emergency and reserve parachute container repair.
5. Repair of an upper or lower lateral band.
6. Major anti-inversion netting (AIN) repair.
7. Basic pattern making
8. Interpretation of plans and drawings.

Thanks to Magnum and Spud's tree landings on the Wooley Creek Fire, I managed to complete all the required repairs on their two damaged chutes alone. I lacked experience in pattern making since our jump suits, harnesses, travel bags, web-gear, and PG bags, already had proven patterns and until a new design became necessary, there wasn't a need to reinvent the wheel. I hoped Boy would cut me some slack in this category since I couldn't see anything that needed immediate improvement.

Boy administered the tests for the FAA. He also selected a special project for every aspiring Master Rigger. From me, he wanted a comprehensive hardbound study guide containing all the information needed to pass both the Senior and Master Rigger's written and oral tests. I had to sift through volumes of FAA regulations, Department of Agriculture directives, as well as the manufacturer's instructional guides.

I elected to take the written and oral tests before starting the study guide and after passing both, I settled into a corner of the training room to start my special project. I had a table large enough to hold all the manuals and a typewriter. I wish I'd paid more attention in my high school typing class because I had to rely on two fingers. I also would've preferred a more secluded location than where the Bitch Board hung—anyone could come in and write anonymous comments on the Bitch Board about anything or anyone—because the damn thing produced a distracting amount of foot traffic next to my workstation.

I took the challenge seriously and often wondering why Boy had given me such an immense project. I figured he'd been trying to impress upon me that a parachute loft needed strict governance and that a person couldn't just walk into a parachute loft and start designing equipment without adhering to the rules and regulations. After all, our lives depended on the equipment we made.

With no fire activity, I became consumed with the project. Unfortunately, it affected my otherwise playful attitude. One morning as I sat down to punch keys, someone had typed on one of my pages: ALL WORK AND NO PLAY MAKES RY A DULL BOY, and not just once, but quite a few times. I'd been working on the project for weeks on end without a fire jump and this put me at wits' end. If I'd discovered who'd done it, I would've dropped a dull Pulaski on their hands. The pressure had me praying to Big Ernie for a break.

*****

Eltapom Fire, Shasta-Trinity National Forest
September 10, 1984

The weather forecasts weren't predicting any lightning storms any time soon, so when the horn sounded twice, it caught us all by surprise. My prayer had been answered. Prior to suiting up, I notice the spotter checking to see if the fire was in a Red Zone. Luckily, it only bordered one, so we flew to the Eltapom Creek drainage on the South Fork of the Trinity River to what we presumed to be a man-caused fire. As we circled, a faint smoke column indicated a small fire. It looked to be a good deal. Boy threw out streamers over a small, lush meadow. He flashes two fingers, Squirrely, and Geo bail at the slap. Hairhat and I move into position. Boy reminded us, "Keep away from the snags," before the slap.

My chute opens cleanly and I follow Hairhat's lead making quarter turns behind him. He sets up perfectly and landed on the edge of the meadow. For me, the trees come up fast and a large pine loomed in front of me too late to make any major steering adjustments. I lifted my feet just enough to miss hitting the top of the tree. As I prepare for a landing roll, my body jolted to a sudden stop. A small section of my parachute hooked on a branch far from the trunk and left me swaying seventy-feet above the ground.

Hairhat yells, "You okay, Ry-son?"

"Fuck no!" I shouted back. "Look at my chute. I'm hanging by a thread."

"Just take it slow and easy coming down."

I prepared for my letdown constantly eyeing the small piece of chute that hooked the branch fearing it would break free and send me into free-fall. Would I scream like others had when burning out of a tree, or would I take another broken back silently like a warrior? As I pulled my letdown rope from my leg pocket, I heard Squirrely yelling to the bros parachuting down, "Keep away from the meadow, it's a bog!"

Parachutes crashed through the trees on the other side of the meadow. A gust of wind filled my canopy, causing me to sway like a pendulum. Bracing for the worst, I heard Hairhat's voice ring out again, "Keep going, Ry-son! You've got to concentrate, man!" I manage to tie off to the parachute and carefully rappelled to the ground. To my surprise and delight, the little sliver of hooked material supported me all the way down. Why it didn't broken loose mystified me. Figuring I could dislodge it from the ground, I give the rope a strong yank. It didn't budge, so I yanked harder, nothing. After five more tugs, I gave up and headed for the fire. As I started to dig line with the others, Squirrely comes crashing through the brush from a recon of the head of the fire, eyes bulging. He looks freaked out and waves us back into a huddle. While looking around nervously, he whispered in a shaky voice, "There's a pot garden up ahead."

No one made a sound. We all scanned the area looking for booby traps, or people lying in wait. Being a first for all of us, we didn't know what to do. We took a knee, and strained to hear or see anything out of the ordinary, but only heard the gurgling creek and the sound of the fire. Squirrely whispered our find into the radio. Within a minute, the district called saying the CAMP team will be coming in the morning with a helicopter to eradicate the plants, but until then, we should secure the site and continue to fight the fire.

The fire burned part way into the plantation, the air smelled of skunk. The plants stood seven-feet tall with huge buds atop every branch. Resin crystals glistened in the sun. Being harvest time, we couldn't understand why someone had started a fire only to leave their valuable crop behind. After combing the area and finding no booby traps, we relaxed.

We cut line all night, taking meal breaks in pairs. When my turn came to eat, I passed through the plants and noticed buds missing from some of the plants. Each time I took a break, I saw more buds missing. By mid-morning, a helicopter landed on the edge of the meadow and a team of machete-wielding CAMP officers attacked the crop. We helped them bundle the plants into a sling. When the helicopter lifted off trailing the load, I talked with one of the cops. "How many busts have you been on this year?"

"Quite a few," the officer said. "This one is unusual though. It's the first one I've been on where there's been a fire. We've found plantations sharing the same water supply and I'm guessing a rival grower may have tried to burn out his competition by torching this site. We're going to recon the area to see if there's another grow on the creek." He eyed Hollywood, Squirrely, and me with obvious suspicion. "It's unusual to see a lot of the top buds missing during a bust. The growers are usually hauling ass out of the area and don't have time to harvest anything like they've done here."

"How strange," I said innocently and shrugged.

The helicopter returned and the CAMP officers loaded up and left. The chopper's prop wash rippled the nylon of a chute in a tall, dead tree. I cringe at the damage and said to Squirrely and Hollywood, "Who's the fuck that landed in that snag? Boy isn't going to be happy."

Hollywood laughed. "I'm the fuck that landed in the snag."

Hollywood looked like a linebacker, clearly over the 200-pound weight limit for jumping and with a blond crew cut, and square jaw, he also looked like a movie star. I remember when he showed up late during his pogue training roll call one morning and none of the overhead said a word because he appeared so intimidating. During roll call someone muttered, 'It's nice to see you made it Hollywood.' The name stuck ever since.

I told him, "Boy isn't going to like that you're becoming a snag magnet."

He made a face and said, "A snag maggot?"

"No, you dumbass," I shook my head and said. "A *snag magnet!*"

Hollywood looked at the snag decorated with blue and white nylon and said, "I may be dumb, but at least I don't have to climb for my chute." He had a point. We didn't climb dead trees for safety reasons, instead, we chain sawed them down. We returned to the fire and mopped through it until the last hot spots disappeared. When Squirrely called it out, it was parachute retrieval time. As the chainsaw ripped through Hollywood's tree,

I'm tugging and pulling on my letdown rope. The little branch still wouldn't let go of my parachute. "Weak attempt, Ry," the guys watching me said. "Is that all you got, you WIMP?"

I pulled, tugged, yanked, and tried different angles, all to no avail. My frustration mounted with each failed attempt. Finally, I yelled, "If you guys think you can do better, why don't you get off your asses and give it a try."

Before I knew it, four guys joined in. It didn't take long before they too abandoned me in frustration. A jumper named JB stood by amused. Seeing how our brute force approach wasn't working, he suggested, "How about tying a loop in the rope and using it as a fulcrum?" He's an avid rock climber and knew ropes and riggings. He came over and tied what looked like a trucker's knot as far up the rope as he could reach, pulled the rope around a second tree and slipped the end through the loop. We all grabbed and pulled, the branch bowed toward us, the tree swayed, but the parachute wouldn't come free. The tree won the tug of war and JB threw his arms up and walked away.

"Where's the damn chainsaw?" I yelled.

Squirrely came over and dropped the climbing gear at my feet, indicating he isn't going to let me cut the tree down. He looked at his watch to let me know I had a time limit. I cursed while slipping into the climbing gear. So, you want to be that way, I thought. What if I'm not out of the tree by the time the helicopter arrives! They couldn't leave without me. I began a slow, deliberate ascent just to piss him off. When I reached the limb holding my parachute, I saw a small stub of a branch, less than an inch thick, had penetrated the nylon just above the lower lateral band. Somehow it had held me in the tree and defeated four men and a fulcrum. It took less than a minute to saw through the branch sending my chute to the ground.

The Eltapom Fire became known as the 'Elta Bud Fire' and later on we learned the CAMP officers did find another plantation down the creek. Instead of eradicating the plants, they staked out the area until the grower returned, and when they arrested him, he admitted to setting the fire to burn out his competition.

I jumped another fire on the Shasta-Trinity three days later. This one on the edge of a red zone also. Four of us landed on the ridge top. While taking a break, we heard something rustling through the brush. I clutched my Pulaski. JB, Buzz, and

Perky did the same. Suddenly, a longhaired, bearded man came out of the bushes with a broken handled shovel. As he strolled toward us, I noticed a pistol on his hip. He didn't look happy to see us, what could we do but stand ready with our hand tools? With no campgrounds in the area, no roads, nothing justified his presence, but pot.

"How's it going?" JB said nonchalantly, trying to break the ice.

Winded from the climb, he took a moment before huffing out, "I wanted to get up here to put the fire out before the woods crawled with Feds. Looks like you beat me to it." Well, we are the *Feds*, but he said it in a non-threatening way and we relaxed. "I saw the parachutes on my way up. They sure did look pretty."

JB told the guy, "We're here to put the fire out. When we're done, we're outta here and we haven't seen a thing." Good move JB. The guy looked us over one more time, turned, and disappeared back into the brush like an animal. Perky let out a sigh and said, "I hate working in these fucking pot infested areas! We're nothing but targets anymore."

"Why so jumpy, Perk?" I said and grinned. "Can't you calm down?"

Perky shot me an angry look. I'd pissed him off earlier in the day when we'd been hauling the fire packs up the mountain. I hid behind a rock and leapt out at him growling like a bear when he passed by. He yelled while backpedalling and cursed me to no end throughout the day. I knew he had a narrow escape from a bear in Alaska and to take advantage of his phobia entertained me.

Now, he's shouting at me, "Calm down? How am I supposed to calm down? I almost got eaten by a bear in Alaska, and now I have pot growers trying to kill me!"

"Nobody's trying to kill you, Perky!"

"Oh yeah, Ry-son?" he commanded. "Where were you a few fires ago? Typing away in the training room? Get this, while waiting for our ride out of my last fire, this van came hauling ass up the road skidding to a stop in front of us. The driver jumps out crying and shaking like she'd seen big foot. Someone had taken shots at her and actually hit the van with a bullet. We had to wait for law enforcement to escort us out. Can you believe that? So don't tell me to fucking calm down! I've had enough!

Let's get out of here!" Perky had it right, sometimes jumping out of planes was the least of our concerns.

CHAPTER 24

A Real Home At Last

Fire Season 1985

I presented Boy with my finished version of the Senior and Master Parachute Riggers Study Guide just before the end of the season. It neared two-hundred pages, and as he flipped through it, he looked satisfied until he came upon a section I dedicated to the BLM's Ram Air parachute system, he raised an eyebrow. Having worked on the damn thing for months and with the end of my goal in sight, I could've done without the drama. I asked him, "Are you going to send in the paperwork for my license now?" He looked over the study guide one more time, which I felt sure to be concise and professionally done. Boy told me flatly, "We don't just give out Master licenses, Ryan. So far, you've done well, but I have reservations about your pattern making skills. I have one more project for you. Meet me in the warehouse."

Pattern making skills? So, it had come down to this after all! Why is he being such a hard-ass on me? I stormed into the warehouse behind him. He pointed to the Stokes litter. "I want you to make an enclosed, custom fitted case for the litter with a shoulder harness system for packing. The top needs to be zippered, allowing easy access. You'll need to make a pattern of it, too."

I stared at the litter, considered the magnitude of the project and glared at him. "You've got to be kidding!"

"And set it up with a detachable parachute harness," he added.

My hopes of becoming a Master Rigger evaporated. I couldn't finish a project like that with so little time left in the season. I felt dejected knowing it would have to wait until next year.

On a brighter note, I had a special side-project of my own. I'd saved enough money for a down payment on a house and set out to find a one. Looking around Redding, the only house I qualified for happened to be a manufactured home in a failed sub-division. Without thinking twice, I put the money down reveling in the fact that there'd be no more barracks, apartments, or rundown slumlord rentals for me. I'm an official homeowner at last.

No sooner had I closed on the house, than my life took a wild turn. The Roach Coach girl told me she's pregnant with my child. This dismayed me because she'd said she was on birth control. How could I get her pregnant? Besides that, our relationship didn't consist of talking about commitment or future plans. I didn't love her to that point, or she with me, so I thought. I'd a couple months off work to settle into my house and think things through. Sylvia lived at her mom's while carrying my baby and that really bothered me. I would've given anything to be there to support her during the pregnancy, but that wasn't going to happen.

I returned to work in February with Hairhat, Squiggly, and Max to finish the winter sewing projects and start on my pattern making nightmare. Equipment changes kept us busy, too. Most of the metal snaps, buckles, and other hardware were being swapped out for plastic. No logical explanation accompanied the order, but those of us who did the retrofitting figured it had something to do with reducing the overall weight of the pack-out bags for the new surge of women entering the ranks. That didn't bother me. Anything that would lighten a pack-out would be worth the trouble.

One day while retrofitting the reserve parachute containers from the heavy bayonet cases to the new nylon knife sheaths, I realized there wouldn't be a place to stow the static line snap anymore. We used to slip them under the rigid knife sheaths. The nylon sheaths were wide enough to accommodate the static line snap and within a few minutes, I sewed a piece of elastic webbing into the borders of the sheath and the snap fit perfectly. I presented the idea to Boy who, to my surprise, liked it. Of course, he ordered me to go through the proper channels by submitting an employee suggestion proposal to the Missoula Equipment Development Center for review.

With the sewing projects finished, I started on the litter case. At first, I glared at it in the hope a light would go off in my head to guide me through the creative process, but by the beginning of April, I'd managed to only make a basic pattern. A few weeks later, I had to put the project on hold again because I had a seat in a military C-141 plane flying to Asheville, North Carolina with a ragtag crew of firefighters.

*****

Vineyard #5 Fire, Nantahala National Forest, North Carolina.

Fires burned throughout the southern states from Florida to Tennessee. We landed in Asheville, North Carolina and on the way to our assignment, someone yelled to the bus driver, "Can we stop at a liquor store?" The driver, a big, bald headed guy with a grumpy disposition turned in his seat at a stoplight looking for the person who had asked. In a southern accent thicker than molasses, he slurred, "Liquor store? Don't you know you's in the Bible belt, California boy!" That settled the liquor store stop.

We crossed the Appalachian Mountains to a Forest Service station in Erwin, Tennessee. With time to kill, I walked to the railway yard and found a small museum with historic pictures of the town. My attention being drawn to a picture taken in 1916, where an elephant hung by its neck from a crane. The caption read:

"Only known execution of an elephant in Tennessee. Mary, the elephant, had killed her handler, Walter Eldridge, in nearby Kingsport. As home to the region's largest railway yard, Erwin was the only community with the means to carry out the death sentence. An estimated 2,500 people turned out at the local railway yard to see Mary hoisted by a crane and hanged by a chain around her neck. The first chain snapped, but a larger one was found and the peculiar task completed. She was hanged for half an hour before being declared dead."

God, am I reading this right? I nervously looked out the window. Later, while eating at the only restaurant in town before heading to a fire, everyone stared at us with disdain. We wolfed down our food and couldn't get out of there fast enough.

At the Forest Service station, a man with a shotgun waited for us. He introduced himself as a Fish and Game warden, said he's going to ride shotgun with us. He also informed us that folks in the back woods were starting fires on Federal lands to chase turkeys onto their farms, where they could shoot them without violating the law. A stiff warning followed, "If you boys stumble upon pot gardens or moonshine operations, get the hell out of there." Had I just entered the Twilight Zone?

We drove through small towns where people peered from behind curtains made of sheets, and kids ran around barefoot with rotting teeth. They'd stop and stare at us like we fell from the sky.

Hardwood leaves crunched under my feet as we hiked to a fire, even the smoke had a maple syrup smell. We joined up with some local good 'ole boys to fight the fire. One of the locals bristled with pride as he raked leaves from the flames, "You boys ain't never tasted nothin' like what I got's cooking back home. If you want, I'll grab a couple bottles for ya'll if we meet up again tomorrow." He went on to say how he made the best moonshine in the county. "White lightning," he called it as he showed me the back of his hands, "It can put hair on your knuckles." I'd often wondered what white lightning might taste like when the good 'ole boy pulled a flask from his pocket, took a big swig and passed it to me. He must've noticed me staring at the bottle top, "No need to wipe, this stuff can kill any germ alive!"

Embarrassed, I took a little sip. It instantly burned in my mouth and all the way down to my stomach. It tasted like rubbing alcohol. Before handing him the flask, I turned my head and spat. It's no wonder their teeth rotted so quickly.

After knocking the fire down, we regrouped in Asheville and flew to the Everglades in Florida. After one fire there, we ended up in Tamiami with a night to ourselves. Hairhat and I went out for a drink. We entered a bar, the only white people there. Latinos strutted around in silk shirts and gold chains dangling from their necks. As they danced to loud Salsa music, we had a quick drink and returned to the motel.

We boarded a contracted DC-3 junker in the morning for the flight back to Asheville. I noticed a grimy pan on the tarmac below the engines catching oil. When the engines fired up, they sputtered and spewed thick white smoke until the cylinders warmed enough to taxi. That lousy plane shuddered the whole way to Asheville. Fire activity suddenly slowed and our group hopped a plane back home. Even though our stay didn't last long, I had enough of an eye-opener in the Deep South to last the rest of my life.

Before I settled back into my stokes project, the Big Valley Ranger District on the Modoc name requested me to build eagle nest platforms for them since Dan and I had done such a good job on the Devil's Garden District. This time Nick 'Knik' Holmes was my climbing partner and we exceeded their target range of platforms by over 50%. We received a nice letter of appreciation from that District Ranger, too.

By May, my son's due month, the jitters set in. I put myself on fire hold. On the second day of the month, the Regional Forester in California received a letter from the Director of Administrative Management indicating that my static line snap stow for the new retrofit reserve knife had been accepted by the Aviation and Fire Management Staff and would be a mandatory fixture on the new FS-12R reserve parachutes, and to top it off, I received a cash award.

By far the most important event that happened that month was the birth of my son on May 14. As I held him, I had mixed emotions. I'd never held a baby before, it felt like holding a priceless piece of china. Being so small and fragile, I dared not drop him. Knowing I had a prodigy in this little bundle, I cried with joy. Knowing my relationship with his mother wasn't improving, I felt fear of losing him. The future made me nervous.

Why couldn't I love her as I did my son? I'd never been so distraught over a relationship. She had so much control over me now. I hoped she wouldn't use my son as a bargaining tool to get back together, or worse, to not allow me to see him. To alleviate the issue on not having the means to care for him, I bought baby clothes, toys, a crib, and decorated a bedroom for him, but he wasn't there unless she agreed on it. That bothered me to no end. I found myself working like a maniac on fires to exhaust the sadness of missing him. I didn't know how long I could live like this.

Once Eric and his mother settled at her mom's place, I went off hold and completed my three qualifying jumps in time to fly to two fires in the high desert of the Toiyabe National Forest bordering California and Nevada. We split the load on two fires, mine went off without incident, but the other jump resulted in three injuries. Coyote hurt his back and Wild Man broke his foot, both out for the season. Slow Jo bruised his heel and returned to work quickly.

Three weeks of inactivity followed, giving me time to work on the dreaded litter case. I had trouble designing some of the features Boy wanted. I consulted JB, who had an extensive background in designing and developing software. His tips proved invaluable, and I started making progress.

An intense lightning storm crossed the Shasta-Trinity forcing me to take a hiatus from the project again. We jumped the whole base out, and McCall boosters flew in. A two-week break followed and by early July, desert fires out of Grand Junction, Colorado had us responding. What I learned from them, I preferred fires in the timber with bears over sagebrush with rattlesnakes. Lightning had fires popping up in Idaho and Montana in the meantime, so we relocated to McCall, where I jumped a gobbler. I ended up in Grangeville and jumped five fires in seventeen days.

My enthusiasm for jumping began to wane due to my custody situation. I couldn't concentrate on fires, always thinking about my son and the unknown. I had stress and fear from not knowing if she'd pack up and leave with him. Guilt for abandoning him wore on me while on fires, and uncertainty about my career took its toll. By early August, I held my son again and I couldn't have been happier. I tried to work things out with his mother when I visited them, but we ended up fighting about child support and visitation. Her wielding him over me had me constantly on defense.

While I had to deal with this, the jump list added eight new names since I'd returned from Grangeville. The Kroger brothers, Pigpen, and Fast Eddie had come home, only this time as BLM jumpers. They rotated on our list, but we didn't go on their fires. This didn't sit well with a lot of the crew. Among the things said, 'They're taking our fires.' 'I'm not jumping out of those run down Volpar's.' 'How long are they going to be here?' 'They should go back to where they came from.'

Gramps had gone to Alaska in the spring to train on the square parachute, and while there, he worked out a deal with Al Dutton. The BLM would stage a crew out of Redding for initial attack to the BLM's Great Basin states of Nevada, Utah, Colorado and Wyoming. They would rotate on Redding's list, jumping rounds on Forest Service fires and squares on BLM fires. They set up their operation in the hangar, our old home. I couldn't understand the animosity, because we went to Alaska regularly to open arms and minds.

*****

Max Fire, Mt. Hood National Forest, Oregon
August 27, 1985

By the end of August, I ended up in Redmond, Oregon, about to reach a milestone. My next jump would be my 150th. When the horn sounded, I boarded a Volpar for the Mt. Hood Ranger District in view of the Three Sisters Peaks. A two-person fire request with Stanly 'Boots' Jones as my jump partner, nothing could've been more rewarding. Boots stood out in his pogue class from day one. At his first roll call, he had his fire pants tucked into a pair of boots so high, they stopped just below his knees. The tallest boots I'd ever seen, and to top it off, he sported a long twisted mustache and a beret. From the waist down, he looked like a storm trooper. From the waist up, he looked like Salvador Dali! Boots hailed from Milwaukee, Wisconsin, where he worked with at-risk teens during the off season. He was an Army vet, who'd been stationed in Bamberg, Germany, a place I'd been to many times. He even spoke a little German. His sense of humor just as offbeat as mine, and I connected with him immediately knowing he respected Oriental Philosophies and martial arts. In our group picture, he painted the WWII Japanese Kamikaze flag on his jump helmet. The red stripes on the white background stood out nicely. Surprisingly, the overhead didn't object.

Flying over my soon to be 150th jump, the fire burned calmly in a patch of dog-hair reproduction, a good deal fire. They didn't come along very often and I intended to enjoy this one. After two streamer passes, the spotter flashed two fingers. I bailed at the slap and concentrated on steering for a small opening surrounded by tall trees. Setting up on the wind line, I let my forward speed carry me to the edge of the opening and

208

while the chute wanted to carry me into the trees, I applied the brakes by pulled down as far as I could on both toggles and settled in the center of the clearing. The braking ability of our new FS-12 parachutes worked well, for if I were flying the old T-10 chute, I probably would've landed in the trees. After a questionable landing roll, I looked up to a pair of boots coming straight at me. I dove out of the way.

"Damn Boots, you trying to kill me on my 150th?"

He laughed as he unsuited. "I'm as surprised as you are, Ry-son. Usually, I'm hanging in the trees." He came over and shook my hand, "Congratulations, man! Let's put this fire out and start the party."

I faintly heard the Volpar; suddenly it streaked overhead so low I thought about diving out of the way. Instead, I looked up to see the spotter in the door pushing our fire pack out. The chute popped open to a cloud of dust and the box swung beneath it. Boots and I watched it fall and just when we thought it would land in the open, an upslope gust of wind blew it into the trees. The box dangled ten-feet from the ground in a little fir. The plane swung around and noticing it in the trees, the spotter radioed, "You want the climbers?"

I looked at Boots, he shook his head no. I replied, "We can get it from the ground." We had a long pack-out waiting and from the look of the tree, it would be an easy shimmy up to the box. We'd chop the tree down with a Pulaski to get the chute.

He answered, "Ten-four, have a good fire," and disappeared leaving us to the beauty of the Mt. Hood wilderness. I looked across the mountain ranges glimmering in the afternoon sun, took in a lung full of the crisp air and said to Boots, "Man, it doesn't get any better than this."

He nodded, "Got that right. It's nice to get out of California's heat for a change."

"And the poison oak," I added.

He looked around, "And the steep ass mountains."

We could've gone on forever making comparisons. I looked up at our supplies dangling and said, "Let's pack our gear to the fire and get the cargo out."

I shimmied up to the box and cut the tie strap. With tools, we had the fire lined and out in four hours and settled in for a night of partying. My flask went back and forth. We toasted to our good fortune, to my milestone, and when the flask went dry,

I radioed a fire across the canyon for another milestone reached that day. Bill Moody, manager of the North Cascades Smokejumper Base, in Winthrop, Washington, had jumped a few more times than me. I keyed the mike, "Congratulations on your 500th, Bill."

He must've known of my benchmark, "Thanks, and you too."

I said to Boots, "Can you imagine? Five-hundred jumps and still going strong?"

Boots said, "I haven't reached fifty yet! Congrats again, Ry. As for that guy, he's a fucking animal."

"It probably took him all of twenty years. That's a long time to stay in jumping shape. I heard he broke his leg once jumping into a dead fire just to see if his guys had lined it properly and cleaned up after themselves."

Boots shook his head, "I guess when you're the boss you can do that sort of crazy shit."

The sun slipped behind the ridge and it started to get cold. I looked over the jump request. By the map, it looked like a ten-mile pack-out to a road. I looked up at the cargo chute hanging from the tree and decided we'd better cut it out before morning since we had such a long way to go. I grabbed a Pulaski and began whacking on the tree. Within minutes, it fell, but it hung up in another tree. I hollered, "Shit!"

Boots watched from the fire. He stood up. "My turn."

After chopping through his tree, it did the same damned thing. "Fucking dog hair," he muttered.

We chopped through five trees before getting our hands on the cargo chute. Boots looked at the dominos of trees, laughed and said, "I hope no one sees this mess."

I stoked the warming fire and heated some water. Boots put on his jacket and settled in. He took a sip of coffee and asked, "How much longer you going to jump, Ry?"

I watched the instant coffee dissolve in my metal cup. "I don't know, Boots. I haven't given the end much thought. I came close four years ago when I broke my back, but if that wasn't enough to make me quit, I don't think anything can. Besides, I just bought a house and have a baby. All I know is firefighting. Figure I *need* to keep jumping now."

"How's that going," he asked cautiously. "The baby? The mother part?"

"If I'd known I could get a girl pregnant while on birth control, I would've kept my pants on."

He had a pitiful look on his face, "I wish you the best of luck."

"Amen to that," I said feeling doubtful about my future. "How long you plan on jumping?"

He stirred the coals. "I'm a vagabond. Feels like it's getting close to move on time again. I'd like to try out the squares. Maybe I'll apply to Alaska next year."

"Alaska! I've wanted to transfer up there for the past eight years."

"Why haven't you?"

"I don't know. I think it has to do with being raised a military brat. All my life, my dad was told where and when to move, always a uniform dictating our lives. I grew tired of moving, of being told what to do and when to do it without explanations all the time. I want to settle in for a change, put out some roots, you know." I thought of something else. "I know I butt heads with Boy, but deep inside, I'm still a military brat. Guess I'm used to structure to tame my wild side. This might sound strange, but I actually like Boy for being the hard-ass he is. Maybe I'm afraid Alaska will turn me totally free, and I might become too wild for my own damn good."

Boots laughed. "I liked your Zen of Flying Chutes. It actually helped me learn to fly."

"Oh yeah?" I grinned. "Then why do you hang up so much?"

Boots laughed, "I guess I like the sound of breaking branches. It can't be replicated anywhere."

"Or the feeling," I added. I pulled my jump suit from my pack-out bag and made a mattress next to the warming fire. The night settled down around us. "Just think about this Boots, if you go to Alaska, you won't be able to find trees big enough to hang up in."

He laughed and made his bed, too. Just before turning in, he said, "This is the best fire I've ever been on, Ry. Congratulations again on 150. I hope mine will be in such a nice spot."

I slipped into my paper sleeping bag and thought about my future. Ever since I'd become a father, everything about my life felt clouded with uncertainty. Would Sylvia try to keep my son from me? Would I end up in a messy court battle over visitation? Uncharted territory surrounded me, one minute I wanted to run away from it all, the next, I'm gearing up for a fight. As I closed my eyes to the crackling of the fire, the only thing I knew for sure, this is where I loved being.

CHAPTER 25

The Spiral

I finished the Stokes litter cover and by the end of September signed the Airman Certificate for my Master Parachute Riggers License. Boy congratulated me. I was proud. He'd made me earn it the hard way. I presented him with a prototype of my elastic webbing static line keeper system I'd been working on ever since learning about the Regennitter fatality, and to my surprise, he liked the idea and allowed me to outfit a few deployment bags with it. It worked well during practice jumps. I also outfitted my jump suit with the emergency tie off device I'd come up with in Alaskan since narrowly escaping burning out of a tree on a jump out of Grangeville, my mind set centered on having it on my suit. Boy caught me stitching the pouch to my jump pants and the shit hit the turbines.

"You can't come in here and make whatever you want!" he laid into me. "We have protocols here. You're a Master Rigger now. You should know better, Ryan."

I shouted back, "When I'm dangling by a thread, I'd rather have something that'll save my ass than have to think about protocols from a hospital bed!"

"I don't care," he shouted. "You know the proper channels."

"Fuck the channels," I said and stormed out of the loft through the drying tower. I kicked the door; it banged open just as the base manager walked by. The look I saw on his face froze me in my tracks. I knew trouble was coming, irreparable consequences. I walked past him across the parking lot, into the BLM jumper's office. I plopped in a chair in front of Kroger and pleaded, "Mark, I think I fucked up for the last time over there. I don't want to be crucified. I need a job. Can you help me out?"

Kroger grinned. It reminded me of the good old days where he had his ass chewed many times, and I felt a rush of relief as he calmly said, "No problem. You're one of us as of now."

It seemed too easy. I had to ask, "You sure?"

"I'm sure," he said. "The question is, are you? You have an appointment with them, right?"

"Yeah, I have an 18/8."

"I'll call Alaska and see if we can keep you in that status. There shouldn't be a problem. If you're serious, I'll tell Gramps that you just switched sides."

Just like that, my life changed. I stared vacantly through Kroger as Pigpen strolled into the office. "Hey, Dog Egg, finally had enough of the Nervous Center? I heard about the fireworks in the loft. We don't suppress creativity here. We embrace it."

"I can't believe I'm here begging for a job," I said desperately.

Pigpen chuckled, "You're not begging, we're offering."

I went home a mental mess, my comfort zone completely shattered. Twelve years with the Forest Service and suddenly I'm a bastard child. I cranked up Buddy Guy on the stereo and drank myself into oblivion holding the bottle like it was the only friend I had in the world.

I struggled through a tough winter of not being able to see my son on a regular basis. Knowing I'd be leaving for Alaska in the spring, I put aside my inward distrust of Sylvia and offered her to move in with me. She accepted and even though our relationship remained tumultuous, at least my son and I shared the same roof for a few months and it turned out to be an enjoyable time.

When I returned in the spring, the Kroger brothers, Pigpen, and Fast Edie greeted me with a surprise. Boots, Hollywood, and Coyote had also jumped ship and joined the BLM. My apprehension about my future in Alaska evaporated instantly knowing I wasn't going to be alone on this new journey.

*****

Alaska Smokejumper Training, Fairbanks, Alaska
1986

I'm standing at the top of the training tower as the instructor yelled out a succession of malfunctions through a bullhorn. "Drogue in tow?"

I yelled back, "Cut away and deploy the reserve."

"Horseshoe?"

"Try to free the canopy from your body. If it doesn't work, cut away and deploy the reserve."

I heard Boots and Hollywood clomp up the stairs. With all the malfunctions covered, the instructor looks at us and smiled. "Good job. Who says Forest Service jumpers aren't smart enough to pull a ripcord?"

We jumped, and as we climbed up the tower again, Boots said in a labored voice, "When you walked across the parking lot to the BLM hangar after sparring with Dave, everyone in the loft looked on in shock. When you didn't come out right away, I knew something was up."

"I didn't know what to do, man. I felt like a trapped tiger. Kroger had gone through the same kind of shit before he left, and when he offered me the job, I couldn't fucking believe it."

Boots stopped to catch his breath. "Well, look at it this way, you've finally made it to Alaska, you're going to be flying a high performance parachute, and you can be as creative as you want without being scrutinized for it. I'm happy for you. Besides, look what you started. We wouldn't be here if you didn't make it look so easy."

I patted his shoulder. "You don't know how good it is having you guys here. It's made all the difference in the world."

Before we reach the top, Boots asks, "How are things on the home front?"

"She moved in and now she says she's pregnant again."

He shook his head. "So much for keeping your pants on!"

"And she was on birth control, again!" I grumbled

He slapped my helmet. "So much for learning from your mistakes. So when's the new baby due?"

"September."

The instructor yelled, "Come on girls, we don't have all day." When he seemed satisfied we had the exit and malfunction procedures down, he smiled and said, "Okay, guys, you're ready. Tomorrow you'll be jumping squares."

*****

Nervousness hung over us like fog in the training room. Pigpen came in and eyed each one of us closely. It seemed like a dream. Here stood the first smokejumper I'd ever met on a fire in southern California, and by doing so inspired me to follow my dream. Now, he'd trained me to fly a cutting edge parachute thousands of miles from our first meeting. I couldn't help but believe karma had something to do with it and for me the bond would last forever. Pride flowed through me as strong as my admiration for him. He hollered, "Okay, Dog Eggs, you ready for this? Let's go through the four-point check." We reviewed every procedure until Pigpen smiled and said, "Okay men, I think you have it. It's time to suit up. You'll be jumping once today with a radio in your leg pocket. If we see you screwing up, you'll be given instructions to get you back on course."

Glimpsing the ground through a light layer of clouds, the jump spot was barely visible. From 6000 feet it looked so different from the standard 1500 feet—the standard jump altitude for the Forest Service. I watched as Coyote set up in the door. I hear the spotter's final briefing, "There's 150 yards of drift up high. The ground wind is calmer. Listen to your radio. Whatever you do, make sure you land into the wind. You're clear. Get ready. We're on final."

Coyote had a smile that reflected our achievement and he went out the door with a joyous yell. The spotter looked at me and put up one finger. I secured my drogue static line snap to the cable and set my foot on the step. At the slap, a new world gripped me. I fall like a rock while the drogue chute flutters madly above me. I went through the jump count, and when 'pull thousand' came, I yanked the ripcord handle so hard, the cable whizzes past my facemask. I looked up and see a jumble of nylon pop into a rectangle of red and white. I yelled out joyfully.

Landing a square is similar to landing a plane. You have the downwind leg where you run with the wind past the jump spot, and then you make the base or crosswind leg to line up on the spot. Once you're on the wind line, you make the final leg by turning into the wind and approach the spot.

I followed the instructions blaring from the radio inside my leg pocket: "Make your downwind leg now!" Being left-handed, I preferred to have the jump spot to my left. I sailed with the wind, keeping the spot in sight. When "Make your base leg!" sounded, I pulled on the left toggle and flew crosswind until, "Turn on final," had me turning left again. I flew toward the spot with the wind in my face. "Ease on and off the brakes!" I pulled down on both toggles a few times to see how the chute braked. It responded immediately and I played with the toggles to find the right braking position to get me close to the spot. Coming in to land, I instinctively pulled down on both toggles as if I were still flying a round. My body swings upward just as my feet were about to touch the tundra, then I swing downward crashing into the tundra back first. The impact knocked the air from me. An instructor ran over yelling, "You flared too early. This program depends on you guys walking away from the jumps, not being carted away."

My body hurt. I lifted myself up in a daze. I said to the trainer, "I'm not used to brakes that work. It won't happen again." I meant it, that landing proved too painful to repeat.

A brutal critique followed. We'd all done something that needed improvement. At the end of the ass-chewing, Pigpen said, "Tomorrow you'll get three jumps, so think about everything we've told you."

I learned to fly the square better with each successive jump. On our sixth, Pigpen said they had a treat in store for us. Our jump altitude would be at 10,000 feet so we could see what a square could do. The jump spot appeared as an indistinguishable location from that height and it felt like an icebox inside the plane. When I felt the slap from the spotter, I jumped and did the count. Nothing could be more exhilarating than falling at ninety-miles-per-hour and when I pulled the ripcord, I looked up to watch the chute deploy. It fluttered around before taking shape and when it popped open, my body swung around for a few seconds, and I started flying. The wind flowing around the slider gave me a sense of my air speed, by the noise it made, I was hauling ass across the sky. My hands felt like ice, especially the one holding the metal ripcord handle. I tucked them under my arms, and not hearing anything from the radio in my leg pocket, I let the parachute fly me toward Fairbanks. The city and the Chena River looked so small, like a toy city. I could see for miles!

When I felt I'd gone far enough, I turned and let the chute fly me back toward Fort Wainwright. I came over the Birch Hill landing zone with just enough altitude to get into the spot. An instructor ran up to me livid as a frustrated coach yelling, "Didn't you hear the radio?"

I pulled it from my pocket, looked it over and mumbled, "Someone must've messed with it, because it's off."

The instructor laughed, "We sent a pickup into Fairbanks looking for you!"

I shrugged my shoulders and said, "Guess I saw what a square could do."

*****

Before we could finish our seventh and final training jump, fire season began. I jumped fire A-024 out of Ruby. After two shifts, native crews flew in to take over and we returned to Fairbanks for the final training jump. I settled into the parachute loft, where I found receptive overhead. When I showed them my prototype of the static line stow device—that I'd coined the 'Safety Stow'—they appeared as excited about it as I was, and before I know it, I'm outfitting quite a few deployment bags with it. I also learned how to rig the squares, the sweet thing about it, you didn't need a rigging table to pack them, any flat surface would do including the ground. A planeload of squares could follow a thunderstorm and jump fires in remote regions of Alaska without having to return to Fairbanks or a spike base to get fresh chutes. You could spend weeks in the bush chasing fires with the same parachute, and that's exactly what I did.

CHAPTER 26

Fire Storm

Fire #A-125, Circle, Alaska
June 29, 1986

Circle City, Alaska, was a settlement carved into the bush in the late 1800's as an outfitter town that flourished on the bank of the Yukon River supplying gold miners in the region. When they discovered gold in the Klondike, the miners packed up and left. The first miners called it Circle believing it rested on the Arctic Circle. The Steese Highway terminated there and Circle became known as the 'End of the Road' in Alaska. I heard they had a hot spring and flying over town to the fire, all I thought about was soaking my bones.

In the distance, I saw flames dance wildly off the black spruce forest. A mile long swath of orange and red consumed everything in its path. An apocalyptic black smoke boiled into the sky, even the towering thunderclouds that produced the inferno couldn't escape the expanding convection column. The sky: gray and churning. A haunting shadow swallowed the land.

A jump spot opened up by the fire and Fast Eddie sent four bros out. While we monitored their decent, the fire sucked at the plane in its hunger for oxygen. It became so fierce, the wingtips rocked up and down, while the fuselage jerked from side to side. The engines strained with power as I looked into the cockpit where our pilot wrestled with the controls. Smoke rushed into the cabin and heat radiated through the windows. My body shuddered with the plane as my stomach tightened to a knot. I said to no one, "This is fucking crazy!"

The pilot wasn't breaking his orbit. The plane kept circling. With my legs straining to anchor my body to the fuselage, and my hands gripping cargo box straps, I forced my face to the window. My bros under canopy struggled against the pull of the fire. Fast Eddie yelled above the roar, "Goddamn it. Keep bucking the wind! Fight it, guys! FIGHT IT!"

The remaining four of us had other thoughts on our minds. Is this firestorm going to rip the plane apart? Are we going to die? I clung to my seat and stared out the window at the four parachutists trapped in the convection column's pull. Suddenly, one of them executed a hard turn. His canopy went horizontal, spinning in a tight circle. He lost altitude quickly and while I'm thinking he's going to crash into the heart of the fire, his chute suddenly flares out and lands in a smoldering area. His jump partners executed the same maneuver and within minutes, I see all of them running from fire. That's when our pilot banked out of the inferno's grip. The calmer air settled my nerves. We found a new drop zone further upwind. Fast Eddie signaled us to hook up and get in position. He yelled into his headset, "Get us up to three-thousand." He briefed my stick as the plane climbed. "Don't spend a lot of time in the air. Get down quickly. We have air tankers and another load of jumpers coming."

When the Volpar leveled out, Eddie stuck his head out the door to locate the exit point. I looked out and saw hills of varying shades of green peppered with dark Alaskan spruce. They stretched as far as the eye could see. Sunlight glinted off tiny lakes like shards of broken glass accenting the distant mountains with a heavenly touch. That's where I wanted to fly.

Eddie pulled his head in. "We're on final!"

I had to leave that beautiful expanse for the fire. Eddie slapped me into reality. I pushed away from the plane. The propeller blast spun me. The world became a blur. I fell to earth with the wind whistling through my facemask. I extended the count until exhilaration turned to concern. My hand shot across my chest like an arrow, pulling the ripcord releasing the drogue. I looked up to see it unfurl as a battle between wind and nylon filled the air. The chute popped open to silence. I smiled, looked at my distant mountains and rode on the wind yet again. I wanted it to last forever, to fly the endless sky of the last frontier with absolute freedom, but fire exploding through a stand of spruce below gripped me. I felt its pull and reefed down as far as possible on my left toggle. The parachute went horizontal into a bomb turn with my body following. The sky turned sideways, everything spun around me and in a matter of seconds I dropped eight-hundred feet. I turned into the wind at last and applied the brakes hard with both toggles, the tundra crunched beneath me, and I leapt to my feet with a yell of pure relief.

The first four jumpers hurried over the tussocks toward us. Happy to see them safe, I hollered, "You guys scared the shit out of us! It looked like a hell of a ride from the plane."

"Yeah, what a crappy way to start a fire!" Sean Cross bellowed.

Tim Pettitt added, "I need to change my fucking underwear!"

On the other hand, a jumper named Sulinski looked as calm as if it were another day in the bush.

A Volpar streaked overhead, then climbed sharply to allow an air tanker to assault the flames. A trail of red, slimy retardant rained down along the edge of the fire we were about to attack smothering it into white whispers of smoke. When the tanker cleared out, the Volpar returned. Eight jumpers streamed out the door and the sky filled with canopies and hoots.

I fashioned a firefighting tool from the top of a spruce with my Woodsman's Pal, and began swatting at the burning tundra. Minutes turned to hours while my clothes became drenched in sweat. Air tankers lumbered in and out, dropping load after load of retardant. After twenty hours of initial attack, Sean appeared through the smoke like an apparition. He'd been directing the operation and noticing our fatigue, said, "Ryan, Decoteau, Clouser, Pettitt, take an hour, get some food and rest. You've done a great job, we're making progress." He disappeared back into the smoke.

I slumped against a spruce tree and lethargically chewed on a trail mix bar, too exhausted to have an appetite, but knew I'd need the energy later and forced myself to eat two more. Exhausted, I thought about my son and my soon to be born child. I missed them like I missed my dad when he shipped off to three wars while growing up. Do I want to spend my career thinking about my babies? Do I want them to feel the same way I did growing up? It's a tough business to be in as a father and more so in a rocky relationship. I felt very alone and fell asleep with food in my mouth. After what seemed like seconds, I'm being shaken awake: "Time to get going, Ryan!"

Stiffness impeded me. Sweat had dried to itchy salt stains that covered my clothes and face. I grabbed a packet of instant coffee and poured it between my lip and gum. An instant rush fired throughout my body, it helped me to my feet. When I pulled my Woodsman's Pal out of its sheath, sunlight glinted off the blade. We fought fire for another eighteen hours, showing no mercy to it or ourselves.

Sean found us in the evening. "We're getting this puppy whipped, boys. Let's take a break at the jump spot."

We trudged into camp to the aroma of fresh coffee and sat on cargo boxes wolfing down freeze-dried meals. I pulled out my flask and poured whisky into my coffee and passed it around. We were beyond exhaustion, in that mental state where sleep isn't possible. I felt rummy, everything came in waves. Soon enough the whisky lightened our mood, and the stories began.

Smokejumper stories usually began with, 'And there I was.' The tales that follow were amazing. Parachuting, firefighting, for us it's one in the same. After all we'd experienced it's a wonder we're still around to talk about it. Sean Cross told a new one about his jump, "I felt the heat through my jump suit as the fire sucked the breath from my lungs. The fucking wind pulled on me so hard, my parachute wasn't responding. The goddamned flames wanted me."

Pettitt helped him out, "Fucking crazy! When I saw you go into the bomb turn, I knew it was the right move, but I flared out too late and crunched into the tundra. Knocked the fucking air right out of me!"

Around and around it went, each jumper counting his salt points as another story unfolded. My thoughts began to drift. How long would I be able to sit around a warming fire with my bros telling stories? Smokejumping had me questioning my sanity so many times that I didn't know what lie ahead, except uncertainty. My head needed clearing and then I felt it, the call of the wild. I left the pack and trudged to a hill overlooking the vast wilderness and our warming fire. I toyed with a wild flower growing from the tundra amazed at how it could survive the harshness of this country. It dawned on me that this flower had to be one with the universe, the same premise my martial arts training stressed. I felt oneness with this country, with my bros, and if I could maintain this state of awareness everything else would fall into place, but I knew better. It's easy to feel this way in Alaska. It allowed my mind to travel freely without distractions. I feared this euphoric experience would be lost once I returned home. I'd have relationship issues to deal with, custody issues, and job issues where rumor had it our Redding home would be moved to Boise, Idaho next year. My world would be cluttered with distractions. I'd lose the peace this country brought me. My intuition from being raised a vagabond signaled change was about to happen, but in what form? I cleared my head, took long breaths, and gave in to my surroundings. An hour passed when I heard hoots. They must've been worried about me, so I hooted back and returned to camp. Pettitt's voice pulled me back to the circle. "Someone ought to write this shit down." That's not a bad idea, I thought, as I crawled into my hootch.

District personnel and native crews soon arrived in mass and we demobe to Circle, where I did get to soak my weary bones in the spring. From there, we flew to fires in the Tanana District, then to the Bettles District, on to the Fairbanks district, back to Tanana, and finally to Galina. In a span of twenty days, I jumped six fires across the state without seeing a bed, feeling a hot shower, or having clean clothes. Exhaustion set in, both physically and mentally.

When the fires in Alaska slowed, I boarded a plane to McCall. We didn't jump any fires while there and being August, I became antsy. My son was to be born in September and I wanted to be close to home. I kicked the idea around until I mustered the nerve to tell Neal, McCall's base manager, and friend, about my concerns. I can't describe the elation I felt when he said, "We'll get you on a plane home tomorrow, and tell Gramps I said hi."

The next morning, I flew home in a small Cessna. I hadn't realized how much I missed my son until I held him at last. He'd grown so much in the months I'd been gone and for the time, his mom and I got on well. I merged onto the Redding jump list and worked in the loft. Boy didn't seem upset with me and I held no animosity. I still had the upmost respect for him.

I jumped three fires while on the Redding list and had to fly a round chute. I realized I'd become spoiled by the squares because the rounds seemed too cumbersome and boring. On my last jump, I landed in a rock pile and injured my elbow. While nursing it, my second son, Sean, was born.

My BLM bros filtered down to Redding for the Great Basin season and a few days after my son's birth, I jumped a fire in the Nevada desert with Coyote. While waiting for a helicopter to pick us up, he filled me in. "I heard the BLM has taken over the Forest Service facility in Boise and that our operation in Redding is over after this season."

I chuckled, "Hell, just as well, they don't want us there anyway. They made a T-shirt with a square and the universal do not enter symbol over it. That speaks volumes."

"Are you going to Boise?" he asked.

"It's not looking good for me. I have a house and two sons. While in Alaska, my neighbor kept an eye on my place and she said this guy was always hanging around. I haven't mentioned it to her and now she's talking about moving to Reno where her sister lives, I see a major custody battle brewing because she's not taking my sons!"

"Sorry to hear that, Ry. If you don't make it north, I'll miss you bro."

*****

1986 ended my smokejumping career. Since I had a permanent position, I tried to secure a local job with the Forest Service, but they were on a 'consent decree' program at the time, and I had to stand at the end of the line even though I had fourteen years of firefighting experience. I walked away from firefighting never to look back again. I continued to visit the jump base since I have friends there. As the years turned into decades, my visits continued. The pogues, officially renamed 'R-5 Rookies,' have invited me to their parties ever since and I've formed new friendships. As I look back, and up every time I hear jump ships fly over my home in the mountains, I feel blessed for having been associated with smokejumping and especially the bros and sis's who have shared the experience. Once a bro, always a bro!

Pettitt's words, "Someone ought to write this shit down," swirled in my head for decades and I've written this book to show those who might be curious what smokejumping is all about. I don't believe there's a better job or people in the world and even though we all know the inherent dangers associated with jumping and fighting wildland fires, we still did it. The Mann Gulch Fire in 1949 took the lives of fifteen smokejumpers. The South Canyon Fire in 1994 took fourteen firefighters, three of which were smokejumpers. In 1970, the California Smokejumpers lost Steven Grammer and Tom Regennitter in the line of duty.

In 2006, I lost my two true idols. Richard 'Hurricane' Tracy, our beloved base manager from 1968 to 1982 passed away, and six months later, my dad passed from the same illness. I can't thank either of them enough for being a major influence in my life and I hope I did them proud.

Tragedy and sadness struck the California Smokejumpers again on Monday, June 10, 2013, when Luke Sheehy was killed by a falling branch while fighting the Saddle Back Fire in the Warner Wilderness, Modoc National Forest. I pray for his family and his fellow bros and sis's. He personified smokejumping and left us way too early. With a heavy heart, I'm dedicating this book to his memory.

GLOSSARY

Air Attack. The planes and people that coordinate air operations over a fire.

Air Tanker. Large aircraft that drops fire retardant chemicals.

Anchor Point. An advantageous location from which to start fire line construction. Minimizes the chance of being out flanked by a fire.

Backfiring. A tactic associated with indirect attack, intentionally setting fire inside the control line to purposely influence the direction or rate of fire spread.

BIFC. Boise Interagency Fire Center, Boise, Idaho.

Big Ernie. The mythical god of firefighters.

Black line. Denotes a condition where there is no unburned material between the fire line and the fires edge.

Blowup. Sudden increase in fire intensity or rate of spread sufficient to preclude direct control or to upset existing control plans.

Buddy Check. The last minute check of jumper's gear, performed by jump partner prior to jumping.

Burnout. A tactic associated with direct attack by intentionally setting fire to fuels inside the control line to strengthen the line.

Bush. General term for the Alaskan wilderness.

Bust. Intense period of lightning fire activity.

Canopy. The uppermost branch layer of a tree, or the term used for a fully opened parachute.

Contained. A fire is contained when its spread has been halted by control lines or natural barriers.

Controlled. A fire is controlled when there is no chance of it escaping the fire lines.

Crown fire. A fire burning hot enough to continuously spread through the tops of trees.

Demobe. Short for demobilization. The action of leaving a fire once it is out.

Dozer Line. Fire line constructed by a bulldozer.

Drift Streamers. Weighted pieces of colored crepe paper used to determine wind drift before jumping a fire.

Drogue. The small parachute that first stabilizes jumpers as they fall from the plane; then pulls the main canopy out of the deployment bag once the drogue release handle is pulled.

Drogue Handle. Also known as a ripcord.

Drop Zone. The area around and immediately above the target, applies to retardant, jumper, and paracargo drops.

Dry Run. A trial pass over the target area, or not jumping a fire for various reasons.

Extended Attack. Work done after the initial effort has failed to stop the fire. For jumpers, usually the second or third day.

Firebrands. Large embers or chunks of burning, airborne material.

Fire Break. Any natural or constructed break in a fuel bed utilized to segregate, stop and control the spread of fire or to provide a control line from which to suppress a fire.

Fire Box. A cardboard box parachuted to jumpers with food, water, and tools for fire suppression.

Fire line. A loose term for any cleared strip used in control of a fire.

Fire Retardant. Any substance except plain water that by chemical or physical action reduces the flammability of fuels or slows the rate of combustion.

Fire Shelter. A personal protective item carried by firefighters which forms a tent like shelter of heat reflective material often referred to a 'Shake-n- Bake.'

Firestorm. A mass conflagration of fire, a blowup.

Flanks. The side boundaries of a fire.

WILDFIRE

Flare Up. Any sudden acceleration of fire spread or intensification of the fire. Usually short lived and it doesn't radically change existing control plans.

Fusee. Railroad flares used to light burnouts and backfires.

Ground Fire. A fire that consumes the organic material in the soil layer.

Ground Fuels. All combustible materials below the surface litter, including duff, tree or shrub roots.

Head. Hottest and most active part of a fire, determines the direction the fire is moving.

Helitack. Fire suppression using helicopters.

Hootch. Sleeping arrangement, tent, rain fly, parachute, etc.

Hot Shot. Highly trained organized fire crew, used mostly on large, long term fires.

Hot Spot. A partially active part of a fire.

Indirect Attack. A method of suppression in which the control line is located some distance from the fire's active edge. Usually done in the case of a fast spreading, or high-intensity fire.

Initial Attack. First effort in controlling a fire.

Jump List. A rotating list that determines the order in which jumpers are assigned to fires.

Jump Ship. Smokejumper aircraft.

Jump Spot. A selected landing area for smokejumpers or helijumpers.

Lead Plane. Aircraft flown to make trial runs over the fire and used to direct the tactical deployment of air tankers.

Litter. The top layer of the forest floor composed of loose debris of dead sticks, branches, twigs, and recently fallen leaves or needles.

Loft. Room where parachutes are rigged and repaired.

Lower 48. Alaska term for the contiguous United States.

Mop Up. The final stage of fighting a fire where all the hot spots are put out.

Mud. Aerial fire retardant dropped by aircraft. Also called retardant, slurry, or Phos-chek.

On final. For aircraft, the final flight path before jumpers exit. For jumpers, the final flight path as they descend into a jump spot.

Ops. Operations desk. The nerve center of any smokejumper base.

Paracargo. Anything intentionally dropped or intended for dropping from aircraft by parachute.

PG Bag. Personal gear bag.

Pogue. A first year jumper candidate, exclusively used by the California Smokejumpers.

PT. Physical training. As part of their daily routine, smokejumpers do one hour of PT each morning.

PT Test. The physical test administered each season to pogues and returning jumpers and must be passed in order to jump.

Pulaski. Firefighting tool. An ax with a grub hoe on the opposite end.

Rappeller. A firefighter that descends down a rope from a hovering helicopter.

Rappelling. The process of delivering firefighters by descending down a rope from a hovering helicopter.

Rate of Spread. The relative activity of a fire in extending its horizontal dimensions. The forward rate of spread at the fire front or head is usually what is meant by this term.

Rats. Army rations, K-rations, C-rations, MRS's (Meals ready to eat).

Ready Room. A room in the smokejumper facility where jumpers suit up for departure to fires.

Re-burn. A fire that is declared out, then later rekindles.

Safety Zone. An area, usually a recently burned area, used to escape in the event the fire line is outflanked.

Scratch Line. A minimum line hastily established or constructed as an initial measure to check the spread of a fire.

Situation Report. Daily report of current fires, personnel assigned, and resource allocations. Also includes weather forecasts.

Slash. Debris left after logging operations. Could include limbs, cull logs, treetops, and stumps.

Sling Load. Equipment and supplies prepared and transported by cables suspended from a helicopter.

Slop over. A place where the fire crosses an established control line.

Snag. A dead tree, still standing.

Speed Rack. Racks on which jump gear is pre-positioned to facilitate fast suit up times.

Spot fire. A fire set outside the perimeter of the main fire by flying sparks or embers.

Spotter. Person who directs the jumping and cargo dropping from the plane.

Spotting. Behavior of a fire producing sparks or embers that start new fires outside of the main fire.

Spruce bough. The top cut from a small spruce used to swat down flames on Alaska fires.

Standby Shack. The main smokejumper building in Alaska including the loft, ready room, tool room, weight room, paracargo bay, etc.

Steering Lines. The right and left lines used to steer a parachute.

Streamer. Fully malfunctioned parachute.

Strip Firing. Setting fire to more than one strip of fuel providing for the strips to burn together. Frequently done in burning out against the wind where inner strips are fired first to create drafts which pull flames and sparks away from the control lines.

Swamper. A worker who pulls brush behind the chain saw operator, or one who works on a dozer crew pulling winch lines and walking ahead of the dozer to guide the operator in constructing fire line.

Tie-In. To connect a control line with another line coming from the opposite direction.

Undercut Line. A fire line below a fire on a slope. Should be trenched to catch rolling material, also called under slung line.

Zulie. Missoula smokejumpers.

ABOUT THE AUTHOR

Ralph Ryan grew up a military brat with his four brothers and his sister. He lived in six different states and spent fifteen years collectively in Europe. After attending high school for four years at the Berlin American High School, he returned stateside and acquired an AA degree in Natural Resources Management and began his fourteen-year wild land firefighting career. Ralph served on Engines, Initial Attack Helishot crews and ultimately, ten years as a California BLM Smoke Jumper.

After reluctantly leaving Smokejumping, he gained employment with the City of Redding and spent twenty-five years in the Parks and Water Departments. He acquired an AA degree in Horticulture at Shasta College and fathered two sons, Eric and Sean. He built a home on a mountain top overlooking Shasta Lake and recently relocated to the city of Redding.

The written word always fascinated Ralph and he began writing short stories and attended Creative Writing classes at Shasta College. One of his instructors, journalist and author Tony D'Souza, saw promise is his work and became Ralph's mentor as he turned a short story into a novel. *Wildfire* is Ralph's first self-published work and he currently has two fiction novels in the works. *The Crossroads: A Journey of Discovery* is nearly completed, and *Freedom* is close behind.

Ralph retired from the City of Redding in 2013 and is now focused on writing, riding his motorcycle and bringing back life to an old house.

Made in the USA
Middletown, DE
04 February 2015